MUSIC IN THE BIBLE

CHARLES JIRKOVSKY

Music in the Bible

First Edition

Copyright © 2023 by Charles Jirkovsky (1989-).

GMAR Publishing. San Diego, California.

All rights reserved, including the right to reproduce this book or portions thereof in any form whatsoever. For more information, inquire at info@musicinthebible.com.

ISBN 979-8-9885094-0-0 (print)
ISBN 979-8-9885094-1-7 (ebook)
ISBN 979-8-9885094-2-4 (audiobook)

For Michelle

מָצָא אִשָּׁה מָצָא טוֹב וַיָּפֶק רָצוֹן מֵיְהוָה

Proverbs 18:22

Contents

Chapter 1
Music in the Bible 1
Introduction 1
What is Music? 3
What is the Bible? 5
Research Approach 13
Translation and Transliteration 19
Music in Each Book of the Bible 21
Table 1: Musical References in
    Each Book of the Bible 22
Table 2: Books of the Bible in Order of
    Musical References 24
What is the Purpose of this Book? 24
Acknowledgments 25

Chapter 2
Vocal Music 27
Table 3: Hebrew Terms Translated as
"Singing" in the Bible 30
Table 4: Vocal, Instrumental, and Other
    Musical References 31
Table 5: References to Singing in English
    Bible Translations 32
Shir 34
Vocal Music in the Bible and
    Other Terms for Vocal Music 37
Vocal Music in the Torah (Pentateuch) ... 37

- Vocal Music in the Book of Genesis 38
- Vocal Music in the Book of Exodus 39
- Vocal Music in the Book of Deuteronomy 41

Vocal Music in the Nevi'im (Prophets) 42
- Vocal Music in the Book of Judges 42
- Vocal Music in the Book of Samuel 43
- Vocal Music in the Book of Kings 44
- Vocal Music in the Book of Isaiah 47
- Vocal Music in the Book of Ezekiel 49
- Vocal Music in the Book of the Twelve 49
  - Vocal Music in Amos 50

Vocal Music in the Ketuvim (Writings) 50
- Vocal Music in the Book of Psalms 50
  - *Mizmor* 52
  - *Maskil* 53
  - Psalms with More Than One Heading 53
  - *Michtam* 55
  - *Shushan* 55
  - *Shiggayon* 57
  - *Lehazkir* 58
  - *Ma'alot* 58
- Vocal Music in the Book of Job 59
- Vocal Music in the Song of Songs 60
- Vocal Music in the Book of Ezra-Nehemiah 61
- Vocal Music in the Book of Chronicles............ 62

Chapter 3
Stringed Instruments 69
    Kinnor 69
    Nevel 103
    Asor 108
    Gittit and Minnim 109

Chapter 4
Wind Instruments 114
    Shofar 114
    Table 6: Notes of the Overtone Series on a *Shofar* 118
    Chatzotzerot 133
    Table 7: *Chatzotzerot* Signals 141
    Ugav 149
    Chalil 152
    Machol 152
    Alamot 156

Chapter 5
Drums and Percussion 160
    Tof 160
    Metziltayim and *Tzeltzelim* 165
    Shalishim and *Mena'anim* 167
    Pa'amonim and *Metzilot* 169

CHAPTER 6
INSTRUMENTS OF KING NEBUCHADNEZZAR'S COURT 171
- *Karnah* 172
- *Mashrokita* 173
- *Kateros* 173
- *Sebbekha* 175
- *Pesanterin* 178
- *Sumponyah* 179
- Musical Instruments in the Bible 181
- Table 8: Confirmed Israelite Musical Instruments . 182
- Table 9: All Confirmed Musical Instruments in the Bible (Including Babylonian Instruments) 183
- Table 10: All Possible Musical Instruments in the Bible (Including Babylonian and Unconfirmed) 184

CHAPTER 7
FUNCTIONAL MUSIC IN THE BIBLE 185
- Table 10: Analysis of Functional Music in the Bible 189
- Table 11: Analysis of Functional Music in the Bible (with all worship functions incorporated)........ 191
- Musical Functions in the Bible 193
- Worship 193
    - General Worship 194
    - The Temple Orchestra 196
    - *Mizmor* 200
    - Thanksgiving 202
    - *Ma'alot* 203

- *Maskil* 203
- Lament 203
- Shabbat... 205
- *Michtam* 206
- *Shushan* 206
- Mercy Plea 206
- Ritual 207
- *Lehazkir* (Remembrance).................................... 207
- Covenant 208
- Personal Worship 208
- Corporate Worship 209
- Warfare 209
- Metaphor/Simile 211
- Babylonian Court 211
- Victory 212
- Civil 212
- Historical 212
- Celebration 213
- Coronation 213
- Dedication 213
- Instrument Construction 214
- Prophetic 214
- Music Therapy 215
- Wedding/Love Song 216
- Fanfare.. 216
- Priestly Attire 216
- Mnemonic 217
- Recreation 217
- Send-off 218

Rosh Hashanah	218
Yom Kippur	219
Homecoming	219
Insurrection	219
General Signal	220
Messianic	220

CHAPTER 8
THEORETICAL MUSIC TONALITY 221

CHAPTER 9
BIBLICAL MUSIC NOTATION 236
    The Masoretic Text 239
    A Brief History of Western European
        Music Notation 245
    The Biblical Te'amim and
        How They are Interpreted Today 249
    Suzanne Haïk-Vantoura:
        La Musique de la Bible Révelée 260
    Table 12: Haïk-Vantoura's Scale Degrees 264
    Chironomy 268
    Reactions to *The Music of the Bible Revealed* 271
    Conclusions 274

CHAPTER 10
ECHOES OF THE PAST IN MUSIC TODAY 276
    Musical Instruments and Styles 277
    Stringed Instruments 278
    Wind Instruments 279

    Drums and Percussion Instruments 280
    Digital Instruments 280
    Table 13: Contemporary Meanings of
            Biblical Instrument Names 283
    Functional Music 284
    Tonality 285
    Notation 286

DEFINITION OF TERMS 288
APPENDIX 297
NOTES 322
SELECTED BIBLIOGRAPHY 343

CHAPTER 1

MUSIC IN THE BIBLE

INTRODUCTION

The LORD is my shepherd; I shall not want...though I walk through the valley of the shadow of death, I will fear no evil...I will dwell in the house of the LORD forever.

Excerpts from Psalm 23
Attributed to David

Have you ever wondered how this beautiful psalm originally sounded? Have you imagined the notes of this lyrical melody, or the tone and timbre of David's lyre? What about the 4,000 instrumentalists and singers of the Temple Orchestra, the court music of King Nebuchadnezzar, the exuberant and musical Psalm 150, or Solomon's epic Song of Songs?

In May of 2018, I was a twenty-nine-year-old doctoral student researching worship practices in the Bible from an ethnomusicological perspective. I found myself considering these very questions, and many others. As a lifelong musician, I could not help but consider how the music mentioned in Scripture originally sounded, as well as the nature of the instruments described.

Surely, David's harp bore little to no resemblance to a modern concert harp, but *what exactly did it look and sound like? How was it played?* To my disappointment, a satisfactory answer was seemingly inaccessible. This topic had been addressed to some extent by scholars, but information was hard to come by. Further, in academia, sources no more than five years old are preferred, so it was concerning that much of the available literature on this topic was more than fifty years old. When I posed questions about biblical music to my colleagues, fellow university professors, and biblical scholars, they almost unanimously suggested that virtually nothing of substance was known about music in ancient Israel, nor could definitive conclusions about biblical music ever be proven. I rejected their assumptions, and refused to believe that the music of millennia past was inaccessible, or worse still, forever lost to history.

I spent the years that followed researching and learning as much as I could about music in Israel and the ancient Near East—from Egypt to Babylon, throughout Asia Minor, Europe, northeastern Africa, and even as far as India and the cultures of Southeast Asia. I carefully read every line of Scripture in its original language, gleaning invaluable clues, information, and answers inaccessible from an English Bible alone, in which the accuracy, authenticity, and integrity of the descriptions of music are reliant on the English translators' own understanding of both ancient and modern music. Using the modern tools and practices of ethnomusicology, I sought to create a historical ethnography of biblical music. Though I successfully defended my doctoral thesis in 2020, I continued my research until I believed I had created a resource that satisfied my own curiosity.

It is my hope that other students, teachers, scholars, religious leaders, people whose interest in ancient music is secularly-rooted, as well as people of faith will all find this book to be a useful and interesting resource.

WHAT IS MUSIC?

Before one can study music in the Bible, a few parameters and working definitions must first be established. Namely, *What is Music?* and *What is the Bible?* Perhaps surprisingly, neither of these terms carry the same meaning to everyone. In fact, their definitions can be quite diverse.

Defining "music" is important because the biblical descriptions of what qualifies as "music" or a musical instrument may differ from person to person. For example, more than 165 small bronze bells have been discovered by archeologists throughout Israel in recent decades.[1] Few people would argue that a bell choir does not meet the standard of "music," but what about a set of wind chimes suspended on a front porch? Do those qualify as producing "music?" Perhaps it is the pitches that matter. Some enthusiasts might say that carefully selected wind chimes, perhaps those with the pitches of a Major Pentatonic Scale (C D E G A) qualify as music, but randomly selected pipes which produce pitches that are dissonant or out of tune are just "making noise." In the Bible, both priests and military horses wore garments adorned with golden bells. (Exodus 28:34, Zechariah 14:20) Do those rise to the standard of "music?"

What about the *shofar*, the hollowed-out ram's horn blown like a trumpet? An average person playing a *shofar* is only capable of producing one or two pitches. Even a skilled musician can likely only produce three or four pitches. Despite a given *shofar's* limited number of possible pitches, they always sound harmoniously, arpeggiating a Major chord. Some might say this narrow range means that the *shofar* cannot be classified as a musical instrument, but before the invention of the piston valve in the early 19th century, European classical trumpeters performed virtuosically while facing a similar limitation.

Maybe *how* the instrument is being used makes a difference. Perhaps when a *shofar* is sounded to signals troops in battle, it is not a musical instrument, but when that same *shofar* is sustained harmoniously over songs of worship, it *is* a musical instrument.

The Oxford English Dictionary defines music as "the art of combining vocal or instrumental sounds (or both) to produce beauty of form, harmony, and expression of emotion."[2] Musicians and musicologists have long struggled to define "music" because none of the definitions offered seem to adequately describe the music of Plainchant, Ludwig van Beethoven, Peking Opera, the Beatles, Ghanaian drum ensembles, Karlheinz Stockhausen, AC/DC, Eminem, John Cage, Miles Davis, and Billie Eilish, yet all are considered to be great examples of music by their fans.

The most problematic aspect of the Oxford definition is the highly subjective term "beauty." Tastes and examples of excellence in Oxford's noted criteria—form, harmony, and emotion—are often unique to the cultures that produce a specific variety of music. Some fans of Beethoven are all too often left more confused than moved following their first exposure to Peking Opera. How many times have you heard someone say that heavy metal or rap *isn't music?* When I explain to my university music students that Karlheinz Stockhausen, Brian Wilson, Paul McCartney, and John Lennon were pioneers in the approaches that would later lead to the hip-hop genre (which I always follow with a performance of Stockhausen's "Studie I" or the Beatles' "Revolution 9"), I often hear a retort along the lines of "that isn't even music."

So where does one draw the line between *sound* and *music*? The only way to move forward using the term *music* with any universality is to simply accept that sounds become music when listened to by people who *take those sounds to be music*. In conducting research for this book, the sound examples that *I* took as music were any instances in the Bible in which sound was *controlled*. This included plucking and strumming stringed instruments, blowing wind instruments, striking or shaking drum and percussion instruments, as well as singing, chanting, or heightened speech of any kind. However, it should be noted that context is of critical importance. The *shofar* may not sound like music to some listeners when it is used as a civil or military signal, but no one listening to Israeli musician Yonnie Dror play a *shofar* with the Yamma Ensemble would question that it is undeniably a musical instrument capable of conveying great emotion and musicality in the right hands.

What is the Bible?

The Bible, as most people understand it, is the central religious text among all Jews and Christians, as well as an important contribution to the foundation of Islam. The Bible originated as a collection of sacred texts of the Jewish People of Israel, and recounts the story of God's relationship with humanity through the narratives of Adam and Eve; Abraham, Isaac, and Jacob; Moses and the Ten Commandments; the Israelite Kingdom under Saul, David, and Solomon; the exile in Babylon; and the return to Judah, to name a few. In the Christian addition of the New Testament, the texts describe the ministries of Jesus and the apostles, including the many letters of Paul, among others. Certain narrative aspects and figures of the Bible are even recognized within Islam, such as Adam and Eve, as well as Abraham as the father of Ishmael and Isaac.

Despite all believing in the God of the People of Israel, a Jew, Protestant Christian, Catholic, Eastern Orthodox Christian, and a member of the Church of Jesus Christ of Latter-Day Saints, often referred to as "Mormons," all have a different Bible or scriptural canon. In short, the contents and book order of the Bible differs dramatically between Jews and various Christian denominations.

The word "Bible" comes from the Greek *"biblia"* meaning book, yet the Bible is *not* a single book. Rather, it is a collection of books—best understood as a small library or anthology. The individual books of the Bible were originally scrolls made of long stretches of rolled parchment. The modern definition of a "book," as pages sewn or glued together between two covers, more accurately describes a "codex." Some scholars posit that the invention of the codex arose in response to ancient biblical debates among early Christians.[3] If two people were debating a particular biblical verse, it would have been cumbersome to unfurl a lengthy scroll and begin a search for a given passage. It was far easier to cut the scroll into uniform pieces and sew them together. The codex is more compact than a scroll, and the reader may simply flip through the pages to find a relevant section.

The invention of the codex led to some important decisions regarding which books were to be included in the Bible, as well as the order in which they should appear. When scrolls were kept in a basket in the Temple in Jerusalem or in a synagogue, it was easy to decide that the Book of Daniel, for example, should be included in the collection of Holy Writings one day, then change one's mind the next day and take Daniel out of the basket, and later change one's mind again the following day and put it back in. However, once the pages had been sewn together, such choices suddenly had an air of finality. This led to the establishment of a biblical canon—an official list and order of the books that are included in the Bible.

The Jewish canon, which is to say, the Bible according to Jews, contains twenty-four books arranged into three sections:

Torah (Law)	Nevi'im (Prophets)	Ketuvim (Writings)
Genesis	Joshua	Psalms
Exodus	Judges	Proverbs
Leviticus	Samuel	Job
Numbers	Kings	Song of Songs
Deuteronomy	Isaiah	Ruth
	Jeremiah	Lamentations
	Ezekiel	Ecclesiastes
	The Twelve^א	Esther
		Daniel
		Ezra-Nehemiah
		Chronicles

The books of Samuel, Kings, Chronicles, and Ezra-Nehemiah were each originally one book telling a single, unified story. Later, due to limited scroll length, they were split into two separate scrolls. Samuel, Kings, and Chronicles were divided into "first" and "second" volumes, though they should still be read and understood as one literary work. Ezra-Nehemiah was also split into two scrolls, though the first scroll was titled Ezra and the second titled Nehemiah. They, too, should be read and understood as one work. The same is not

---

^א One collection containing the books of Hosea, Joel, Amos, Obadiah, Jonah, Micah, Nahum, Habakkuk, Zephaniah, Haggai, Zechariah, and Malachi.

true of the Christian New Testament. Books of the New Testament with names such as 1 Corinthians and 2 Corinthians, or 1 John, 2 John, 3 John, represent individual letters that were written at different times, though Christian tradition has attributed them to the same author or audience.

These three sections of the Jewish Bible—Torah, Nevi'im, and Ketuvim—are often abbreviated in Hebrew with the acronym "TNK," or its more pronounceable variant, *Tanakh* (tah-nah-kh). When a person refers to the *Tanakh*, they are referring to the complete Jewish Bible. The use of the Greek term "Pentateuch" or the Hebrew term "Chumash" should only be understood as the collection of Genesis, Exodus, Leviticus, Numbers, and Deuteronomy.

When the books listed above were translated into the Greek collection known as the *Septuagint* (often abbreviated as LXX, marking the tradition that seventy translators produced this version of the Bible), they were arranged into a codex and given a different order. This is the order that would come to be known as the Christian "Old Testament." These are the same books as the Jewish Tanakh, but in a different sequence.

While the following list contains the same literature as the Jewish Scriptures, the books of Samuel, Kings, Chronicles, and Ezra-Nehemiah were each divided into two separate books. For example: 1 Samuel and 2 Samuel. The Book of the Twelve was divided so that each of the twelve prophets were separated into individual books.

Listed below is the book order as it appears in Protestant Bibles:

Pentateuch	Historical Books	Wisdom Literature
Genesis	Joshua	Job
Exodus	Judges	Psalms
Leviticus	Ruth	Proverbs
Numbers	1 Samuel	Ecclesiastes
Deuteronomy	2 Samuel	Song of Solomon
	1 Kings	
	2 Kings	
	1 Chronicles	
	2 Chronicles	
	Ezra	
	Nehemiah	
	Esther	

The Major Prophets	The Minor Prophets
Isaiah	Hosea
Jeremiah	Joel
Lamentations	Amos
Ezekiel	Obadiah
Daniel	Jonah
	Micah
	Nahum,
	Habakkuk
	Zephaniah
	Haggai
	Zechariah
	Malachi

While the aforementioned books comprise the Old Testament as it appears in Protestant Bibles, Catholic Bibles include the additional books of Tobit, Judith, 1 Maccabees, 2 Maccabees, Wisdom, Sirach, and Baruch. The Eastern Orthodox Church and Latin *Vulgate* also include those seven texts, as well as three more: 1 Esdras, the Prayer of Manasseh, and Psalm 151. Lastly, the *Vulgate* additionally includes 4 Esdras (2 and 3 Esdras are Ezra and Nehemiah), and 3 and 4 Maccabees.

Additionally, Christian Bibles contain the collection of books known as the "New Testament." The New Testament was written centuries later, during the Greco-Roman occupation of Judah (also called Judea). Unlike the Hebrew Bible which was written in Hebrew (and occasionally Aramaic), the New Testament was written exclusively in Greek. In total, the biblical canon can range from twenty-four to fifty-one books, depending on whether it belongs to the Jewish tradition or one of the Christian denominations of Protestant, Catholic, or Eastern Orthodox.

The Greek texts of the Christian New Testament describe the ministries of Jesus and the apostles. These texts are:

Gospels/Historical	Epistles	Eschatological
Matthew	Romans	Revelation
Mark	1 Corinthians	
Luke	2 Corinthians	
John	Galatians	
Acts of the Apostles	Ephesians	
	Philippians	
	Colossians	
	1 Thessalonians	
	2 Thessalonians	
	1 Timothy	
	2 Timothy	
	Titus	
	Philemon	
	Hebrews	
	James	
	1 Peter	
	2 Peter	
	1 John	
	2 John	
	3 John	
	Jude	

Later still, the canon was expanded by Joseph Smith, an American who established the Church of Jesus Christ of Latter-Day Saints (LDS) in 1830 C.E. The LDS canon includes the English additions of:

Book of Mormon
Doctrine and Covenants
Pearl of Great Price

To more than two billion people, some combination of these books is held as Scripture or "holy writings." But just as "sound only becomes music to a person who *takes it as music*," written works only become Scripture to those who *take them as Scripture*.[4] The New Testament is not Scripture to the Jewish People, nor is the Book of Mormon Scripture to Protestant, Catholic, or Eastern Orthodox Christians. This book will focus exclusively on the collection of books that are revered as Scripture to *all* Jews and Christians. This collection, known as the *Tanakh* or as the "Old Testament," will henceforth be referred to using the theologically-unbiased term "Hebrew Bible." At times, the terms "Bible" and "Scripture" will also be used for linguistic variety to refer to the aforementioned collection of twenty-four books (or thirty-nine books by the Christian division) which are common to all Jewish and Christian religious groups.

Research Approach

The first phase of this research was critically and carefully reading the Bible in its entirety in English, noting and analyzing every reference to music. However, it quickly became apparent that this was not the most effective way to study a biblical subject as technical and specific as music. The problem is that when comparing multiple translations, such as the Jewish Publication Society (JPS),⁽ᴬ⁾ New Revised Standard Version (NRSV), New International Version (NIV), ArtScroll's Stone Edition (Stone), King James Version (KJV), New King James Version (NKJV), New American Standard Bible (NASB), New Living Translation (NLT), et cetera, there are numerous translation discrepancies. For example, the first two instruments mentioned in the Bible are found in Genesis 4:21. In the KJV, one of the oldest English translations of the Christian Bible, the two instruments are listed as "harp and organ." In the NIV, they are listed as "stringed instruments and pipes" (notice the plural names). In the NASB, they are called "lyre and flute." Results are equally inconsistent in Jewish English translations. The JPS uses the names "lyre and pipe" while the Stone writes "harp and flute."

In short, none of the translators seem to agree on what these instruments actually were. There seem to be a few contributing reasons for translational differences.

The first reason is the available resources during the translation process. When the King James Version was first printed in 1611, its translators had access to far fewer documents

---

ᴬ In this book, the terms "Jewish Publication Society" and its abbreviation "JPS," will always refer to the the New Jewish Publication Society translation first published in 1985, not the original Jewish Publication Society translation printed in 1917.

and resources than translators today. The translators of the KJV all too often anachronistically inserted their own contemporary instruments, such as the organ, sackbut and cornet, into the biblical text.

The second reason is that many translations are theologically charged. Verses have been, at times, interpreted and translated to fit the theology of the translators. Examine, for instance, the wildly varying language of Psalm 22:16 or Isaiah 7:14 throughout different translations based on the theological motivations (or lack thereof) of the translators.

The third reason is that some Bible translations are simply not concerned with such technical accuracy for a legitimate and understandable reason: they want the text to be accessible to all readers. In order to comprehend the biblical text, there are Bibles published with simplified and/or modernized language for new readers or those at a lower reading level. Some Bible versions aim for word-for-word translations, while others opt to convey more general ideas, such as thought-for-thought paraphrasing. On the spectrum of Bible translations, those which employ a *word-for-word* translation are referred to as "formal equivalency," while those that attempt a *thought-for-thought* translation are referred to as "dynamic equivalency." An extreme example of dynamic equivalency in a Protestant Christian Bible would be the Message Bible (MSG) or The Living Bible (TLB). Moving toward Formal Equivalency, the New Living Translation (NLT), followed by the New International Version (NIV) are moderate, but still considered part of the Dynamic Equivalency spectrum. While translations such as the English Standard Bible (ESV) and New American Standard Bible (NASB) are examples of Formal Equivalency, an "interlinear Bible," which displays the text in its original language, a transliteration of the original language ("transliteration" means writing the word phonetically using

English letters), and the English equivalent of that word. Both translation approaches have benefits as well as deficiencies. The seemingly clumsy syntax of extreme Formal Equivalencies often prove difficult to read, but the extreme Dynamic Equivalencies often distort the actual text in favor of readability for new or young audiences.

miz·mō·wr	lə·ḏā·wiḏ;		Yah·weh	rō·'î,	lō	'eḥ·sār.
מִזְמוֹר	לְדָוִד	.	יְהוָה	רֹעִי	לֹא	אֶחְסָר׃
A Psalm	of David		Yahweh [is]	my shepherd	not	I shall want
N-ms	Prep-l | N-proper-ms		N-proper-ms	V-Qal-Prtcpl-msc | 1cs	Adv-NegPrt	V-Qal-Imperf-1cs

An interlinear version of Psalm 23:1.[5]

With these three points to consider, the most reliable English translation for scholarly research is 1) modern enough that it utilizes all of the available sources, 2) theologically unbiased, aiming to convey the true and unadulterated meaning of the text, and 3) one that is between moderate and formal on the spectrum of Dynamic and Formal Equivalency. Based on these criteria, the two best translations for this research are the Jewish Publication Society (JPS) and the New Revised Standard Version (NRSV). The former is a Jewish translation, while the latter is from a Christian perspective, but both fulfill the requisite criteria for the purposes of this research.

These two English Bibles have served as the cornerstone translations for this research. However, reading these translations side-by-side led to the identification of a fourth cause of translational discrepancies: that all translations—antiquated and modern, Jewish and Christian, theologically-charged and academically objective—make the critical mistake of describing music from a strictly contemporary Western perspective. When any modern citizen of the Western world reads the word "harp," they likely imagine some variation of a concert harp, such as the one shown here.

A modern concert harp.

To see an example of this anachronistic Eurocentrism, look no further than Domenico Zampieri's 1619 painting "King David Playing the Harp," which shows a fair-skinned David playing a 17th century European harp.

"King David Playing the Harp," Domenico Zampieri

In actuality, David's instrument shared almost no similarities with the concert harps of Europe. Similarly, there were no tambourines or timbrels in ancient Israel, yet those are the terms which most translators use to describe the instrument of Miriam. (Exodus 15:20) To fully understand and appreciate biblical instruments as they actually existed, readers must remove the Western lens through which all English translations portray music in the Bible. To do this, one must engage with the scriptural texts in their original languages, which led to phase two of my research.

The second research phase was studying the Bible in Hebrew (and occasionally Aramaic) in order to read musical passages in their original language and context and identify all 547 musical references. Through this process, I developed an original translation of the musical references contained in the Bible based on a musicological approach. Throughout this book, I have incorporated my own music translations of the Hebrew into English when appropriate, although I am a fervent advocate for using the original names of instruments, rather than those of their closest European cousin. This is because musicians and music scholars use the vernacular/vocabulary of any given culture when referring to its musical instruments. For example, the Peruvian *cajón* is not referred to as a "box drum." The Indian *sitar* and *tabla* are not called a "guitar and drums." The Chinese *pipa* is not called a "lute." Why, therefore, should the instruments of ancient Israel be referred to by the names of their European counterparts? Among other goals, the following pages aim to familiarize audiences with the true Hebrew names of all biblical instruments.

The third phase of this research project involved reading all available literature on this topic. Surprisingly, relatively little has been written on the subject of biblical music. One exception is Jonathan L. Friedmann, who has made significant contributions to the field of bibliomusicology over the last decade. While there is a small collection of indispensable bibliomusicological books from the last 100 years, the two that were most pertinent were *Music in Ancient Israel* by Alfred Sendrey (1969) and *Music in Ancient Israel/Palestine* by Joachim Braun (1998). Additionally, *The Music of the Bible Revealed* by Suzanne Haïk-Vantoura (1976) is one of the most interesting bibliomusicological reads in the field. In terms of general biblical scholarship, the works of Richard Elliot Freidman, Christine Hayes, and Gary A. Rendsburg are worthy of study. Despite this book's focus on the Hebrew Bible, New Testament scholars Dale B. Martin and Bart D. Ehrman also played a significant role in understanding the music of ancient Israel during the Greco-Roman era (4th Century B.C.E. to the 4th Century C.E.), particularly for their ability to describe Second Temple Judaism and the Greco-Roman influence on Judea with detailed brevity. Ancient authors, including Josephus, Plutarch, Philo, and Tacitus, as well as the Scribes of ben-Asher, Rashi, and the authors of the Talmud similarly provide indispensable accounts of biblical music, as well as perspectives from various historical periods.

TRANSLATION AND TRANSLITERATION

Unless otherwise specified, all English Bible *translation* quotes in this book are sourced from the Jewish Publication Society, or, in the case of musical terms, are the product of my own translation.[6]

Most *transliterations* herein, including all musical terminology, are the author's own, and are based on modern Hebrew pronunciation. The only exceptions are commonly used English transliterations and spellings, such as "Moses," "Bethlehem," "Solomon," and "Esther," instead of *Moshe*, *Beit Lechem*, *Shlomo*, and *Ester*, respectively. Readers may notice that some transliterations differ from those used by prominent biblical music scholars like the aforementioned Alfred Sendrey and Joachim Braun; for example, the transliteration of נֵבֶל as *nevel* instead of *nebel*. All transliteration decisions were made to accurately portray a modern phonetic English representation of Hebrew words.

Some guidelines for reading Hebrew transliteration:

- In this book, silent consonant letters will always be transliterated based on the associated vowels from the Masoretic text.
- ח (chet) will always be represented with the letters "ch" and should be pronounced as a harsh "h" sound, as though clearing one's throat, as in "Johann Sebastian Ba*ch*," "*Ch*anukah," or "*ch*utzpah."
- כ (kaph) without the dagesh, will always be represented with the letters "kh," and should also be pronounced with a harsh "h" sound.

MUSIC IN EACH BOOK OF THE BIBLE

Throughout this book, each musical topic will be described in biblical chronological order. However, to add context to those descriptions, the following two tables outline the number of musical references in each book of Scripture. There is a total of 547 musical references throughout the Hebrew Bible. In this study, a "musical reference" is any musical word. This includes names of instruments, words related to playing music, descriptions of singing, and adjectives which describe music. Some verses contain more than one musical reference. For example, Genesis 4:21, the first musical verse of the Bible, contains two musical references. These will be represented in the Appendix as Genesis 4:21 A and Genesis 4:21 B. However, on a few occasions, when two musical words combine to create one musical idea, such as *nevel asor* (ten-stringed harp) or *Shir Ha'Shirim* (Song of Songs), they are treated as a single musical reference. The tables that follow also list the total musical percentage accounted for by each book in relational to all 547 musical references in the Bible.

(see next page)

TABLE 1:
MUSICAL REFERENCES IN EACH BOOK OF THE BIBLE

Book	Occurrences	Percentage
Torah/Pentateuch	**42**	**7.70%**
Genesis	5	0.91%
Exodus	15	2.74%
Leviticus	3	0.55%
Numbers	15	2.74%
Deuteronomy	4	0.73%
Nevi'im/Prophets	**126**	**23.03%**
Joshua	16	2.93%
Judges	14	2.56%
1 Samuel	14	2.56%
2 Samuel	16	2.93%
1 Kings	8	1.46%
2 Kings	6	1.10%
Isaiah	24	4.39%
Jeremiah	7	1.28%
Ezekiel	7	1.28%
Hosea	3	0.55%
Joel	2	0.37%
Amos	6	1.10%
Obadiah	0	0%
Jonah	0	0%
Micah	0	0%
Nahum	0	0%
Habakkuk	0	0%
Zephaniah	1	0.18%
Haggai	0	0%
Zechariah	2	0.37%
Malachi	0	0%

Ketuvim/Writings	**377**	**69.17%**
Psalms	236	43.30%
Proverbs	0	0%
Job	8	1.46%
Song of Songs[2]	1	0.18%
Ruth	0	0%
Lamentations	0	0%
Ecclesiastes	0	0%
Esther	0	0%
Daniel	27	4.94%
Ezra	3	0.55%
Nehemiah	15	2.74%
1 Chronicles	49	8.99%
2 Chronicles	42	7.68%

---

[2] Song of Songs is listed as one musical reference, but with 117 verses, it is one of the longest musical examples in the Bible, second only to the Book of Psalms.

TABLE 2:

BOOKS OF THE BIBLE IN ORDER OF MUSICAL REFERENCES

1.	Psalms	236	43.14%
2.	Chronicles	91	16.64%
3.	Samuel	30	5.49%
4.	Daniel	27	4.94%
5.	Isaiah	24	4.39%
6.	Ezra-Nehemiah	18	3.30%
7.	Joshua	16	2.93%
8.	Exodus	15	2.74%
9.	Numbers	15	2.74%
10.	Judges	14	2.56%
11.	The Twelve	14	2.56%
12.	Kings	14	2.56%
13.	Job	8	1.46%
14.	Jeremiah	7	1.28%
15.	Ezekiel	7	1.28%
16.	Genesis	5	0.91%
17.	Deuteronomy	4	0.73%
18.	Leviticus	3	0.55%
19.	Song of Songs	1	0.18%
20.	Proverbs	0	0.00%
21.	Ruth	0	0.00%
22.	Lamentations	0	0.00%
23.	Ecclesiastes	0	0.00%
24.	Esther	0	0.00%

WHAT IS THE PURPOSE OF THIS BOOK?

Music in the Bible addresses the instrumentation, functionality, tonality, and notation of music as described in the Bible. The biblical narrative is augmented with extrabiblical sources when appropriate. This book's goal is to provide the most complete and accurate portrait of music from the biblical era as possible, based on all available sources. From the onset, this is not a *religious* book. Rather, it is about the depiction, historical background, and context of music in a collection of texts revered as holy writings by roughly one-third of the world's population.

This book aims to accept the Bible at face value and explore corroborative evidence in the Bible's own historical context. Braun writes that the Bible is a work of mythology.[7] While he is not alone in his position, this statement is problematic. To millions of Jews and Christians around the world, the Bible holds inherent truth. Readers who take the Bible as Scripture have been without a scholarly resource of serious academic merit that describes music's roles in biblical Israel. In this text, I do not comment on any aspect of historicity that is not related to music in the Bible or that cannot be supported by archeological evidence or corroborating sources. Biblical stories will be examined as literature and placed in their original historical context when appropriate. My intent is that readers who take every word of Scripture as literal truth, as well as readers who are not religious, but interested in biblical music from an anthropological or musicological perspective, will all find this book accessible, respectful, and interesting.

Acknowledgments

I am hardly the first person to study and write about this topic. This work would not have been possible if not for the landmark contributions of men and women like the late Alfred Sendrey, Joachim Braun, Suzanne Haïk-Vantoura, Solomon Rosowsky, Jeremy Montagu, John Stainer, Abraham Idelsohn, Saul Levin, nor the modern contributions of Emanuel Rubin, John H. Baron, Jonathan L. Friedmann, and Joel Gereboff. I, along with the entire field of bibliomusicology, am indebted to these scholars for their invaluable contributions.

I must also acknowledge my amazing colleagues, friends, and family who read various drafts of this book, offering insight and clarity along the way. In alphabetical order:

Rabbi Benj Fried, M.Div.

Corey H. Marco, M.D., J.D.

Joni Marco, J.D.

Pastor Andy Lopez, M.A.

Dafna Meller, M.A.

Taylor Smith, Ph.D. (Musicology)

I would also like to thank my wife, Michelle, for embarking on this research project with me and providing thoughtful and thought-provoking questions. Her background as a concert harpist and her degree in Art History from Stanford University both provided me with an indispensable home resource.

These readers each brought a unique perspective to this text and undeniably improved and enhanced the final manuscript.

Listen to advice and accept discipline, and at the end,
you will be counted among the wise.
Proverbs 19:20.

CHAPTER 2

VOCAL MUSIC

Music played an important role throughout the biblical narrative and was equally important within ancient Israelite society. There are an astounding 547 references to music throughout the Bible (though 261 [48%] of the references specifically describe instrumental music). This figure should not come as a surprise when one considers that music has been documented in every culture which has ever been studied.[8] Dr. Norman M. Weinberger, a Ph.D. and professor of neurobiology and behavior at the University of California, Irvine, notes that:

> . . . Our fondness [for music] has deep roots: we have been making music since the dawn of culture. More than 30,000 years ago, early humans were already playing bone flutes, percussive instruments and jaw harps—and all known societies throughout the world have had music. Indeed, our appreciation appears to be innate. Infants as young as two months will turn toward consonant, or pleasant, sounds and away from dissonant ones. And the same kinds of pleasure centers light up in

a person's brain whether he or she is getting chills listening to a symphony's denouement or eating chocolate or having sex or taking cocaine.[9]

Any person who has witnessed a crying baby's calm when her father sings to her, or a toddler bopping along to a rhythmic groove, cannot deny that music is innate. The universality of music within the human experience goes even further: every culture has vocal music. This is as true for the ancient Israelites depicted in the Bible as it is for any culture. Learning to play a musical instrument is a skill that takes years to master, but anyone and everyone can sing. Further, when your instrument is your own voice, you always have your instrument with you.

It is difficult to determine exactly how many instances there are to vocal music in the Bible because in biblical Hebrew, the words for "music," "song," and "sing" all share the same root word of *shir*. In some instances, *shir* refers to singing, but in others, it clearly refers to instrumental music. Therefore, the question must be refined in two ways:

1) How many times are specific Hebrew words associated with vocal music used?

2) How many times does a given English Bible interpret and translate a passage as relating to singing?

There are two primary Hebrew root words related to music and singing. The first, *shir*, can describe any type of song. The second, *zamer*, specifically describes a sacred song. Additionally, the word "psalm" is used in English Bibles in place of the Hebrew word *mizmor*, which is a derivative of *zamer*.

Interestingly, the root word *shir* can serve as a noun or a verb, and can even be conjugated to convey numerous musical meanings. Below is a short collection of the many ways in which *shir* can be conjugated to mean a variety of musical terms.

Shir	JPS Tranlation	Chapter:Verse
shirim	music/songs	Genesis 31:27
ya'shir	sang (or "will sing")	Exodus 15:1
shirah	song/poem	Exodus 15:1
shiru	sing	Exodus 15:2
va'tashar	will sing (or sang)	Judges 5:1
la'shir	singing	1 Samuel 18:6
sharim*	singing	2 Samuel 19:36
shir	song	2 Samuel 22:1
sharim*	musicians	1 Kings 10:12
shirahyikh	songs	Ezekiel 26:13
mesher'rim	singers	Nehemiah 12:28
meshem'im	playing	1 Chronicles 15:28
meshre'rim	singers	2 Chronicles 5:12
meshrarim	singers	2 Chronicles 20:21
meshorarim	singers	2 Chronicles 23:13
mash'me'im	playing	1 Chronicles 15:28
" "	sound	1 Chronicles 16:42
m'shorer	sung	2 Chronicles 5:42

TABLE 3:
HEBREW TERMS TRANSLATED AS SINGING IN THE BIBLE

1. Shir
2. Zamer
3. Rata'an
4. Lemor
5. Odekha
6. Mon
7. Portim
8. Oreh
9. Kol
10. Higayin
11. Ranu
12. Tehilla
13. Hallel
14. Huyeldot
15. Mesherim
16. <u>Lehedot</u>

TABLE 4:
VOCAL, INSTRUMENTAL, AND OTHER MUSIC REFERENCES

Vocal	152
Instrumental	293

Additionally, all 99 musical headings found within the Book of Psalms indicate singing. Of those 99, the 57 which are labeled as a *mizmor* also indicate stringed instrumental accompaniment.

Mizmor	57
Other musical Psalm headings	42

These additions bring the totals to:

Vocal	251	45.9%
Instrumental	350[7]	64.2%
Other	3	0.5%

---

[7] Remember that *mizmor* counts toward both vocal and instrumental and therefore, there is some crossover between the two.

TABLE 5:
REFERENCES TO SINGING IN ENGLISH BIBLE TRANSLATIONS

Jewish Publication Society	203
New Revised Standard Version	200
King James Version	201
Average	201.3

The fact that these figures are relatively close—203, 200, and 201 in English leads to two important observations for studying music in the Bible: everyone *generally* agrees, but no one agrees *completely*. This book will evaluate the discrepancies which have led scholars and translators to arrive at different conclusions, as well as empower readers to arrive at their own conclusions about music in the Bible.

Music may be part of every culture, but let's examine why *vocal music* is so prevalent across human history.

1) As mentioned above, the human body, including the voice, is the one musical instrument that a person always has with them. Unlike a drum, lyre, or horn, people can sing anytime and anywhere. The same is also true of body percussion, such as clapping and stomping. Freddie Mercury, Brian May, Roger Taylor, and John Deacon of Queen fully understood this, as is evident by their recording of "We Will Rock You"—a song that never fails to generate audience participation from an entire stadium.

2) Communal singing offers an important form of social bonding. In the above example of "We Will Rock You," audience members at a Queen concert or professional sporting event often feel a sense of unity experienced upon participating in a synchronized, 10,000-person strong

stomp-stomp-clap, stomp-stomp-clap, and join together in a raucous chorus of *"We will, we will rock you!"*ה In fact, thanks to the real-time data on brain activity provided by Functional Magnetic Resonance Imaging (FMRI) and Positron Emission Tomography (PET), neuroscientists who studied musicians playing music observed that the musicians' brains "simultaneously [process] different information in intricate, interrelated, and astonishingly fast sequences" across the visual, auditory, and motor cortices, as well as across both hemispheres of the brain.[10] Additionally, a 2020 study conducted as a collaboration between East China Normal University, Harbin Conservatory of Music, and the Karolinska Institutet in Stockholm, showed that when a group of musicians perform together, not only is the musicians' brain activity synchronized, but so is the brain activity of the audience listening.[11] Whether it is an audience singing along with Queen at Wembley Stadium, or the Israelites worshiping at the Temple in Jerusalem, every person in attendance is neurologically aligned with synchronized brain activity for the duration of the musical experience as a result of making music together.

ה The Bible also describes musical clapping in Psalm 47:2 (or 47:1, depending on the translation.

3) Singing, or the closely related "heightened speech," can convey far greater emotion and drama than speech alone. Imagine one of your favorite songs that always moves you. Would you experience the same sensation by only reading the lyrics as you would listening to a recording of the song itself? The power of melody, harmony, and rhythm can transform the recitation of text into a powerful, emotional, or cathartic experience.

4) The final reason that singing plays such a critical role in music around the world, and especially in social and communal music, is that amateur singers may participate without a high degree of skill or specialized training. As long as they can match pitch and keep a steady beat (and even if they can't in many cases), a congregation of people can always join together in song.

SHIR

Despite its ninety-eight occasions being most frequently translated as "music," the Hebrew root word שִׁיר or *shir* (pronounced "sheer") held a far broader definition in ancient Israel than the word "music" holds for modern English speakers. Remember that The Oxford English Dictionary defines "music" as "vocal or instrumental sounds (or both) combined in such a way as to produce beauty of form, harmony, and expression of emotion."[12] The Hebrew word *shir* certainly encompasses that meaning, but *shir* can also mean "song." In English, "music" and "song" are not interchangeable. As most people understand the terms, a "song" has more specific parameters and is a concrete, identifiable expression of music. Formally trained musicians also differentiate "song" to mean music with sung lyrics, while music that is solely instrumental is not a "song," but rather a "piece." For example, "Come Together" by the Beatles is a song, but Niccolò Paganini's violin solo "Caprice No. 5 in A minor" is a piece of music.

As mentioned earlier, the word *shir* appears in the Bible ninety-eight times. Throughout numerous English translations of the Bible, *shir* is at times rendered as "poem." Now the differences in meaning are more pronounced. Despite her impassioned and moving delivery, no one would listen to Youth Poet Laureate Amanda Gorman's recitation of her work "The Hill We Climb" and think to themselves, "That was a such moving *song*." The middle ground between spoken word and singing is an ancient practice called "heightened speech." When reciting text with heightened speech, the speaker will impart their words with a musical and rhythmic cadence. The speaker may even linger on specific, identifiable pitches, offering to the text an air of melody.

To modern ears, heightened speech lies somewhere in between speech and song. To ancient Israelites, as well as all other Near Eastern and Middle Eastern cultures, heightened speech was one of the primary means of public scriptural recitation and prayer. Therefore, even a "poem," a text that was not perceived as "music," per se, would still have been delivered in a manner that might be indistinguishable from singing to the modern ear. Further, every line of text from the Hebrew Bible is accompanied by a system of musical notation called *te'amim,* the primary focus of Chapter Nine. When a pastor reads from the Hebrew Bible or "Old Testament" in a church today, the text is simply read aloud. Perhaps done so with great passion and animation, but nonetheless read as one would read from any other book. However, when those same lines of Scripture are recited by a rabbi or cantor in a synagogue, they are always sung based on the ancient melodies preserved in written record by a group of scribes called the Masoretes more than 1,000 years ago.

One way to reconcile this translational challenge is to accept that vocal music was so ubiquitous in ancient Israel that if someone referred to "music," unless otherwise specified, *of course* singing was involved. Therefore, throughout the rest of this chapter, I will highlight instances in which an alternative word has been translated as "singing." However, I will ask you to accept that for the Israelites, singing and the performance and recitation of music were one and the same because singing was nearly always an essential component of music.

The text of Scripture is intended to be recited in song, rather than read like any other book. For more than 1,000 years, every single word, verse, chapter and book of the *Tanakh*, known as the "Old Testament" to Christians, has featured musical notation below the text. Let that sink in. There is a *notated melody* included below every line of Scripture within the Hebrew Bible.

As an example, consider this excerpt from Deuteronomy 6:4:

שְׁמַ֥ע יִשְׂרָאֵ֖ל יְהוָ֣ה אֱלֹהֵ֑ינוּ יְהוָ֥ה ׀ אֶחָֽד׃

Based on the ancient musical tradition, this melody would be recited today as:

Hear, O Israel! The LORD is our God, the LORD alone.

In this excerpt, C is the tonal center. Notice the lack of a time signature or bar lines. This reflects the secondary role rhythm plays to melody in the ancient Near East. The rhythm would follow the natural flow of the text.

Some readers may notice that this is not one of the "traditional" melodies used to sing the *Sh'ma* in many synagogues. One of the most commonly recited melodies today was written in the 19th century by Austrian composer Salomon Sulzer. Sulzer's *Sh'ma* arrangement was introduced in his *Shir Tziyon* (Songs of Zion) collection, written and published between 1840 and 1865 C.E. As Debbie Friedman and numerous others would do 150 years later, Sulzer sought to modernize Jewish liturgical music with refreshing, contemporary melodies and chord progressions. His original melodies are not related to or based upon the trope or *te'amim*.

Salomon Sulzer's "Sh'ma"

VOCAL MUSIC IN THE BIBLE AND OTHER TERMS FOR MUSIC

VOCAL MUSIC IN THE TORAH (PENTATEUCH)

The following pages will chronicle every instance of vocal music in the Bible, examine the specific Hebrew word utilized, and explain its context within the biblical narrative. This section will proceed through Scripture in the chronological Jewish order found in all Hebrew language versions of the Bible. When a particular book contains no references to vocal music, I will write, for example: "The Book of Ruth contains no mention of vocal music." If your preferred version or Bible translation *does* mention singing other than the instances recounted within this chapter, that indicates a translational discrepancy in which translators inserted a mention of singing that does not actually exist. Perhaps surprisingly, such additions do occur frequently in some English versions. For a complete list of musical passages in the Bible, see the Appendix on page 297.

VOCAL MUSIC IN THE BOOK OF GENESIS

The first biblical reference to singing is in Genesis 31:27. Jacob, the son of Isaac and the grandson of Abraham, is fleeing from Laban, the father of Jacob's two wives, Leah and Rachel. Laban confronts Jacob for leaving without notice and for taking Laban's daughters. Laban asks Jacob,

> *Why did you flee in secrecy and mislead me and not tell me?*
> *I would have sent you off with festive shirim (music/songs),*
> *with tof (drum) and kinnor (often translated as "lyre").*[1]
>
> Genesis 31:27

This use of the word *shirim* is indicative of the challenges of defining the root word *shir*. Remember, *shir* means both "music" and "singing." In the JPS translation above, the translators used the word "music." However, the NRSV, Stone, and KJV all translate *shirim* as "songs." The NIV and NLT use the broader "songs and music." The mention of a *tof* (drum) and *kinnor*

---

[1] In the instance of Genesis 31:27, *kinnor* would more accurately be transliterated as *khinnor*. The rational for maintaining the *"kinnor"* spelling will be described in Chapter 3.

("lyre") inform the reader that, in this example, singing is accompanied by musical instruments. This verse is the only mention of singing in the Book of Genesis.

Vocal Music in the Book of Exodus

The next two examples of singing both come from Exodus 15:1, after Moses and the Israelites escape Pharaoh's army via the Reed Sea (often mistranslated as "Red Sea"). The chapter opens with:

Then Moses and the Israelites sang this song (ya'shir) to the LORD. They said: I will sing (et ha'shirah) to the LORD, for He has triumphed gloriously; Horse and driver He has hurled into the sea.

Exodus 15:1

As previously mentioned, the entire Hebrew Bible includes the *te'amim* musical notation, and should be sung, not merely spoken. However, Moses's "Song of the Sea," as it has come to be known, is the first example of a "song" as modern people understand the meaning. However, neither its form nor its structure resembles a modern song. There are no repeated sections, no AABA or verse-chorus arrangements. Exodus 15 offers a prime example of a "song" in the ancient world.

The "Song of the Sea" is the source for two of the most important Jewish liturgical texts: the "Mi Chamocha" (Who is Like You?) (Exodus 15:11) and "Ozi v'Zimrat Yah" (The LORD is my Strength and Song) (Exodus 15:2). The "Mi Chamocha" prayer is recited in synagogues during both evening and morning Shabbat services and on major holidays. Curiously, the phrase "*Ozi v'zimrat Yah*" is often translated as "The LORD is my strength and *might*," despite the fact that the root of *"zimrat"* is *"zamer,"* which means "song of praise."[13] Even though practically every English Bible translation continues to write "might," scholars unanimously agree that "The LORD is my strength and *song*" is the more accurate translation. The fact that "song" and "might" are interchanged in some translations could speak to the power of music in the eyes of the biblical authors and translators. This exact phrase is echoed in Psalm 118:14. These two music-themed prayers, the "Mi Chamocha" and "Ozi v'Zimrat Yah," are very important in Judaism. So much so, in fact, that the Shabbat that corresponds with the week when Exodus 15 is studied and read aloud in synagogue is called *Shabbat Shirah* or "The Shabbat of the Song."[14]

When read in a Torah scroll, the "Song of the Sea" appears with a beautiful text pattern to represent the parting waves of the Reed Sea.

The Song of the Sea is featured in the middle column.

Immediately after Moses's song concludes, his sister, the prophetess Miriam, "led all of the women" in their own song of worship celebrating the Israelites' deliverance out of Egypt. (Exodus 15:20-21) In this example of singing, two Hebrew words are used for "sing:" *rata'an* and *shir*. Some English versions translate both terms as "sing," while others translate *rata'an* as "chant." Miriam and the women accompany the song with drums and dancing. Note that in this story, set 3,000 year ago, the *women* are worshiping by singing and playing instruments, not just the men. (Exodus 15:20-21) Both textual and archeological sources corroborate the notion that women were active participants in singing and the playing of instruments in the ancient Near East.[15] Numerous clay figurines of women playing musical instruments—drums, harps, and lutes—have been excavated throughout Israel.[16] (See Chapters Three and Five)

There is no mention of vocal music in the Books of Leviticus or Numbers.

VOCAL MUSIC IN THE BOOK OF DEUTERONOMY

Singing is not mentioned again in the Bible until the end of the Book of Deuteronomy. The Hebrew word *shirah*, a noun variant of *shir,* appears four times from Deuteronomy 31:19-21. After a written record of the Torah is completed, the Israelites are instructed to gather every seven years to listen to a public recitation of Genesis, Exodus, Leviticus, Numbers, and Deuteronomy in their entirety. God tells Moses that he, Moses, is about to die, but gives him one final task. Moses writes down the words to one final *shirah*—forty-three verses—and joins

Joshua as they recite the song to the people of Israel. The Song of Moses, as some call it, takes up the entirety of Deuteronomy 32. This *shirah* of worship praises God and warns about straying from the lessons and laws outlined in God's commandments. The Song of Moses is structured into two columns within Torah scrolls, the only such instance within the entire Bible.

The Song of Moses, Deuteronomy 32

VOCAL MUSIC IN THE NEVI'IM (PROPHETS)

There is no mention of vocal music in the Book of Joshua.

VOCAL MUSIC IN THE BOOK OF JUDGES

The next reference to singing appears in the Book of Judges and introduces a new variation of *shir:* "tashar," which is universally translated as the past tense "sang." (Judges 5:1)

Interestingly, *tashar* means the future-tense feminine, "will sing," to modern Hebrew speakers. The Israelite judge and leader Deborah is joined by her military commander Barak as they sing a song following Israel's victory over the Canaanite king, Jabin. This passage (all of Judges 5), has come to be known as the "Song of Deborah." The "Song of Deborah" is noteworthy is that many leading scholars posit that it may likely be the oldest text in the entire Bible, with the other contender being the Song of the Sea. This is due to its inclusion of Canaanite and Akkadian words and language which pre-date the rest of the biblical vernacular.[17] Within the song, in Judges 5:3, the term *shirah* is used once again, but a new term, *zamer*, appears for the first time. *Zamer* is the root word of *zimrat* used in *"Ozi v'zimrat Yah"* from Exodus 15:2. This word represents another perfect example of the challenges associated with translating musical terms from Hebrew into English; the JPS translates *zamer* as "hymn" or "sacred music," the NRSV and ESV translate it as "melody," the NIV as "song," the NLT as "music," and the KJV as "praise."[†]

VOCAL MUSIC IN THE BOOK OF SAMUEL

Though not an example of vocal music specifically, another term for music, *nagan*, is first used in 1 Samuel 16:18. When rendered as a verb, *nagan* means "to play music." However, it can also be used as a noun to mean "musician." In this first

---

[†] *"Zamer"* is also the root of Klezmer, a 19th century Eastern European Jewish musical style marked by its iconic use of clarinet, violin, and the Hebraic Scale, (see Chapter 9). When the Hebrew word *kle*, meaning "tool," or in this context "instrument," is combined with *zamer*, meaning "music," the result is *kle zamer*, meaning musical instrument.

appearance, *nagan* is used as a verb to describe David playing for Saul. This story will be detailed further in the next chapter on stringed instruments.

In 1 Samuel 18:6, David returns from killing Goliath to sounds of *shir*, dancing, and the playing of instruments, as Israel rejoices and celebrates its victory over Philistia at the hands of the young future king, David.

Later, in 2 Samuel 19:36 (or 19:35, depending on the translation), David has been King of Israel for some time. He meets King Barzillai of Gilead to assist the eighty-year-old ally of Israel in crossing the River Jordan into the Holy Land. Barzillai tells David that due to his advanced years, he has lost his hearing and can no longer listen to *sharim*.

In 2 Samuel 22, readers are introduced to David's "Song of Praise," as it has been designated in some Bibles. Reading like a psalm of thanksgiving, 2 Samuel 22 is a *shir* comprised of fifty-one verses of worship. David expresses his gratitude for God protecting him from his enemies, including Saul. In 2 Samuel 22:50, the term *odekha* is translated as "sing" in some English Bibles, but simply as "praise" in others, though it actually means "to give thanks." *Zamer* is also used in 2 Samuel 22:50, once again as a "hymn" or "sacred song."

Vocal Music in the Book of Kings

By chapter ten of the Book of 1 Kings, David has long since died, and his son Solomon reigns over Israel. Solomon may be most well-known for his wisdom and for realizing David's vision of constructing the first Holy Temple in Jerusalem, but he was also a prolific songwriter to whom 1,005 songs are attributed. (1 Kings 5:12) In a reaction to Solomon's regional fame, the Queen of Sheba, a country which many scholars suggest was likely the Arab country of Saba in modern-day

Yemen,[18] visits Solomon and brings gifts including highly coveted algum wood.[ח] This exotic wood was used to craft musical instruments for the *sharim* or "musicians." Although *sharim* is often translated as "singers," in the case of 1 Kings 10:12, it specifically and clearly refers to instrumentalists.

There were many historical developments in Israel between the previous reference to vocal music in 1 Kings 10:12 and the next references in 2 Kings 3:15. These developments carry with them some changes in terminology, specifically with regard to the name "Israel." To avoid confusion, allow me to briefly fill in some history. The word "Israel" is first used in Genesis 32:29 when Jacob is renamed *"Yisrael"* (Israel), which means "wrestles with God"—a fitting description of Jacob's narrative, as well as that of the Jewish people. Because Jacob's twelve sons were the namesakes for the Twelve Tribes, all of the Tribes are known collectively as the People of Israel or the Nation of Israel. Following the Exodus, the Israelites conquer the land of Canaan.

King David is a descendant of Judah, one of Jacob's twelve sons. After seizing Canaan, David unifies the twelve tribes into a Kingdom called "Israel." The region of Judah, which includes Jerusalem, was just one of twelve areas within Israel. David and Batsheva bear a son named Solomon, who eventually succeeds David as king. As good, godly, and wise as Solomon was as a young king, he spends the latter years of his reign marrying 700 wives for political alliances with other nations, taking on 300 concubines (1 Kings 11:3, 1 Kings 7:8, 1 Kings 11:1), adopting the worship of those women's Gods, accumulating wealth, and using slave labor for building projects. In short, Solomon breaks all of the commandments outlined for an Israelite monarch in Deuteronomy 17. Solomon dies at the end of 1 Kings 11, and

---

[ח] Many scholars agree that algum wood was most likely sandalwood.

1 Kings 12 begins with Solomon's son, King Rehoboam, acting just as his father had. The northern tribes revolted in 930 C.E. under the leadership of Jeroboam, resulting in the north seceding and Israel dividing into two nations: The Northern Kingdom of Israel and the Southern Kingdom of Judah. Jeroboam is anointed king of the north in Israel, while King Rehoboam continues as monarch in Judah. Judah retains the capital city of Jerusalem, while Israel eventually establishes Samaria as its capital.[ʊ]

The story of the famous prophet Elijah and his protégé Elisha takes place three generations after the Northern Kingdom of Israel's secession. In 2 Kings 3:15, Elisha is prophesizing for King Jarom of the Northern Kingdom of Israel. Elisha asks for a *menagen*. Some translations use "musician" while others choose something along the lines of "someone who can play the harp." In the same sense that *shir* can mean both "music" and "singing," *menagen* can mean "musician" or "string player." Stringed instruments such as the *kinnor* and *nevel* (often translated as the "lyre" and "harp") were so ubiquitous with instrumental music in ancient Israel that, more often than not, to be a musician was to be a string player. Another example is in the introduction to Psalms 54 and 55, which both begin with the instruction *bi'neginot*. Some English translations write "with instrumental music," yet others write "with stringed instruments." To audiences in antiquity, these were one and the same.

[ʊ] Most scholars and historians agree that Israel and Judah did indeed split in approximately 930 B.C.E. The nation and people of Israel would not be united again in their ancestral homeland until the establishment of the modern state of Israel in 1948 C.E.

Vocal Music in the Book of Isaiah

The Book of Isaiah opens with a message of God's judgement and a warning. Within the narrative, leaders in Jerusalem and throughout the Southern Kingdom of Judah have rebelled against God's covenant with their idolatrous ways and must be punished. This opening also offers a hopeful reminder that God will indeed fulfill His covenant promise to Abraham. In Isaiah's series of warnings, he sings (*ah'shirah*) a metaphorical song (*shirah*) in which the nations of Judah and Israel are God's vineyard, and the people are the grapes which God is growing for wine. (Isaiah 5:1) Though he expected sweet grapes, they are bitter (rebelling against God), and Isaiah rhetorically asks what he could have done differently, while knowing he did everything he could.

Later, in Isaiah 23:15-16, the prophet metaphorically describes a harlot's song and uses the term *shir,* which is rendered into English as "ditty" or "song." The Oxford English Dictionary defines a "ditty" as "a short, simple song."[19] The decision to use "ditty" here is interesting, since the Hebrew term used, *shir*, means simply "song." This may suggest a distinction between the unskilled music of the metaphorical harlot described by Isaiah when compared with the highly-skilled musicians of the Temple Orchestra, who were trained in the tradition of David.˙ The verb *nagen*, meaning "to play," also appears in this passage, and is followed by *shir*.

˙ Throughout the ancient Near East and Middle East, there was a tradition that prostitutes played stringed instruments, such as the harp and lyre. (Braun, 84)

The verse reads:

Take a kinnor ("lyre"), go about the town, Harlot long forgotten; Sweetly nagen (play), make much shir (music), To bring you back to mind.

Isaiah 23:16

After describing the anguish and despair that will engulf Israel, Isaiah pivots to a happier note, expressing God's enduring love for the people of Israel despite their rebellion against Him.

Isaiah 30:29 reads:

For you, there shall be singing as on a night when a festival is hallowed; There shall be rejoicing as when they march with chalil (a double-reed woodwind), with tuppim (drums/timbrels), and with kinnorot ("lyres") To the Rock of Israel on the Mountain of the LORD.

Isaiah 30:29

A quick aside for anyone following along in their own Hebrew language version of the Bible: If you compare Isaiah 30:29 to an English translation, you may be surprised and confused to see that there is absolutely no mention of *tuppim* or *kinnorot* in the original Hebrew. Some translations include these two additions, while others do not. An explanation is offered in the footnotes of *The Jewish Study Bible*, which describes that "'with timbrel and lyre' was brought from verse 32 for clarity."[20] Adding to the confusion, many English versions of verse 32 makes no reference to either instrument, but the Hebrew version of verse 32 does indeed include the words *b'tuppim u'v'kinnorot*, which mean "with drums and with lyres." Some translations leave these instrumental references in their original location of Isaiah 30:32, while others relocate them to Isaiah 30:29.

Lastly, in Isaiah 51:3, the prophet calls upon the people of Israel to trust in the LORD, and describes songs of thanksgiving filling the air. Here, the Hebrew word *zimrah*, a variant on the previously-used *zamer*, is translated as "music."

There is no mention of vocal music in the Book of Jeremiah.

VOCAL MUSIC IN THE BOOK OF EZEKIEL

In Ezekiel 26:13, God uses the prophet Ezekiel to condemn the prideful kings of Egypt and Tyre, the two regional superpowers with whom Israel's kings had aligned, for asserting themselves as gods. In describing Tyre's impending demise at the hands of Babylon, God declares:

> *I will put an end to the mon (murmur/music) of your shirahyikh (songs), And the sound of your kinnorayikh ("lyres") shall be heard no more.*
>
> Ezekiel 29:13

This moment, like the famous Psalm 137, describes music as an essential aspect of life. To say that their music will be heard no more is to say that the entire kingdom and its people will perish.

VOCAL MUSIC IN THE BOOK OF THE TWELVE

There is no mention of vocal music in the writings of Hosea nor of Joel.

Amos

The prophet Amos lived one hundred and fifty years after the northern and southern kingdoms divided. He was a shepherd and fig tree farmer from a town in Judah near the border of Israel. In Amos 6, the prophet accuses Israel's leaders of idolatry and religious hypocrisy, and warns that God will send a nation to destroy them. In particular, Amos condemns people in Jerusalem and Samaria who live extravagant, luxurious, and worry-free lives, all while ignoring the needs of their countrymen and the commandments of the Torah. In Amos 6:5, the prophet criticizes those who "sing trivial songs to the sound of the *kinnor* and fancy themselves musicians like David." (NLT) This passage introduces two new Hebrew terms related to music. They are *lifrot* and *al pi*. *Lifrot* is translated as "humming" or "singing songs," though in modern Hebrew, it is understood as a verb meaning "to play stringed instruments." *Pi* is translated as a "tune" or "sound," with *al pi* meaning "to the tune of" or "to the sound of," or literally, "by mouth."

There is no mention of vocal music in the writings of Obadiah, Jonah, Micah, Nahum, Habakkuk, Zephaniah, Haggai, Zechariah, or Malachi.

<u>Vocal Music in the Ketuvim (Writings)</u>
Vocal Music in The Book of Psalms

The Book of Psalms is often thought of as a collection of songs and/or hymns. The psalms are divided into 150 "chapters," one for each psalm. However, a variety of literary styles is represented, so to call them all "songs" or "hymns" is an over-simplification. The word "psalm" is Old English, and is derived from the Greek *psalmos*, which the Oxford English Dictionary defines as "[A] 'song sung to harp music', from *psallein* 'to pluck.'" However, the original Hebrew name for Psalms was *Tehillim* (teh-hee-leem) (תְּהִלִּים), which means "praises."[21] The term *tehillim* is derived from the root *hallel*, which means "to praise." Another example of *hallel* is *hallelu-Yah* ("Hallelujah"), meaning "Praise Yah" or "Praise the LORD."

This tapestry of poetic prayers was composed by numerous authors over hundreds of years. It is positioned within the Bible as the first book of the Ketuvim (Writings). Adele Berlin and Marc Zvi Brettler posit that this placement could be because of its impressive length, or simply because its status as an authoritative library of texts was established early in the biblical canonization process.[22] Berlin and Brettler go on to assert that the Psalms were used in the liturgy of the Second Temple, and were perhaps, in the case of the oldest psalms, utilized in the First Temple.[23] Of the 150 psalms, seventy-three are attributed to David (48.6%), twelve are attributed to Asaph (8%), eleven to the children or progeny of Korah (7.3%), two to Solomon (1.3%), one to Moses (.6%), one to Heman (.6%), and one to Ethan (.6%). The remaining forty-nine psalms are anonymous, which is why they are also known as "orphaned psalms" (32.6%).[ב24]

Despite the fact that many English Bibles describe all *tehillim* simply as "psalms," in the original Hebrew text of the Bible, the psalms are described with headings that include terms such as *mizmor, shir, michtam, maskil, shiggayon, shushan, lehazkir,* and *ma'alot*. It was during the translation of the Septuagint between the third and second centuries B.C.E, that these words

---

ב Asaph and Korah were both Levite priests and musicians under King David. Along with David and his son, Solomon, ninety-eight psalms come from the Davidic School.

were often translated and simplified as *psalmos*, or "praises." [25] This is why, to this day, many English Bibles refer to all 150 *tehillim* simply as "psalms." However, each term has its own specific, unique musical meaning.

מִזְמוֹר

Mizmor

A m*izmor* (meez-mor) is a sacred song with stringed instrumental accompaniment.[26] The term *mizmor* comes from the root word, *zamer,* which is a word for sacred music thought to have developed far later than *shir*.[27] Of the 150 psalms, fifty-seven, or 38% of them, are labeled as a *mizmor*. While the Hebrew word *tehillim* has been translated into English as "psalms," in the phrase "a psalm of David," the word that is translated as "a psalm" is *mizmor*. This means that any psalms in an English Bible which begin with "a Psalm of David" are intended to be recited with stringed instrumental accompaniment. Based on the original meanings of the Hebrew *mizmor* and the Greek *psalmos,* only the psalms with the heading "*mizmor*" should be understood as actual "psalms" in the English sense. The psalms that are designated as *mizmorim* are Psalms:

3, 4, 5, 6, 8, 9, 12, 13, 15, 16, 19, 20, 21, 22, 23, 29, 30, 31, 38, 39, 40, 41, 47, 48, 49, 50, 51, 62, 63, 64, 65, 66, 67, 68, 73, 75, 76, 77, 79, 80, 82, 83, 84, 85, 87, 88, 92, 98, 100, 101, 108, 109, 110, 139, 140, 141, 143

Maskil

Alfred Sendrey [born Alfred Szendrei] (1884-1976), the celebrated American bibliomusicologist, describes that a *maskil* is a didactic song intended to teach a lesson.[28] Didactic songs have been used throughout history and across all cultures, and have proven to be very effective with both children and adults who lack a formal education. Sendrey's sentiment echoes that of the German biblical scholar Heinrich Friedrich Wilhelm Gesenius (1786-1842), who similarly posited that a *maskil* is a didactic poem or song intended to instruct or convey a lesson.[29] Fourteen, or 9.3%, of the psalms are labeled as a *maskil*. Modern secular examples of didactic songs for children include "The Alphabet Song," "Skeleton Bones Song," and "This is the Way (We Wash Our Hands)." The psalms that are designated as *maskilim* are Psalms:

32, 42, 44, 45, 47, 52, 53, 54, 55, 74, 78, 88, 89, 142

Psalms with More Than One Musical Term in the Heading

Many psalms feature more than one musical term in the heading. Psalm 88, which is one of the most interesting from a bibliomusicological perspective, is labeled as a *shir*, a *mizmor,* and a *maskil*. Further, it is attributed to both the Korahites *and* Heman the Ezrahite. This clearly establishes that one psalm can be a *shir*, a *mizmor,* and a *maskil*. But this raises the question: does this mean that, unless specified, a *mizmor* is not a *shir*? Of course not. By their definitions, a *shir* is a "song," while a *mizmor* is a "sacred song with stringed accompaniment," and a *maskil* is a didactic song. Ergo, Psalm 88 is a sacred, didactic song to be performed with stringed accompaniment. If it is implied that a *mizmor* and *maskil* are each songs, why then would the author also choose to include *shir* in the heading? Is this not redundant? The inclusion of *"shir"* within the heading is likely the result of more than one copy of Psalm 88 circulating in antiquity.

At some point, headings were added to Psalm 88's text. One tradition probably associated it with the Korahites, while another associated it with Heman the Ezrahite. One version was likely set to stringed accompaniment, while another was not. One scribe may have found didactic merit in it, while others did not share this sentiment. At some point, perhaps under the reign of King Josiah in the 7th century B.C.E., the psalms were gathered, collated, and organized into a unified collection as the Book of Psalms we know today. When the ancient scribes and priests compiled multiple copies of Psalm 88 with varying headings they likely chose to retain all headings rather than select just one.

This would hardly be the first such example in the Bible. The stories of Adam, Noah, and Abraham all include "doublets," or narratives that are recounted twice, but are slightly different in each telling. The entire Book of Chronicles could even be classified as a doublet, retelling the stories of Samuel and Kings.

When reading psalms with more than one heading, one need not ask which is the "most accurate" or which is "the original." The simple fact is that psalms with multiple musical heading were entered in Scripture as canon, and the headings are not mutually exclusive.

Michtam

A *michtam* is derived from the Hebrew root *chatam*, which originally meant "to conceal," but took on the meanings of riddle, puzzle, or maxim.[30] This led Gesenius to conclude that a *michtam*, like a riddle, has a concealed, deeper meaning.[31] The six *michtam* psalms account for 4% of the psalms.

The six psalms that include *michtam* in the heading, all of which attributed to David, are 16, 56, 57, 58, 59, 60.

Shushan

A *shushan* (often referred to in the plural as *shoshannim*) is an ancient secular melody that has been repurposed for sacred use by setting a liturgical text to the secular music.[32] In its four scriptural instances (2.6%), *"shushan"* is one of the biblical music terms that actually enjoys a general consensus by scholars regarding its meaning.[33] In modern music terminology, a song that uses the melody of a preexisting song but with new lyrics is called an "interpolation." One popular modern example is Ariana Grande's song "7 Rings" (2019), which is an intentional and blatant interpolation of Richard Rodgers' and Oscar Hammerstein's "My Favorite Things" from "The Sound of Music" (1965). A modern religious example is the Christian hymn "Because He Lives" (1971), which is an interpolation or *shushan* because its melody comes from the song "Any Dream

Will Do" from the 1968 musical "Joseph and the Amazing Technicolor Dreamcoat." "Ripple" (1970) by the Grateful Dead also interpolated "Any Dream Will Do." Another example is the 2011 album "A Shabbat in Liverpool" by Lenny Solomon and Schlock Rock, which sets Jewish liturgies to popular melodies by the Beatles.

There are a number of reasons why ancient Jews would have incorporated secular melodies into their liturgies. One is that it is easier to worship together when a tune or melody is widely-known. Or perhaps, just like today, it was a fun way to get children and adults excited, like The Ein Prat Fountainheads' 2012 interpolation of Bruno Mars's "Marry You" (2010), which they repurposed as "Livin' in a Booth." The lyrics were re-written and transformed to be about the Jewish holiday of Sukkot. (Exodus 23:16, 34:22, Leviticus 23:34-43, Numbers 29:12-40, Deuteronomy 16:13-15, Ezra 3:4, Nehemiah 8:13-18.)

Another important impetus for the inclusion of *shoshannim* or interpolated melodies is "syncretism." The Oxford English Dictionary defines "syncretism" as "the amalgamation or attempted amalgamation of different religions, cultures, or schools of thought."[34] This would mean that in an effort to bring Canaanites or some other people group into Israel, the Israelites repurposed existing Canaanite melodies with Israelite texts, traditions, or stories. Syncretism was a common practice under Alexander the Great as he sought to Hellenize the world, and remains a popular practice today among Christian missionaries who seek to evangelize native, aboriginal populations.[35]

There are four psalms designated as a *shushan*. Because of the music notation in the Bible (more about this in Chapter 9), a record of these original ancient melodies has been preserved.

Psalms containing the *shushan* heading are: 45, 60, 69, 80.

SHIGGAYON

There is only one psalm, Psalm 7, with the heading *shiggayon*. According to the Midrash and Rashi, the term refers to an "error" or "fault."[36] Scholars generally agree that *shiggayon* comes from verb *shaggah, which means* "to wander."[37] Some scholars have suggested that this indicates a musical change in meter or melody mid-way through a piece of music, yet the melody of the *te'amim* and the strophic nature of the text make this assertion seem unlikely.[38]

Traditionally, it is believed that Psalm 7 was written by David while he was on the run from King Saul.[39] The word *shiggayon* is assumed to be related to the similar word *shiggionot* found in Habakkuk 3:1. *Shiggionot*, as it appears in Habakkuk, is seemingly related to *shiggayon*, which Sendrey's competing theory suggests refers to "a song of lament."[40] This fits the context of Psalm 7's text. However, the meaning of Habakkuk 3:1's *"shiggionot"* is not unanimously agreed upon by scholars. Sefaria.org, an online database of Jewish texts, even defines *"shiggionot"* as "a song?" — complete with the question mark.[41] As Psalm 7 is the only psalm labeled as a *shiggayon,* no further conclusions can be drawn regarding this word's meaning.

Lehazkir

"*Lehazkir*" appears in the headings of two psalms attributed to David, and means "in remembrance." One interpretation is that these psalms do not call for the people of Israel to remember some event or story, but rather a plea to God not to forget His people and His covenant promise.

Psalms with the heading *"Lehazkir"*: 38, 70

Ma'alot

There are many theories as to the nature of the fifteen *ma'alot,* (10%) or the "songs of ascents" or "song of degrees" as they are known in English. Jewish tradition teaches that these were songs of worship to be offered while ascending Mount Zion (where Jerusalem rests and the Holy Temple resided), or perhaps songs to be sent up to God. Another theory offered by scholars is that each line should be recited as one ascends the stairs to the entrance of the Temple.[42] One less common, but still interesting theory is that the "degrees" refer to ascending scale degrees, and that the melodies were originally composed based on a particular scale.[43] A modern example might be "Do-Re-Mi," made famous by Julie Andrews in "The Sound of Music." The melody of "Do-Re-Mi" is built upon succeeding notes of a Major Scale. Though this theory may seem unlikely to anyone familiar with the modern method of Jewish cantillation, it was a contributing factor when Suzanne Haïk-Vantoura attempted to decipher the *te'amim*.[44]

The psalms of ascent are: 120, 121, 122, 123, 124, 125, 126, 127, 128, 129, 130, 131, 132, 133, 134

There is no mention of vocal music in the Book of Proverbs.

VOCAL MUSIC IN THE BOOK OF JOB

The two references to vocal music in the Book of Job occur exactly in the middle of the story, when Job rhetorically asks "Why do the wicked live on, prosper and grow wealthy?" (Job 21:7) In describing these people, Job opines,

They yisu (lift up/sing to the music) of tof (drum) and kinnor (lyre), and revel to the tune of the ugav (flute). They spend their days in happiness, then eventually die in peace.
Job 21:12

In Job 21:12, the terms יִשְׂאוּ *yisu* and קוֹל *kol* are used. This is the only occasion in which *yisu* is used to describe music. *Yisu* may be best defined to mean "to lift, bear up, carry, or take,"[45] but since this sentence describes "lifting up" a drum, lyre, and flute, it is always interpreted as "making music" or even "singing." The second term in this verse, *kol,* is translated as "tune," as in "to the tune of." This *kol* (קוֹל) is not to be confused with the homophone *kol* (כֹּל), which simply means "all" or "every."

שִׁיר הַשִּׁירִים

Song of Songs

King Solomon may not be remembered as a virtuosic musician like his famous father, but tradition does attribute *Shir Ha'Shirim:* The Song of Songs to him, in addition to 1,005 psalms (1 Kings 5:12). Though often read in English as prose, the ancient Hebrew musical notation described at length in Chapter Nine will demonstrate that Song of Songs is indeed a song. This work is an example of epic love poetry from the ancient Near East. The title "Song of Songs" comes from the Jewish idiom "____ of ____s" which means "the best or grandest example of something." "Miracle of Miracles" from Fiddler on the Roof (1964) describes the *greatest miracle*. Similarly, the "Holy of Holies," describes the inner-most sanctuary and the holiest site of the Tabernacle. (Leviticus 16:2) George Frideric Handel's 1741 oratorio "Messiah" even utilizes this idiom with the refrain "King of Kings and Lord of Lords." Other examples are "servant of servants," (Genesis 9:25) "Shabbat of Shabbats," (Exodus 31:15) "God of gods," (Deuteronomy 10:17), "vanity of vanities" (Ecclesiastes 1:2), and "king of kings." (Ezra 7:12) To call this book of Scripture the "Song of Songs" is to say that it is the *greatest song*.

Song of Songs recounts the story of two lovers. It stands out because it seems unrelated to the rest of the Bible, and does not mention or refer to God or any other narrative element of Torah. Despite its sexual nature, some Jews have historically explained it as an allegory in which the man in the story represents God and the woman represents Israel. Similarly,

Christians have interpreted the story with the man representing Jesus and the woman representing the Church. Dr. Tim Mackie of the Bible Project asserts that as more and more examples of ancient love poetry are discovered, it seems increasingly likely that no deeper meaning to the story was intended by its author.[46] Mackie posits that it was canonized merely as a portrayal of human sexual love: one of the most intimate, and therefore most important, experiences one has in life.[47]

There is no mention of vocal music in the Books of Ruth, Lamentations, Ecclesiastes, Esther, or Daniel.

VOCAL MUSIC IN THE BOOK OF EZRA-NEHEMIAH

The Book of Ezra-Nehemiah recounts the chronological end of the Hebrew Bible. Once the Jews have returned to Judah, they rebuild Jerusalem and erect the Second Temple. Originally a single book with a single author, Ezra-Nehemiah was long ago divided into two separate books to accommodate scroll length: the Book of Ezra and the Book of Nehemiah. In this study, they will be examined in their original, unified context. Despite the book's binary title, the narrative actually follows three leaders: Zerubbabel, then Ezra, then Nehemiah.

Zerubbabel, whose name means "born in Babylon," leads the reconstruction of the Holy Temple. This marks the beginning of the Second Temple period, a term which describes Judaism and the Jewish people from the return out of Babylon until the Temple is destroyed by the Romans in 70 C.E. Along with the reconstruction of the Temple came the reinstitution of the Temple Orchestra, originally established by King David. (1 Kings 10:12) Once the new Temple's foundation had been laid, the new Temple Orchestra commemorated the occasion with the singing of *hallel or* "songs of praise" and the playing of *chatzotzerot* (silver trumpets) and *metziltayim* (cymbals) by Levite descendants of Asaph. (Ezra 3:10-11) Nehemiah 12:8 also describes the Levite priests who joined Zerubbabel's cause singing *yedot* or "songs of thanksgiving."

Nehemiah is a Jewish official serving in the Persian government as the Jews return to Judah. Nehemiah learns that Jerusalem's walls are in ruin, so he prays and gains permission from the Persian King Artaxerxes to rebuild them. Along with Nehemiah's civic project, he is also committed to the spiritual renewal of the Jewish people. Nehemiah and Ezra, the Jewish leader who emphasized a rededication to Torah observance, combine forces to spiritually realign the people of Judah. They first lead a week-long dedication to studying, praying, and reflecting on Torah, followed by the celebration of Sukkot, also known as the "Feast of Tabernacles" or "Feast of Booths." There is an abundance of singing and instrumental music, including six references to singing (Nehemiah 12:27, 28, 29, 42, 46A, 46B). Four of these references introduce a new term for "singers": *"mesher'rim."* The term *bi'kle shir David* or "with musical instruments of David" is also contained in Nehemiah 12:36 to describe the instrumentation of the reformed Temple Orchestra.

Vocal Music in the Book of Chronicles

The final book in the Hebrew Bible is Chronicles, or in Hebrew, *Divrei Ha'Yamim,* which literally translates to "Words of the Days." As with the books of Samuel, Kings, and Ezra-Nehemiah, Chronicles was originally one book that was later divided into two parts, now called "1 Chronicles" and "2 Chronicles." Chronicles is the final book of the Bible in the Jewish canonical order because it serves as a conclusion to the Tanakh, summarizing many of the most important narrative elements of the rest of Scripture. Much of Chronicles seems to retell the stories from the books of Samuel and Kings, but from a different perspective, which is often more positive and flattering to its literary characters. Much of the added content not present in the Books of Samuel or Kings focuses on David's Temple Orchestra. Aside from the Book of Psalms, Chronicles is the biblical book with the most musical references. Chronicles contains ninety-one references to music, accounting for 16.73% of the music in the Bible.

Vocal music is first mentioned in 1 Chronicles 6:16-17 (or 1 Chronicles 6:31-32, depending on the translation) when the word *shir* appears twice. This passage describes the origin of the Temple Orchestra and explains that the Levite musicians who ministered with music and led worship within the tabernacle (in Jerusalem around 1000 B.C.E, not the Tabernacle as described in Exodus) were the same musicians who would later serve as the first members of the Temple Orchestra.

1 Chronicles 13:8 tells the story of David's first attempt at relocating the Ark of the Covenant to Jerusalem. In this passage, David and the people of Israel are celebrating the Ark's impending arrival into Jerusalem with singing *(u'v'shir)* and instrumental music. However, someone touched the Ark, a forbidden action, prompting God to delay the Ark's arrival into Jerusalem.

Jewish and Christian tradition attributes the Book of Chronicles to Ezra. One contributing clue to this assertion can be observed in reading 1 Chronicles 15:16 in which the Hebrew word *mesher'rim* is once again used to refer to singers. Throughout all of Scripture, *mesher'rim* can only be found in the books of Ezra-Nehemiah and Chronicles. *Mesher'rim,* or variations thereof, appears four times in the former and seven times in the latter book.

In preparation for his second attempt to usher the Ark of the

Covenant into Jerusalem, David orders the Levite leaders to "appoint a choir of Levites who were *mesher'rim* (singers) with *bikle shir* (musical instruments) to sing joyful songs with the accompaniment of *nevalim* (often translated as "harps"), *kinnorot* (often translated as "lyres"), *and metziltayim* (cymbals)." (1 Chronicles 15:16 NLT)

In 1 Chronicles 15:22, readers are introduced to a Levite official named Chenaniah (sometimes transliterated Kenaniah). The author writes that Chenaniah was in charge of the music because "he was a master of מַשָּׂא *massa*." (1 Chronicles 15:22) Though the etymology and official definition of the Hebrew word *massa* is uncertain, the passage's context has led scholars to universally agree that it must refer to some type of song or music. Another translation writes that Chenaniah was chosen as the music director of the Temple Orchestra *because of his skill*. This is an extraordinary and important detail to consider. In a society in which a man's line of work was traditionally determined by his father's trade, the Temple Orchestra director was chosen based on skill and merit. The same is true of the Temple Orchestra members—they had to be Levites, but among the Levites, only the most skilled were selected to perform and lead musical worship within the Temple. (1 Chronicles 25:8)

By the time of the next reference to vocal music in 1 Chronicles 15:2-28, the Ark of the Covenant has been successfully delivered to Jerusalem. Chenaniah leads the *mesher'rim* in singing, celebrating, and worshiping with *shofarot, chatzotzerot, metziltayim, nevalim,* and *kinnorot*. Then, King David himself leads a song of thanksgiving, urging all to *shiru* a *zamru* – sing a song of praise to God. (1 Chronicles 16:9) *Shiru* is the first-person plural conjugation of *shir* used for "we sing." *Zamru* is the first-person plural conjugation of *zamer*. Later in his song, David declares "*Shiru* to the LORD, all the earth.

Proclaim His victory day after day...all the trees shall *yeran'nu* (sing/shout) for joy at the presence of the LORD." (1 Chronicles 16:23,33) David follows this verse with the familiar refrain, "His faithful love endures forever." (1 Chronicles 16:34)

1 Chronicles 16 concludes with David appointing worship leaders to various positions in Jerusalem and Gibeon, located just to the north. Asaph is appointed to serve before the Ark of the Covenant, along with Jeduthun's son, Obed-edom, Hosah, and sixty-eight others. Zadok, another Levite priest, will minister at the Tabernacle in Gibeon. The location of Heman's and Jeduthun's ministerial posting is not described, but David assigns the pair to lead Israel in song with the refrain "His faithful love endures forever" once more, *mashem'im* (accompanied by, to the sound of) *chatzotzerot* (silver trumpets), *metziltayim* (cymbals), and other *kle shir* (musical instruments). (1 Chronicles 16:37-43)

When it comes to the musical references mentioned in the Bible, those featured in 1 Chronicles 23-25 are among the most interesting in all of Scripture because they describe the duties and requirements of the Temple musicians. In order to serve in any official ministerial capacity, one had to be a man, a descendant of the tribe of Levi, and at least thirty years old. When the Temple was constructed, there were 38,000 Levites who met these criteria. Of those 38,000 Levites, 4,000 of them were appointed to minister with *kelim l'hallel* (instruments for praise/worship). (1 Chronicles 23:1-6)

1 Chronicles 25:1 describes David appointing the families of Asaph, Heman, and Jeduthun as instrumental musicians leading with *kinnorot* (lyres), *nevalim* (harps), and *metziltayim* (cymbals). These men led worship in the Temple and reported directly to King David. (1 Chronicles 25:6) Between Aspah, Heman, Jeduthun and their collective sons, there were 288 worship musicians. (1 Chronicles 25:7) The author of the Book

of Chronicles describes them as trained, highly-skilled, and learned musicians, who were appointed by sacred lots with no preference as to age or experience. Assuming that a Temple musician met the criteria of being thirty years old and highly skilled in *shir,* he was treated and valued equally amongst his colleagues. (1 Chronicles 25:7-8)

2 Chronicles 5 describes Asaph, Heman, Jeduthun, and their sons leading worship at the Temple. They are joined by 120 *ha'leviyim ha'meshre'im* (Levite singers) who played *chatzotzerot* (silver trumpets). Together, this ensemble was 308 members strong. They worshiped together with the familiar refrain, "He is Good, His faithful love endures forever." At this, the spirit of the LORD filled the Temple. (2 Chronicles 5:12-14)

During the dedication of the Temple, the same refrain "His faithful love endures forever" from Psalms 118 and 136 is echoed again in 2 Chronicles 7:3, and once more as the Levites sing in 2 Chronicles 7:6. In fact, 2 Chronicles 7:6 even describes that the Levites were worshiping "with the psalms of David that they knew." Just as today, the Israelites recited the psalms as a form of prayer and worship. This verse also describes the use of בִּכְלֵי־שִׁיר *(bi'khle shir)*—musical instruments that David made specifically to praise the LORD.

Music is next mentioned in 2 Chronicles 9, which details the visit of Queen of Sheba. 2 Chronicles 9:11 corroborates the account in 1 Kings 10:12 that algum wood was used by the *sharim* to construct *kinnorot* and *nevalim.*

2 Chronicles 20 tells a biblical story which may seem obscure to many readers, but is near and dear to many *musicians* reading the Bible: the story of Jahaziel. Jahaziel was a Jewish musician who lived during the reign of King Jehoshaphat. He was a Levite, a descendant of Asaph, and a member of the Temple Orchestra. After Solomon's death, the northern tribes secede and Israel splits into two countries: Israel in the north and

Judah in the south. A few generations later, Solomon's great-great-grandson Jehoshaphat is reigning as the King of Judah. Judah is at war with the Moabites, the Ammonites, and the Meunites. Jehoshaphat receives news that the enemy army has his men vastly out-numbered. As Jehoshaphat leads his men in prayer, the spirit of the LORD comes upon the young Jahaziel. Jahaziel shares that it is God's Will that the musicians lead the Jewish army in battle while singing and worshiping God. Jehoshaphat agrees and appoints *mesharim* (singers) to the front lines of battle. When the Moabites, Ammonites, and Meunites see and hear the army of Judah singing and worshiping to God, the foreign armies begin fighting amongst themselves. They then turn on their ally, the nation of Seir, and kill every solider before killing their own ranks. The Jews sing out together, "His faithful love endures forever!" (2 Chronicles 20:14-21) Because this compelling story places the musicians as the avant-garde in battle, it is often relayed to ministerial musicians today. It likens musicians to worshiping warriors—fighting on the front lines for the spiritual salvation of their congregations.

2 Chronicles 23 is another example of a doublet, a repeated biblical story, even if from a different perspective. This time, it doubles the story of Jehoiada the priest, the Queen Mother Athaliah and her infant grandson, King Joash, from 2 Kings 11. 2 Kings 11 was not described a few pages ago in the section on Vocal Music in the Book of Kings because the first doublet *does not* mention singing. Vocal music is only described in the second doublet, but Athaliah's attempt to usurp power through killing the living heirs to her son's throne is once again short-lived. She was executed six years after murdering most of her family. Her death is met with celebration from *meshorarim* (singers) playing *bikle ha'shir l'hallel* (musical instruments for praise and worship). (2 Chronicles 23:13) Again, in 2 Kings, only instrumental musicians are named, but in 2 Chronicles,

both instrumentalists *and* singers are mentioned. Doublets often feature subtle differences. This distinction might seem inconsequential, or it might indicate that the terms formerly used (*sharim* and the later *meshorarim*) could perhaps be interpreted as singers or instrumental musicians.

Following the events around Queen Athaliah and her grandson King Joash, Jehoiada the priest makes a covenant between himself, the young Joash, and God. This leads to religious reforms, including a rededication to keeping the Torah and worshiping God with *shir*. (2 Chronicles 23:16-18)

2 Chronicles 29 introduces Hezekiah, who is considered one of Judah's greatest kings. The Temple was temporarily closed under the previous king's reign, leaving the Temple Orchestra unable to lead worship at God's holiest site. Under Hezekiah, the Temple Orchestra resumed its ministry. The musicians used their and *kle David* (instruments of David) to sing *shir YHVH* (a song of the LORD). Hezekiah orders all of Israel to sing and worship using the psalms of David and Asaph. (2 Chronicles 29:26-28)

The final musical reference in all of Hebrew Scripture is found in 2 Chronicles 31:2. This takes place just before Judah is invaded by Assyria. Hezekiah commands the Levites to *lehodot*. Out of context, this term simply means "to give thanks," but as it is delivered to the Levites in the context of their responsibilities within the Temple Orchestra, it is consistently translated as "sing songs of praise and thanksgiving." It is fitting that the final musical instruction in the Hebrew Bible commands the music leaders of Israel to sing and play worshipful songs of thanksgiving.

CHAPTER 3

STRINGED INSTRUMENTS

KINNOR

BACKGROUND, CONSTRUCTION, AND ARCHEOLOGY

The *kinnor* (kee-nor) played by David is the stringed instrument which appears the most often in the Bible, as it is mentioned on forty-two occasions. When reading this instrument's name in the Tanakh, its pronunciation appears as both *kinnor* with a "hard K" (as in "Kansas") and as *khinnor* with a "harsh Kh" (as in the end of "Tanakh"). The difference has nothing to do with the instrument, but rather with sentence structure.

Kaph, the first Hebrew letter in the word *kinnor* receives a dot in the middle of the letter called a *dagesh lene* which softens the pronunciation to the "hard K" under the following circumstances:

1. When it is the first letter of the sentence.
2. When it follows a silent *shva* vowel marker or a closed syllable.
3. When it follows an implied pause.

Instances are divided relatively evenly throughout the Bible, but transliterations within this book will always transliterated as *kinnor* even when the word lacks the *dagesh lene*. This is both for the sake of uniformity and to conform with the accepted transliteration of *kinnor*.

Before discussing the *kinnor,* one cannot examine the biblical history of David's instrument of choice without also considering King David himself. David was the chief musician of the Bible, and is doubtless the most famous *kinnorist* in history, if not the most famous harpist in history. The *kinnor* (plural *kinnorot*) is a hand-held, plucked string instrument. To this day, it remains one of the most iconic musical instruments related to the Bible, Israel, Judaism, and music in general. David was a musician from the Tribe of Judah, hailing from Bethlehem. He was the son of Jesse, the great-grandson of Ruth and Boaz, served as the third King of Israel, united the Twelve Tribes of Israel, established Jerusalem as its capital, and was the first dynastic king of the House of David.

Many scholars and historians agree that a historical David did indeed exist; his reign began around 1000 B.C.E.[48] There are extra-biblical references to David which corroborate his existence because they are dated to within 100 years of his lifetime, including the Tel Dan Stele of Damascus.[49] Some scholars allege the Mesha Stele of Moab[50] and Bubastite Portal at Karnak of Egypt[51] refer to David, as well. Not only is King David often portrayed in artwork holding his *kinnor*, but the *kinnor* is also the national instrument of Israel. The *kinnor* is so important to Israel and her musical history that the Hebrew word *nagan* (נָגַן)(nah-gahn), when rendered as a verb, literally means to play a stringed instrument, but is often used colloquially as a noun simply meaning "music" or "musician," thereby encompassing players of all instruments. (1 Samuel 16:18, 2 Kings 3:15, Isaiah 23:16, Psalm 4:1, Psalm 54:1, Psalm 55:1, Psalm 61:1, Psalm 67:1, Psalm 76:1)

The word "kinnor" is usually translated as either "harp" or "lyre" in English Bibles (note the singular), though it sometimes appears as "stringed instruments" (note the plural). The Stone Edition (Stone), King James Version (KJV), New King James Version (NKJV), American Standard Version (ASV), and New Living Translation (NLT) all use the term "harp;" whereas the Jewish Publication Society (JPS), New Revised Standard Version (NRSV), New American Standard Bible (NASB), and English Standard Version (ESV) use the term "lyre;" and New International Version (NIV) uses the term "stringed instruments." This translation is representative of one of the many discrepancies translators have had to work through when producing English Bibles. To the average person reading the Bible as Scripture, perhaps such distinctions seem trivial. However, for the music historian, musicologist, ethnomusicologist, or even worship leader, the details matter. This begs three questions: 1) Is there a difference between a harp and a lyre? 2) If so, what is the difference? And 3) Which one was the *kinnor*?

Before exploring these questions, we must first place ourselves in the position of the English translator. Despite his or her mastery of an ancient language of the Near East or Asia

Minor, the translator is in all likelihood not an expert in musical terminology, let alone familiar with terms for ancient musical instruments from a non-Western region of the world. The average translator looks at every reference to the instrument, not only within the Bible, but hopefully the Talmud and other ancient writings on Jewish music such as those of Josephus, Tacitus, Philo, and Plutarch. Then, with all available evidence and references, the translator will likely identify the most closely-related instrument in the target vernacular. Through this approach, it seems reasonable that the translator will settle on either "harp" or "lyre" as *kinnorot* admittedly look like they belong in this family of Western instruments.

So what is the difference between a harp and lyre? Both are musical instruments with suspended strings between two points which are plucked or strummed. One prominent theory is that all plucked stringed instruments from cultures across the world, and most notably the harp, likely originated from a bow and arrow. If wound tightly enough to produce a clear and distinct pitch when plucked, any bow is essentially a single-stringed harp. Over time, additional strings allowed the production of polyphonic sounds. These eventually evolved into harps and lyres. The only difference between the two is that a lyre has a bridge while a harp does not. A bridge is the part of an instrument over which the strings are suspended, resulting in three points of contact. For example, a violin has a bridge. The strings are fixed to the body and lay atop a wooden bridge. This raises the strings as they run up to the crossbar of the instrument and make contact with the nut before being tightened with tuners. On a harp, the strings are simply connected at opposite points of the instrument, resulting in only two points of contact. *Kinnorot* come in varieties both with and without a bridge.

Violin Bridge

There are two distinct varieties of *kinnorot* in ancient Israel. The earliest *kinnorot* are examples of what ethnomusicologists refer to as "box lyres." Their namesake is their box-shaped wooden body, which is also called a resonating chamber. Anyone who might think of these instruments as primitive would be mistaken. The fact that these early instrument-builders across the Near East understood that having a resonating chamber, not unlike a modern acoustic guitar, dramatically improves tone and increases volume is evidence of their masterful luthier skills. Even during the millennia leading up to the biblical narrative, lyres had already evolved from an archery bow to intricate, robust instruments capable of beautiful music is a testament to these cultures' engineering, as well as the value they placed on music.

On each side of the resonating chamber, a piece of wood called a "column" extends upward. Together, these two columns support the "crossbar" or "yoke."

A recreation of an early box lyre-style kinnor.

The Jewish philosopher and historian Josephus writes that *kinnor* strings were made from the small intestine of sheep, commonly referred to as "gut" or "catgut" strings.[52♭] The tradition of using gut strings made from animal intestine is thousands of years old, and continues in the finest orchestras today. Throughout history, catgut has also been used for several other worthy purposes, including archery bows, tennis rackets,

---

♭ "Catgut" strings are not made from the intestines of felines. The term may derive from "cattle gut," though strings are frequently made from cattle, sheep, goat, hog, horse, mule, and donkey intestines.

and even surgical sutures.[53]

The strings are made from the outer-membrane that encases the intestines called the "serosa." The serosa is removed, trimmed of fat, and cut into long, thin strips. The strips then rest in water or a saltwater solution for a few days. The individual strands are then grouped together, tied at each end, and allowed to dry over several weeks. The number of strands tied together will determine the gauge of the string. Lower pitches require a thicker string, and therefore, more strands. Even the thinnest, highest-pitched strings require multiple strands for strength and durability. In modern gut string production, strings are tied in groups of three to twenty-three strands. As the strands dry and dehydrate, collagen proteins in the intestines act like glue and bind the strings together.[54]

The strings were knotted and fed through holes in the resonating chamber and pulled taut before being secured on the neck. There, they would have been wrapped around a piece of hard material, such as wood, stone, or bone. These functioned like tuning pegs. They were twisted to tighten or loosen the tension on the string, thereby raising or lowering the string's pitch to the desired frequency or "note." Scholars can say with confidence that the strings were indeed tuned to specific, harmonious, and intentional pitches.[55] In addition to this being a common practice across cultures, the Jewish philosopher, Philo Judaeus (10-15 B.C.E. – 45-50 C.E.), a Greek-speaking Jew, also known as Philo of Alexandria, or simply as "Philo," wrote:

> *For as the* λύρα [lyra, kinnor] *or any musical instrument is out of tune, if even one tone and nothing more be false, but in harmony when a single plucking produces consonant sounds, so it is the same way with the instrument of the soul which is dissonant when stretched too far by rashness*

toward the highest pitch or when it is relaxed beyond measure by cowardice and loosened toward the lowest.[56]

Today, the *kinnor* is almost always thought to have had ten strings. This comes from Josephus' description of the instrument,[57] which is reliable and widely accepted, as well as from the Talmud (Arakhin 13b:12-13, Eruvin 21a:16, Avot D'Rabbi Natan 25:1), but "ten strings" is not specified in the Bible itself. The term "ten-stringed harp" or "ten-stringed instrument" is used in Psalm 92:4 (or 92:3, depending on the Bible version), but the actual Hebrew phrase used is "*al asor v'al navel*," describing a different instrument; not a *kinnor*. The two relevant terms used here are *asor* and *navel*, a variation on *nevel*. Both terms will be explained in detail later in this chapter, but a *nevel* is a lower-voiced string instrument. Additionally, Sendrey asserts that *asor* is an adjective meaning "having ten strings."[58]

In addition to what has become the ten-string standard, the Talmud teaches that "in the days of the Messiah," the *kinnor* will have eight strings. (Arakhin 13b:11) It is also written that *kinnorot* played in the Temple had seven strings, an important and symbolic number in the Bible. (Arakhin 13b:10) "*Asor*" appears only one other time in the text, in Psalm 144:9. While Psalm 92:4 describes that the *nevel* may come in a ten-stringed variety, only Josephus' writings from the Hellenistic-Roman period specify ten strings for the *kinnor*. This is not unlikely given the biblical authors' partiality for certain numbers, such as seven, ten, and twelve, but the *kinnor*, or at least early *kinnorot*, likely featured varying numbers of strings. Keep in mind how difficult it may have been for these ancient Jews to find a replacement string when one or more of the gut strings would inevitably break. This must have been especially true in an era before string protection and coating, when even a humid day could warp a string. Fortunately for David, much of Israel has a desert climate with low humidity.

Any musician will attest that the materials used to craft an instrument have a significant impact on the instrument's tone. This begs the question: what variety of woods were used to construct a *kinnor*? As is the case with most wooden instruments, it probably varied based on preference and availability, but we can narrow it down to three likely varieties. The word "*kinnor*" suggests an etymological connection with the word "*kunar*," the Hebrew word for lotus wood.[59] Even today, lotus wood remains a popular selection for crafting musical instruments. A competing etymological theory suggests that the word *"kinnor"* comes from "*Kinneret*," the Hebrew name for the Sea of Galilee, as well as a city on its shores.[60]

While some *kinnorot* may have been constructed using *kunar*, or lotus wood, the biblical text provides two other alternatives. In 2 Samuel 6:5, it is written that, *kinnorot*, *nevalim*, and *tuppim* (too-peem, drums) were made of Cypress wood. Then, in both 1 Kings 10:12 and 2 Chronicles 9:11, it is written that King Solomon ordered that *kinnorot* and *nevelim* be made from the algum wood imported from Ophir. The identities of both the land of Ophir and algum wood are still debated among scholars. Numerous places have been suggested as Ophir, though the most prevalent theory is that Ophir is the Ethiopian region of "Afar." For this reason, many of the finest modern *kinnorot*, such as those from Harrari Harps in Jerusalem, are constructed from African woods from this region. Numerous study bibles suggest that the "algum wood" mentioned in the Bible was possibly "sandalwood." Some species of sandalwood are native to eastern Africa and have been used to make instruments in many regional cultures. Josephus also discusses the materials used to create *kinnorot*. He wrote, "The [algum] wood which was brought to [Solomon] at this time was larger and finer than any that had ever been brought before…for those we speak of were to the sight like the wood of the fig tree, but were whiter, and more shining.[61]

The method for playing the *kinnor* may have impacted the sound the instrument produced as much as the materials used to construct it. The *kinnor* was played either with the fingers plucking the strings, as David did, (1 Samuel 18:10, 19:9) or with a plectrum akin to a modern guitar pick, as Josephus describes.[62] Artistic depictions of David typically portray him playing with his fingers, and most modern *kinnorists* follow this method. However, the Middle Eastern *oud,* a contemporary of the *kinnor* that is still played today, is typically played with a plectrum. Fingers provide a softer, gentler, and more nuanced tone, but a plectrum allows for greater volume and a far more articulated tone.

A coin depicting how lyres were often held in the ancient world. The left hand holds the instrument while the right hand plucks the strings.

Though many ancient biblical instruments have been unearthed by archeologists, a *kinnor* has yet to be discovered. Without a physical Israelite *kinnor*, musicologists must rely on written descriptions, artwork, and similar instruments from nearby civilizations to understand how the instrument would have sounded. In the case of the *kinnor,* all three types of information are available. In the last one hundred years, contemporaneous box lyres from neighboring civilizations have been discovered.[63] There is also a small treasure of written accounts of *kinnorot* dating back to the Second Temple Era, and even some surviving Israelite artwork featuring *kinnorot*.

As previously stated, the *kinnor* came in two distinct varieties. The early *kinnorot* are depicted in cave etchings in Negev, a city in southern Israel, and date back 5,000 years.[64] The Negev Caves hold a treasure trove of ancient art, with more than two hundred images etched into the inner walls of the caves.[65] These 5,000-year-old etchings, discovered in 1955 by Emmanuel Antai, date back two millennia before the time of David.[66] It should come as no surprise that the *kinnor* is the first musical instrument described in the Bible, considering how old the *kinnor* is estimated to be.[67] (Genesis 4:21)

A modern Israeli coin depicting a kinnor.

Negev Cave etchings of people playing kinnorot.

The Negev Cave etchings depict two people each playing *kinnorot*. Scholars' opinions vary greatly with regard to dating the Negev Cave Etchings. Some people date them as early as the third millennium B.C.E., while others believe they could have been completed during the Greco-Roman Era.[68] These asymmetrical box lyres are clearly shown with one column extending further out than the other at an angle. They are larger than one might expect, about ⅓ to ½ the size of the musicians playing them. This is in line with Egyptian and Sumer-Akkadian artwork which depicts people playing box lyres.[ᵖ] These are also approximately the size of a person's torso, and are played either seated or standing, with the base of the lyre resting on their hip or thigh. Through these ancient artistic depictions, we can also see that the lyres were sometimes played with both

---

[ᵖ] Sumer and Akkad were kingdoms in the north and south of Mesopotamia, respectively, the region also known as Babylon.

the left and right hands plucking the strings, and other times played with one hand supporting the instrument while only the other hand plucks the strings.

Megiddo Jar with a person playing a kinnor, circa 1000 B.C.E.[69]

Another Israelite example can be found on a piece of pottery which depicts a musician playing a *kinnor*. Dating back to the historical time of David (around 1,000 B.C.E.), the *kinnor* depicted here looks practically indistinguishable from the other accounts of *kinnorot*, and is in line with the depictions of the Negev Cave etchings.[70] The jar features a clear and vivid portrayal of a person playing a *kinnor*.[71] Notice the uncanny resemblance to the Negev Cave Etchings. Look at the way the person depicted on the Megiddo Jar is holding the *kinnor*. The *kinnor* is held by the left hand in front of the person's body, while the strings are plucked with the right hand.

The greatest archeological indication of what the *kinnor* would have looked and sounded like, as well as one of the most important musical discoveries of the 20th century, is the excavation of the Babylonian "Lyres of Ur." The four Lyres of Ur were discovered in a royal grave in the Cemetery of Ur by archeologists from the University of Pennsylvania and the British Museum in 1929 C.E.[72] Ur, the birthplace of Abraham, is a city established around 4,000 B.C.E. along the western banks of the Euphrates River, which is located in modern-day Iraq.[73] (Genesis 11:28) Like Israelite depictions of *kinnorot*, the Lyres of Ur are box lyres, featuring the requisite box-shaped resonating chamber.

The four lyres were discovered among ten preserved corpses. One lyre was placed in the arms of the Sumerian Queen Pu-abi (pronounced "poo-ah-bee") with her hand resting over the strings as though strumming. Upon their discovery, expedition leader Sir Charles Leonard "L." Woolley possessed the quick thinking and presence of mind to pour liquid plaster and submerge the lyres, forever retaining the shape of their delicate and perishable wooden frames.[74] While the wood may have decayed over their 5,000-year entombment, the inorganic ornaments of gold and silver were perfectly preserved.[75] The lyres were restored and currently reside separately; one at the National Museum of Iraq, one at the British Museum in London, and two in Penn Museum at the University of Pennsylvania.[76]

The first of the four lyres is known as the "Golden Lyre of Ur." The Golden Lyre is widely considered to be the finest example of the four. Religious readers may find it ironic that this instrument of Babylonian worship is adorned with a golden calf. (Exodus 32) The bull's eyes were fashioned of inlaid mother-of-pearl and lapis lazuli.[77] This first lyre resides in the National Museum of Iraq in Baghdad. Tragically, it was irreparably damaged when the museum flooded during the 2003 American invasion of Iraq.[78] Following this damage, an exact replica (pictured below) was created, which tours the world and is actively played with orchestras and at harp expositions.[79]

Performance on an exact replica made from of the Golden Lyre of Ur.[80]

The second lyre is known as the "Queen's Lyre," as it was found with Queen Pu-abi.[81] This lyre is the only one not covered in sheets of precious metals, but like the Golden Lyre, it also features a golden bull's head with lapis lazuli accents. It is interesting that Queen Pu-abi was buried holding the most understated lyre of the four. Perhaps this particular lyre held a sentimental or special significance to her. The Queen's Lyre resides in the British Museum in London.

The third lyre is known as the "Bull Headed Lyre [sic]," although all four lyres feature a bull's head. The bull's head itself is made of a wooden core, covered in gold, with a beard made of silver and lapis lazuli.[82] Of the four lyres, this is the only one on which the tips of the bull's horns are covered in lapis lazuli. On the front of the lyre, there is a vertical panel depicting four scenes related to Babylonian funeral rituals. The panel is composed of shell inlays on bitumen, which is a black, semi-solid state of petroleum known more commonly today as asphalt.[83] From top to bottom, the panel scenes depicted are: 1) a man wrestling two bulls with human heads, 2) a hyena holding a serving plate and a lion holding a jar, 3) a ram, a bear, and another animal (possibly a donkey), all holding and playing a single large lyre that features a bull's head, and 4), a scorpion-man guarding the gates to the underworld as a man approaches. The wood from this lyre had completely deteriorated by the time of its excavation, but when Sir Woolley filled in the ground imprint with plaster, its shape and dimensions were preserved. The original bull's head and front panel reside at the Penn Museum at the University of Pennsylvania, but a perfect replica featuring a recreated wooden body may be seen at the Iraq Museum in Baghdad.

The fourth lyre is nicknamed the "silver Lyre" after the sheets of silver covering its wooden body.[84] The Silver Lyre, like the others, is adorned with lapis lazuli. Both the Bull Headed and Silver Lyre reside within the Penn Museum at the University of Pennsylvania.

Excavation site at the Cemetery of Ur, 1929.

Sir Leonard Woolley moving the original Golden Lyre from the ground into plaster, 1929.[85]

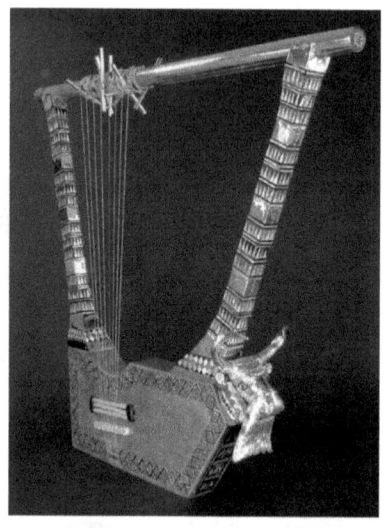

The Golden Lyre
(Exact recreation from a mold of the original)

The Queen's Lyre

The Bull Headed Lyre
(Left: Original, Right: Recreation)

The Silver Lyre

The wood has been replaced on all four lyres. The original wood had completely deteriorated over the last 4,600 years, but the precious metals and gemstone adornments are original.

One interesting note is the presence of local ornamental materials such as gold, silver, and in particular, lapis lazuli used to decorate these lyres. Lapis lazuli is a beautiful blue gemstone with a rich history. The premier mine in the world, which has operated continuously for more than 7,000 years, is located just across the border in modern-day Afghanistan. The presence of lapis on the Lyres of Ur speaks to the region's robust trade which occurred during this time period. Lapis lazuli is mentioned twelve times in the Bible, so we can perhaps assume that this stone was also considered precious to the Israelites. Modern *kinnorot* are sometimes inlaid with lapis lazuli and other gemstones which date back to the description of Aaron's breast plate in Exodus 28:18. Most interestingly, in Genesis 2, the Garden of Eden is located near the land of Havilah, where there is gold and lapis lazuli (Genesis 2:12), perhaps lending a religious connotation to these decorous elements on the lyres.[86]

The Lyres of Ur date back to approximately 2,600 B.C.E.[87] It is fascinating to think about these instruments in their historical context, as they were already preserved in their Mesopotamian graves by the time Abraham is thought to have migrated from Ur to Canaan. Considering their similarities to early Israelite *kinnorot*, the Lyres of Ur may be the closest surviving examples of the *kinnorot* described in the Bible.

Kinnorot of the Greco-Roman Era

As previously mentioned, there are two distinct varieties of *kinnorot*. The first type, including the box lyres, which appeared in the Negev Cave etchings, date back an estimated 5,000 years, and the Lyres of Ur date back roughly 4,600 years. The second variety was played during the 1ˢᵗ century C.E. and is clearly a product of the Greek influence that impacted all aspects of life in Judea³ since at least the 2ⁿᵈ century B.C.E. From 132–136 C.E., Jews in Israel were at war with the Romans in what is now called the Third Jewish-Roman War, or more commonly, the Bar Kokhba Revolt. The Second Temple was destroyed during the Second Jewish-Roman War in Jerusalem in 70 C.E. During the Bar Kokhba Revolt, the Jews minted their own silver and bronze currency. Many of the coins recovered depict palm trees (perhaps a reference to Jericho), the Temple, and three types of musical instruments: *chatzotzerot* (silver trumpets), a *nevel*, and a *kinnor*.[88] The late *kinnorot* depicted on these coins closely resemble the appearance of a Greek lyre. However, these *kinnorot* have no visible bridge. Today, the imagery of these late *kinnorot* can be seen everywhere from modern Israeli coins to statutes and artwork throughout the city of Jerusalem, to the clip-on sheet music holders which marching bands attach to their instruments known as "lyres," as well as numerous music association logos, and even band letterman jacket patches.

---

³ "Judah" was originally the territory inhabited by the descendants of Judah, the son of Jacob. When the Northern Tribes seceded, the southern half of Israel became known as the Kingdom of Judah. When Roman General Pompey seized Jerusalem in 63 B.C.E., the land of Judah became known as the Roman Province of "Judea," which included Judah, Samaria, and Idumea.

*Kinnorot depicted on coins from
the Bar Kokhba Revolt, 132-136 C.E.*

Today, many musical instrument companies produce *kinnorot* modeled after both early box lyre styles and late Greco-Roman-era styles. Instruments inspired by *kinnorot* from this era, from the entry-level beginning *kinnorot* manufactured by a company called Mid-East Instruments; to the many American luthiers and private craftsmen who will create a modernized *kinnor,* complete with an electric pick-up to plug the instrument into an amplifier or sound system; to the professional *kinnorot* of the highest caliber from Harrari Harps located just outside of Jerusalem, are available for any musician who desires to play the instrument of David, at many different price points. Almost all modern *kinnorot* are made with ten strings.

KINNOR TUNING

We do not know how *kinnor* strings were tuned in the time of the First and Second Temples. I will offer my best educated guess in Chapter 8: Theoretical Music Tonality, but the world will likely never know this information with absolute certainty. However, the most common tuning for modern ten-string *kinnorot* is, from low to high:

Low ← →High
E – F# – G – A – B – C – D# - E – F# – G

Some readers will likely recognize this as an E Harmonic Minor Scale. This is an accurate description, but when playing the *kinnor,* the most commonly-used tonality is the Hebraic Scale. The Hebraic Scale, in the Key of B, is:

B – C – D# - E – F# - G – A – B

With this modern *kinnor* tuning, B is the tonal center of a piece of music as often or more often than E is the tonal center. This will be discussed in greater detail in Chapter 8.

A less common modern tuning is:

C – D - E – F - G – A – B – C – D - E

This tuning has obvious appeal for Americans and other Western players.

I personally use three different tunings. Approximately one-third of the time, I play the *kinnor* in the standard tuning of:

E – F# – G – A – B – C – D# – E – F# – G

I never tune the *kinnor* strings to different "letter" pitches, in that I would never tune my low string to C, but about approximately one-third of the time, I tune the strings to C Major/A Minor like:

E – F – G – A – B – C – D - E – F – G

Some musicians may be tempted to call this Phrygian tuning, but I never think of E as the tonal center. In this tuning, I usually think of A as the tonal center, or, sometimes, C.

The final third of the time, I still keep the "letter" of the pitches the same, but like a modern harpist adjusting her foot pedals, I adjust the pitches to match the key signature of a song I'm playing. With this approach, I never need to adjust a string more than a half-step, which is far better for the strings than changing the lowest note of the *kinnor* to match the tonal center of a key.

For example, if a song is in D Major with an F# and a C#, the *kinnor* strings are tuned to:

E – F# – G – A – B – C# – D - E – F# – G

If a song is in F Minor with B♭, E♭, A♭, and D♭, I tune the *kinnor* to:

E♭ – F – G – A♭ – B♭ – C – D♭ - E♭ – F – G

One final option that is quite useful for using the *kinnor* to perform glissandi is to tune the *kinnor* to an open C6 chord by lowering the F to E and raising the B to C. Because these changes constitute only a half-step, the strings are not overly stressed.

$$E - F\flat - G - A - B\sharp - C - D - E - F\flat - G$$

Which is the same as:

$$E - E - G - A - C - C - D - E - E - G$$

Like a modern harp from the European tradition, the F and C strings on a modern *kinnor* are often colored: black/blue for F and red for C. As with many modern harps, *kinnor* strings are usually made of catgut. Unfortunately, like all harps that lack either pedals or levers, changing the pitch of a string can be a long and tedious process to make sure the strings maintain their pitch. Chromaticism outside of the ten pitched strings is entirely out of the question. However, harmonics are playable, and produce a beautiful, pure, bell-like ringing sound. Many composers trying to capture the sound of "Israel" or "the Near East," rather than writing for *kinnor,* which is the most authentic option, may instead compose music to be played on a nylon string guitar to achieve a similar timbre.

KINNOROT IN THE BIBLE

The word "*kinnor*" appears forty-two times throughout the Bible. In Genesis 4:21, the *kinnor* is the first musical instrument mentioned in the Bible, followed immediately by the *ugav* (flute).

Scripture reads:

> *And the name of his brother was Jubal; he was the ancestor of all who play the kinnor and the ugav.*
>
> Genesis 4:21

Jubal and his brother Jabal are in the eighth generation of people listed in the Bible, beginning with Adam and Eve in the Creation narrative, and descended from the line of Cain. (Genesis 4:17-21) This is interesting in that the *kinnor* and *ugav* are the only two biblical instruments to receive an explanation of their origin. Jubal and Jabal also have two half-siblings: Tubal-cain and Naameh. Jewish tradition teaches that Jubal created the *kinnor*, while Tubal-cain is described as one who "forged all implements of copper and iron." (Genesis 4:22) The lineage that leads to Noah, Abraham, and eventually David stems from Adam's and Eve's third son, Seth, who was the brother of Cain and Abel. No further descendants of Cain are mentioned after Jubal's generation. As the verses in this passage of Genesis conclude with Jubal and Tubal-cain as the originators of two of the most important musical instruments and metalwork, it seems that the author included these details for no other reason than providing a historical record. This speaks to the importance of music in biblical societies.

The only other reference to the *kinnor* in the Torah is in Genesis 31:27. In this passage, Laban confronts Jacob for fleeing with his daughters Leah and Rachel. Laban says to Jacob:

> *Why did you flee in secrecy and mislead me and not tell me? I would have sent you off with festive music, with tof (drum) and kinnorot.*
>
> Genesis 31:27

At this point in the biblical narrative, all the reader knows about the *kinnor* is that it is a very old instrument attributed to Jubal (a figure about whom the Bible describes nothing more), and that it was used to play music for a send-off. Note that at this point in the Bible, the *kinnor* has not yet been specified as a musical instrument of worship.

After the two references in the Torah, the *kinnor* is next mentioned in the stories of David and Saul. Saul was the first King of Israel. Despite God's urging toward the contrary, the people of Israel demanded a king in order to be like other nations. (1 Samuel 8) Samuel, a prophet of God, crowns Saul as king and anoints his head with oil. (1 Samuel 10:1) Shortly afterward, Samuel describes a group of prophets who play musical instruments, including the *kinnor,* while prophesizing. The other instruments are a *nevel* [harp], *tof* [drum], and *chalil* [double-reed woodwind]. (1 Samuel 10:5)

Despite Saul's many military victories, he is tormented by depression, anxiety, and fear. Saul's advisors suggest procuring a musician who could play music to sooth Saul's spirit. In Bethlehem, a young man named David was well-known for his skill in playing the *kinnor*. In fact, the Talmud explains that David so loved the *kinnor* that he slept with it hanging above his bed. (Berkhot 3b:29) David was the son of Jesse and the grandson of Ruth and Boaz. Young David plays the *kinnor* for King Saul as an early example of music therapy. Through listening to the sweet sounds of the *kinnor*, Saul's psychological torments temporarily cease. (1 Samuel 16:16-23) Saul is pleased with David, and David accepts a resident position as Saul's personal music therapist. (1 Samuel 16:14-23) The benefits of music therapy are widely acknowledged today, but this story of David and Saul demonstrates that music has been used in this capacity for millennia.

King Saul ultimately disobeys God, and in consequence, God revokes His blessing. Following God's instruction, Samuel preemptively anoints David as the future king. David defeats Goliath; becomes a warrior for the Israelite army; befriends Jonathan, Saul's eldest son; and completes his tenure in Saul's army in devoted service to his king. Saul's episodes with depression and fear persist, but David is no longer able to sooth his spirit with music.

Saul becomes increasingly paranoid that David seeks to dethrone him. Despite Saul's multiple attempts on David's life, David always spares Saul's life. Saul may have tried to have David killed many times, but when presented with an opportunity to exact revenge on Saul, David always declines since Saul is his king who was chosen by God. Eventually, Saul is defeated in battle by the Philistines. Three of his sons, including Jonathan, are killed in battle, and Saul is gravely injured. As Saul falls on his sword, his death marks the end of the would-be dynasty. Saul's surviving son, Ish-bosheth, briefly reigns as the second King of Israel, but David enjoys the support of the people of Judah, and after two years, he becomes their king. David unites the tribes of Israel and establishes Jerusalem as the capital.

During this time, David brings the Ark of the Covenant to Jerusalem. The Ark's arrival is celebrated with music and dance, including the performance of *kinnorot*, as well as a *shofar* (ram's horn), *chatzotzerot* (silver trumpets), *metziltayim* (cymbals) and *nevalim* (harps). (1 Chronicles 15:28)

When David establishes the Temple Orchestra, the *kinnor* is one of the "instruments of David" deemed worthy of and appropriate to be played to accompany and facilitate worship in the Temple. Of the 4,000 Levite musicians in the Temple Orchestra, 288 of then are selected for the *kinnor*, *nevel* (harp), and *metziltayim* (cymbals). The *kinnor* is so important to Temple worship that even though Shabbat is a holy day of rest, during which people are not permitted to do any kind of work, they were still permitted to play the *kinnor* to express their musical worship. And if a *kinnorist* is playing in the Temple on Shabbat and a string breaks, he may tie a new string onto his instrument, even though this is technically considered "work." (Eruvin 102b:14, 103b:6, 105a:10) The notion that a string may be replaced even on Shabbat demonstrates the critical role the *kinnor* played in Sabbath worship.

The prophet Isaiah mentions the *kinnor* four times, but always as part of a parable or metaphor warning against the Israelites and Judahites who have strayed from God's path. (Isaiah 5:12, 16:11, 23:16, 24:8) Ezekiel also references the *kinnor* as part of a metaphor. (Ezekiel 26:13). None of the other prophetic books mention the *kinnor*.

Moving on to the books of the *Ketuvim,* or "Writings," the *kinnor* is mentioned by name in thirteen of the 150 psalms. It is first referenced in Psalm 33:2, in which righteous readers are encouraged to "Praise the LORD" with the *kinnor* and the ten-stringed *nevel*. The *kinnorist* and *nevelist* are instructed to "Sing a new song for God" and "to play sweetly." (Psalm 33:3)

One of the most important passages in the Bible for readers seeking to better understand how to worship God is the anonymous Psalm 43. This psalm is the only example of instrumental music used to accompany personal worship in the Bible. There are numerous instances of instruments being used in communal or "corporate" worship, but this is the only example in which the author writes:

> *Send forth Your light and Your truth; they will lead me; they will bring me to Your holy mountain, to Your dwelling-place, that I may come to the altar of God, God, my delight, my joy; that I may praise You with the kinnor, O God, my God.*
>
> Psalm 43:3-4

Other passages may imply or apply to personal worship, such as Psalm 33, but Psalm 43 is the most explicit in its application of personal, instrumentally accompanied worship. Keep in mind that, as previously stated, any of the fifty-seven psalms that begin with the heading *"mizmor"* would have originally been recited along with instrumental string accompaniment.

David, the most famous musician in the Bible and the most famous *kinnorist* in history, is traditionally attributed as the author of seventy-three psalms, two short of half of the collection. Despite this figure, David only mentions the *kinnor* once in the book of Psalms in Psalm 57. The story of Psalm 57 takes place before David was anointed as King as he was hiding in a cave on the run from King Saul who sought to have him killed. David writes of singing and chanting for God. David goes on to write that the music of the *kinnor* and *nevel* will awaken his soul. David repeats that he will praise God through music. (Psalm 57:8-10)

In Psalm 49:5 (or 49:4, depending on the translation), the author, a Korahite, writes about how empowered he is as a believer in and follower of God. He writes that this melody should be set to music and played on the *kinnor*.

After 145 psalms that address joy, sorrow, thanksgiving, and the coming Messiah, among other topics, the final five psalms read like the grand finale of a great symphonic masterwork of worship. Each of these five final psalms concludes with the command to Praise the LORD, *"Hallelu-Yah!,"* or the more familiar spelling, "Hallelujah!" The *kinnor* is right at home in Psalm 149:3 and in Psalm 150:3. In the latter instance, it is joined by the *shofar*, *nevel*, *tof*, *minim*, *ugav*, and *tziltzel*. Psalm 150 is doubtless one of the greatest musical passages in the entire Bible.

The *kinnor* is next mentioned in the Book of Job. The *kinnor*, along with the *ugav* (flute), are mentioned in both Genesis, the chronological beginning of the Bible, and in Job, the book which some scholars suggest takes place contemporaneously with Abraham. In Job 21:12, Job asks why the wicked lead prosperous lives, celebrating and playing music on *kinnor*, *tof* (drum), and *ugav*. In Job 31:30, Job describes his own anguish, stating:

So my kinnor is given over to mourning,
my ugav, to accompany weepers.

Job 30:31

Ezra-Nehemiah is not the final book in either the Jewish or Christian canons. However, it is the chronological narrative end of the Hebrew Bible. The Book of Ezra-Nehemiah describes the construction of the Second Temple to replace the First Temple, which was destroyed by Babylon in 586 B.C.E. The establishment of the Second Temple also signaled the return of the Temple Orchestra. Just as the Ark of the Covenant's entrance into Jerusalem was celebrated with *kinnorot*, *nevalim*, (harps) and *metziltayim*, (cymbals) (1 Chronicles 13:8) these instruments were also played during the dedication of the Second Temple in Ezra-Nehemiah. (Nehemiah 12:27) The Temple Orchestra is re-established, and the "musical instruments of David" once again comprise the Levites' preferred instrumentation, even centuries after David's death. (Nehemiah 12:36)

As described in the previous chapter, the Book of Chronicles presents a treasure trove of insight into the music of the Holy

Temple, as well as information about the *kinnor's* role therein. The *kinnor* is first mentioned in 1 Chronicles 13:8, which describes the initial unsuccessful attempt to bring the Ark into Jerusalem, as well as in 1 Chronicles 15:28, which describes the successful second attempt. The *kinnor* is played to celebrate the Ark's arrival on both occasions. However, there are two *kinnor* references that occur between these two events. In 1 Chronicles 15:16, David commissions the creation of the Temple Orchestra. Many of these early Temple Orchestra members had served God through David as ministerial musicians, but the Temple Orchestra is now an official institution under the direction of Chenaniah. (1 Chronicles 15:22) The Levite musicians are singers, but are also commanded to accompany worship with *kinnorot, nevalim* (harps), and *metziltayim* (cymbals). Mattithiah, Eliphelehu, Mikneiah, Obed-edom, Jeiel, and Azaziah are Levites who were specifically designated in the text as *kinnorists*. This same list is reiterated a few verses later in 1 Chronicles 16:5.

Jeduthun was the Levite priest who, along with Asaph and Heman, was appointed by David to lead their families in proclaiming God's message through their musical ministry. (1 Chronicles 25:1, 2 Chronicles 5:12) The three Levites are commanded to accompany worship with *kinnorot, nevalim,* and *metziltayim.* (1 Chronicles 25:1) Chronicles' author writes that "Jeduthun accompanied on the *kinnor*, prophesied, praising and extolling the LORD." (1 Chronicles 25:3) In this passage, readers are introduced to the last of sixteen specifically named biblical figures directly associated with the *kinnor*. They are Jubal, David, Asaph, Heman, Jeduthun, Mattithiah, Eliphelehu, Mikneiah, Obed-edom, Jeiel, Azaziah, who were the Temple *kinnorists;* and finally Jeduthun, Gedaliah, Zeri, Jeshaiah,[◦] Hashabiah, and

---

[◦] Some manuscripts list a sixth son, Shimei.

Mattithiah.[y] (1 Chronicles 25:3, 25:6)

2 Chronicles 5:12 reiterates that Asaph, Heman, and Jeduthun are to lead their families in musical worship accompanied by the *kinnor,* among other instruments.

2 Chronicles 9:11 is a doublet of 1 Kings 10:12, which describes the *kinnor's* construction from algum wood.

2 Chronicles 20:28 takes place right after the story of Jahaziel and Judah's victory over the armies of Ammon, Moab, and Mount Seir. When the Judahite army returns to Jerusalem, they marched to the Temple playing *kinnorot, nevalim* (harps), and *chatzotzerot* (silver trumpets).

The final mention of a *kinnor* in the Bible describes King Hezekiah's purification and rededication of the Temple. Hezekiah orders that the Temple Orchestra, which had briefly suspended its duties, immediately resume. Meanwhile, he places Levite musicians, including *kinnorists,* at their posts to lead musical worship. (2 Chronicles 29:25)

For more information on the *kinnor,* consider reading the excellent book, *Kinnor: The Biblical Lyre in Biblical History, Thought, and Culture* by Jonathan L. Friedmann and Joel Gereboff (2021).

---

[y] There are two *kinnorists* named Mattithiah.

Kinnor references in the Bible:

Genesis 4:21, Genesis 31:27, 1 Samuel 10:5, 1 Samuel 16:16, 1 Samuel 16:23, 2 Samuel 6:5, 1 Kings 10:12, Isaiah 5:12, Isaiah 16:11, Isaiah 23:16, Isaiah 24:8, Ezekiel 26:13, Psalm 33:2, Psalm 43:4, Psalm 49:5 (or 49:4 depending on translation), Psalm 57:9 (or 57:8 depending on translation), Psalm 71:22, Psalm 81:3 (or 81:2 depending on translation), Psalm 92:4 (or 92:3 depending on translation), Psalm 98:5 (mentioned twice), Psalm 108:3, Psalm 137:2, Psalm 147:7, Psalm 149:3, Psalm 150:3, Job 21:12, Job 30:31, Nehemiah 12:27, 1 Chronicles 13:8, 1 Chronicles 15:16, 1 Chronicles 15:21, 1 Chronicles 15:28, 1 Chronicles 16:5, 1 Chronicles 25:1, 1 Chronicles 25:3, 1 Chronicles 25:6, 2 Chronicles 5:12, 2 Chronicles 9:11, 2 Chronicles 20:28, and 2 Chronicles 29:25.

NEVEL

BACKGROUND, CONSTRUCTION, AND ARCHEOLOGY

The *nevel* (plural: *nevalim*) is another member of the plucked string family. A *nevel* is essentially a larger, lower-voiced cousin of the *kinnor*. This relationship to the *kinnor* is akin to a viola and cello, or a guitar and a bass guitar, since, in modern performance at least, the *nevel* is tuned one octave lower than the *kinnor*. Bibilomusicologists believe that the *nevel* was played in a lower register than the *kinnor* for two reasons: 1) Both the *kinnor* and *nevel* are stringed instruments, but the *kinnor*'s gut strings were made from the small intestine of a sheep,[89] while the lower pitched *nevel*'s gut strings were made from a sheep's large intestine.[90] (Mishnah Kinnim 3:6) 2) When examining coins from the Bar Kokhba Revolt, one of the stringed instruments appears to be much larger than the other. Like a double bass, a tuba, or a bassoon, larger instruments tend to have a lower range of playable notes. The thicker string gauge of the *nevel*, combined with its larger body size, have led scholars to reasonably conclude that between the *kinnor* and the *nevel*, the *nevel* was the lower-pitched instrument of the two.

Bar Kokhba Coins.
Left: Kinnor; Right: Nevel, 132-136 C.E.

Like the *kinnor*, the *nevel* seems to have been constructed in varieties both with and without a bridge. Evidence of *kinnorot* pre-date *nevalim* significantly, perhaps an indication that the *nevel* was developed as a lower-register variation of the *kinnor*. While etymology can sometime help to determine an instrument's origin, this is not the case with the *nevel*. Sendrey writes that *"nevel"* means "to inflate" or "to bulge."[91] He posits that this may describe a plectrum used to play the instrument, but this theory is at odds with the writings of both Amos and Josephus. In the Book of Amos, the verb *parat*, which means "to pluck fruits," is used to describe how the instrument is played. (Amos 6:5) Most scholars take this to mean that the *nevel* was plucked using one's fingers. The 1st century C.E. Jewish historian Josephus explicitly states that the *nevel* was played with one's fingers.[92] Examining the image of the *nevel* on the Bar Kokhba coin above, it appears as though the "inflation" or "bulge" more likely refers to the body shape. Today, high-quality acoustic guitars are constructed with a curved back, which results in a better tone. Since the *nevel* appeared long after the *kinnor*, perhaps the string instrument was improved after the *kinnor* was developed, and ancient luthiers found that the slightly bulbous shape depicted on the Bar Kokhba coins improved the *nevel's* tone. This is usually achieved by hyper-hydrating the wood, then bending it and allowing it to dry in its newly-contoured shape.

The *nevel* is described twice in the Bible with the Hebrew adjective *asor*, which Sendrey explains signified that it had ten strings.[93] (Psalm 33:2, Psalm 92:4 [or 92:3 depending on translation]) Yet Josephus describes the *nevel* as having eight strings,[94] and the ancient rabbis who penned the Talmud wrote that a *nevel* could have as many as twenty-two strings, perhaps an association with the twenty-two letters of the Hebrew alphabet.[95] In reality, the number of strings on the instrument likely varied.

The terms "lyre" and "harp" are often used interchangeably, with almost no consistency, when translating the Hebrew terms *kinnor* and *nevel*. A modern *nevel* and a guitar share the same lowest string of E2. The *nevel* is seemingly the lowest-voiced instrument in the Temple Orchestra, as well as the lowest-pitched instrument of ancient Israel.[96]

Along with the *kinnor*, the *nevel* was constructed from the algum wood of Ophir. (1 Kings 10:12, 2 Chronicles 9:11) Also along with the *kinnor*, the *nevel* is also depicted on the coins recovered from the Bar Kokhba Revolt from 132 C.E. The basic design of these late *nevalim* have inspired many modern designs for both *kinnor* and *nevel* body shapes.

NEVALIM IN THE BIBLE

The *nevel* is mentioned twenty-three times throughout Scripture. It is almost always listed as an instrument of worship alongside the *kinnor*. As mentioned, the *nevel* may be a more recent musical instrument than the *kinnor*. The *kinnor* is mentioned in Genesis and Job, which chronologically are the earliest in the biblical narrative, while the *nevel* is not mentioned until 1 Samuel 10:5, shortly after Saul is anointed as the first King of Israel.[ס] The story describes a band of prophets descending from the place of worship playing a *nevel*, a *tof* (drum), a *chalil* (double-reed woodwind), and a *kinnor*.

Amos 6:5 is one of the few examples from Scripture in

[ס] Despite Genesis and Job taking place at the beginning of the biblical story, many scholars suggest that the Book of Job and the first ten chapters of Genesis were among the final additions to the Hebrew Bible.

which the *nevel* is listed apart from other instruments. In this verse, the *nevel* is described as accompaniment to a drinking song.

In every other instance, the *nevel* is always listed as part of a worship ensemble, including the Temple Orchestra. In Psalm 94:4, the *nevel* is described as an instrument played on Shabbat. As evidenced by Psalm 94 and Eruvin, a Talmudic tractate in the Order of Moed, both the *kinnor* and the *nevel* were permitted to be played on Shabbat. In its final scriptural reference, the *nevel* functions as an instrument of both war and worship. In 2 Chronicles 20:28, it is used to celebrate the victory over the Moabites, Ammonites, Meunites, following the story of the musician Jahaziel.

A set of Israeli coins from 1967.
The gold coin on the lower right depicts a nevel.

The instrument pictured above is marketed by Mid-East Instruments as a "kinnor," though by comparing it to the Bar Kokhba coin depictions, it is clearly modeled after a nevel.

Nevel references in the Bible:

1 Samuel 10:5, 2 Samuel 6:5, 1 Kings 10:12, Isaiah 5:12, Amos 6:5, Psalm 33:2, Psalm 57:9 (or 57:8 depending on translation), Psalm 71:22, Psalm 81:3 (or 81:4 depending on translation), Psalm 108:3, Psalm 150:3, Nehemiah 12:27, 1 Chronicles 13:8, 1 Chronicles 15:16, 1 Chronicles 15:20, 1 Chronicles 15:28, 1 Chronicles 16:5 (or 16:4 depending on translation), 1 Chronicles 25:1, 1 Chronicles 25:6, 2 Chronicles 5:12, 2 Chronicles 9:11, 2 Chronicles 20:28, and 2 Chronicles 29:25.

Asor

The term *asor* comes from עֶשֶׂר (*eser*), which means "ten." The word *asor* is used in a musical context three times in the Bible. (Psalms 33:2, 92:4[or 3], and 144:9) When rendered as an adjective, as in the case of two of its biblical appearances, *asor* implies the number ten, denoting an instrument's ten strings. For example, Psalm 33:2 includes the phrase "*b'nevel asor*," or "with a ten-stringed *nevel*." When used musically as a noun, therefore, context suggests that *asor* means "a ten-stringed instrument."[97] For instance, in Psalm 144:9, *asor* is used as a noun, and is not attached to another instrument such as a *nevel* or a *kinnor*. Despite Psalm 144:9's lack of a specifically-named instrument, it is usually translated into English as "ten-stringed harp." A modern example of this usage is when a guitarist says she "plays the twelve-string" in reference to her twelve-string guitar. The word "guitar" was not used, but context makes her meaning clear. Even though the Talmud and Josephus agree that the *kinnor* was produced in a ten-string variety, in the Bible, *asor* is only associated with the *nevel*.

Asor references in the Bible:

Psalm 33:2, Psalm 92:4 (or 92:3 depending on translation), and Psalm 144:9.

גִּתִּית   מִנִּים

GITTIT AND MINNIM

In this section, the *gittit* (gee-teet) and the *minnim* (mee-neem) have been grouped together. Both are possible Hebrew names of an instrument that scholars and archeologists know existed in ancient Israel, but have been unable to positively identify: the lute, or more accurately, the *oud* (pronounced "ood"). Archaeologists have excavated figurines of lutists, the earliest of which date back to approximately 1600 B.C.E, 600 years before the time of David.

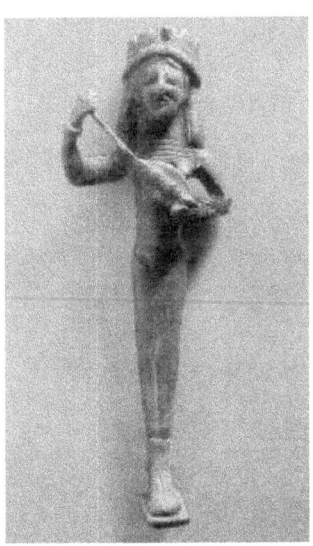

Israelite lutist figurine, Braun describes as being female, 1600-1400, B.C.E.[98]

A lute is a string instrument with a pear-shaped body which is flat on top, yet bulbous on the back. It is usually about two feet long with a neck like a guitar, a bridge and nut, and a headstock angled backward at approximately ninety degrees. In antiquity, lutes and *ouds* had as few as three strings, but thirteen strings have become the standard today. These strings are usually in pairs which are tuned in unison, or in octaves called "courses." A modern twelve-string guitar and a mandolin both feature "courses" as well.

When the term "lute" is used, it should be understood as a uniquely European variant that was derived from the much older Middle Eastern *oud*.[99] The lute, violin, and brass trumpet are all instruments which many associated with Europe, but migrated there from the ancient Near East and Middle East.[100] The lute and the *oud* are incredibly similar. The primary difference is that a European lute has frets like a guitar, while a Middle Eastern *oud* is fretless like a violin.

An oud.

Oud is an Arabic word (العود). Curt Sachs posits that the term refers to a piece of thin, flexible wood used as a plectrum, akin to a guitar pick.[101] Another theory is that it comes from the Persian word *rud* (pronounced "rood"), meaning "strings." Dumbrill argues that both terms come from the Sanskrit word *roudi,* meaning "musical instrument."[102] The term made its way into Hebrew as *oud* (עוּד). This Hebrew version has the same phonetic pronunciation as in Arabic, though its meaning refers to the more generic term "stick."

Only mentioned three times, the *gittit* (gee-teet) is one of the least understood biblical stringed instruments. (Psalms 8, 81, and 84) The JPS, NRSV, and KJV do not attempt to translate this instrument's name, and instead, simply transliterate it from the Hebrew. This indicates that the translators were unsure of the *gittit's* identity.

The words *"gittit"* and "Gath," one of the five major Philistine cities, share the same etymological root. This commonality led Sendrey to assert that the *gittit* is associated with this locality.[103] The Bible relates that David spent time in Gath, so Sendry posits that either David or the Israelites could have brought the *gittit* back to Israel and introduced it into Israelite music. (1 Samuel 27:2 and 29:3) Competing theories exist as well, such as that of Redslob and Gesenius, who agree that the *gittit* was a stringed instrument, but insist that its etymology comes from the Hebrew *nagen,* or its infinitive variation *"genet,"* which means "to play strings.[104]

The *gittit* is not the only unknown string instrument in the Bible; the other is the *minnim*. Sendrey writes that *minnim* is the plural variant of *men* and means strings from the Greek *nema*.[105] Thought the term apparently appears in the plural, contextually, it applies to a singular instrument. It is described only twice: once in Psalm 45:9 as *"minni"* and again in Psalm 150:4 as "*minnim.*" The JPS translates both of these as "lute," whereas the NRSV simply uses "stringed instruments" and "strings." The KJV uncharacteristically ignores the *minnim*. Usually, when the KJV translators were unsure of an instrument's identity, they made an educated guess and inserted the name of a contemporary instrument from the early 17th century C.E. which might be similar. In this case, these scholars were so unsure as to the identity of the *minnim* that this instrument was omitted completely in the King James Version.

The *minnim* makes an appearance in one of the greatest musical passages of the Bible: Psalm 150.

> *Hallelujah. Praise God in His sanctuary; praise Him in the sky, His stronghold.*
> *Praise Him for His mighty acts; praise Him for His exceeding greatness.*
> *Praise Him with blasts of the shofar; praise Him with nevel and kinnor.*
> *Praise Him with tof and dance; praise Him with* **minnim** *and ugav.*
> *Praise Him with tziltzel-shema; praise Him with tziltzel teruah.*
> *Let all that breathes praise the* LORD. *Hallelujah.*
>
> Psalm 150

While we cannot definitively link either the *gittit* or the *minnim* to the lute, lutes were utilized in ancient Israel.[106] There are numerous archeological artifacts that depict Israelite musicians playing lutes,[107] but for some reason, lutes were not explicitly described in Scripture. Nor were the *gittit* or *minnim* described in great detail within the Bible or in extrabiblical sources. *Minnim* may refer to some type of Israelite lute, or this word may be a general term referring to all stringed instruments, as Sachs suggests.[108] The *gittit* may also have been perhaps a closely related Philistine variety of box lyre. Between the archeological discoveries of terracotta art and figurines depicting lutes and the evidence of lutes in the civilizations and cultures in areas surrounding Israel, it seems improbable that lutes were not part of ancient Israelite music. More likely, they were part of secular culture, rather than religious ritual, and were therefore simply not mentioned in Scripture. Notice the female figure playing a lute pictured on page 109. Throughout the ancient world, prostitutes were often musicians, and specifically string players. If the lute was associated with prostitution or as a pagan instrument, it may not have found a place in the biblical narrative.[109]

Gittit references in the Bible:
Psalm 8:1, Psalm 81:1, Psalm 84:1

Minnim references in the Bible:
Psalm 45:9, Psalm 150:4

CHAPTER 4

WIND INSTRUMENTS

SHOFAR

BACKGROUND, CONSTRUCTION, AND ARCHEOLOGY

Imagine standing in the deserts of ancient Israel 3,000 years ago. It was a very quiet place compared to today. There were no cars, household appliances, humming fluorescent lights, cell phones, radios, or construction. Shepherds and farmers likely heard the same noises every day: people walking and talking, herds of bleating sheep, and the sounds of nature, such as thunder and wind. Then, a man picks up a *shofar*—a hollowed out ram's horn that has been fashioned into a trumpet—and blasts it at full volume! What an incredible and powerful sonic sensation it must have been! It is no wonder ancient Jews described its sound as divine.

MUSIC IN THE BIBLE 115

With individual references,[z] the mighty *shofar* is the most commonly mentioned instrument throughout the Hebrew Bible. Throughout the Bible, *shofarot* (plural) are used extensively for worship rituals, warfare, and civil signaling/communication. The *shofar* also holds the distinction of being the only instrument still in regular liturgical use in Jewish religious rituals and is even utilized in some Christian settings.[110]

Organic horns such as the *shofar* and conch shell were the predecessors of later brass instruments like the trumpet, trombone, and tuba.[111] In fact, *shofarot* and modern brass instruments are essentially played the same way: the player

---

[z] Sendrey and Braun both write that *"shofar"* appears seventy-four times in the Hebrew Bible, rather than seventy-two. These authors may have included *"yobel"* (another name for a *shofar*), *"teruah"* (a variety of *shofar* call), or some other alternative in the count, as the term *shofar* and variations thereof appear only seventy-two times. The terms *yobel* (6), *teruah* (6), *tekiah* (4), *noaru* (1), and *reotem* (1) all also refer to the *shofar* or a *shofar* blast.

buzzes his or her lips together against a small opening or mouthpiece. The natural conical shape of the horn functions like an amplifier, increasing the volume as the instrument's diameter expands before exploding out of the opposite end. The conical shape of the animal's horn allows for "impedance matching."[112] This means that the vibrating air molecules produced by one's buzzing lips expand as they pass through the *shofar*, matching its expanding shape. These vibrating air molecules then exit the horn, creating a far greater volume of air, and therefore sounding much louder.

Every *shofar* begins as a *keren,* the anatomical name for a "ram's horn," and both terms are used throughout the Bible. *Keren* is described in such cases as the horn of the ram that was stuck in the thicket when Abraham almost sacrificed Isaac. (Genesis 22:13) A *keren* is only designated as a *shofar* after a four-step process. First, the horn must be humanly taken from a *kosher* animal. This means that it is holy and worthy of sacred use because the animal has a cleft hoof and chews the cud. A male ram that is at least one year old is usually used for this purpose. Second, the tip is cut off to form a mouthpiece. Next, the horn is hollowed out by removing the cartilage. And lastly, the mouthpiece is straightened using heat to temporarily soften the keratin of which it is composed.[113] (Leviticus 11:3-8, Deuteronomy 14:4-8) If the horn survives this process without being damaged or cracked, then it is deemed *kosher* and is ready to be blown in worship or rituals.[114] It should be noted that the term *keren* is used only once to describe a fashioned *shofar* in Joshua 6:5.

The possible pitches or musical notes that can be produced on a *shofar* are based entirely on the harmonic overtone series (Intervallic Relationships: P1, P5, P8, M10, etc.), but there are still limitations for each individual musician.[115] A virtuoso performer may be able to combine their embouchure tension and air velocity to produce five or even six overtone partials (notes in the order of the overtone series), whereas a less-experienced performer may be limited to one or two partials. Whether or not a *shofar* player, called a "master blaster," was trained in music, such as the Temple Orchestra musicians (1 Chronicles 25:7), versus the seven priests circling Jericho, to whom the Bible does not imbue with any indication of musical prowess, (Joshua 6:4) may have had a significant impact on the tone and range produced by any given *shofar*.[116]

Most horn and brass players, even those who are quite accomplished, begin playing in the second partial of the overtone series. The lowest pitch a horn is capable of playing is called its "fundamental pitch." If a specific *shofar's* lowest pitch is E3, that means most players will be able to produce sound beginning with the second partial one octave higher at E4. That specific *shofar* can produce E4, B4, E5, G#5, B5, E6, et cetera, following the overtone series. This can be thought of as a major triad arpeggio, with the minor seventh theoretically added in the upper partials to produce an implied, arpeggiated dominant seventh chord. Bear in mind that producing sound at the minor seventh scale degree would require an unusually long *shofar* and a phenomenally-skilled player.

Players can also manipulate their embouchures to raise or lower pitches. Virtuoso players might even modulate the pitch as far as multiple semi-tones, though from a practical perspective, expectations should be limited to the second through fifth partials which make up the scale degrees of 1-5-8-10.

Keep in mind that each individual *shofar* has a different fundamental pitch based on its length and interior diameter. Therefore, just like a 17th century trumpet player in a European orchestra, if a musician acquired multiple *shofarot* in different keys (that is to say, *shofarot* with different fundamental pitches), then the player could play chromatic music. A *shofar* with C as its fundamental pitch can produce C G C E. A *shofar* with B♭ as its fundamental pitch can produce B♭ F B♭ D, etc. If a modern *shofar* player possessed *shofarot* with fundamentals of five consecutive chromatic pitches, he or she could perform all twelve chromatic Western pitches.

TABLE 6:
NOTES OF THE OVERTONE SERIES ON A SHOFAR

	Tonic	P5	P8	Maj3(10)
Shofar in C:	C	G	C	E
Shofar in C#/D♭:	C#/D♭	G#/A♭	C#/D♭	E#/F
Shofar in D:	D	F#/G♭	D	A
Shofar in D#/E♭:	D#/E♭	A#/B♭	D#/E♭	Fx/G
Shofar in E:	E	B	E	G#/A♭

Notice that all twelve chromatic pitches are accounted for.

Due to the organic and perishable nature of *shofarot*, no surviving specimens have been excavated in Israel. However, unlike most ancient instruments which have been nearly lost to history, rams' horns are still readily available around the world. By examining a 3,000-year-old ram-headed sphinx unearthed in Egypt in February of 2019, it appears that there have been no evolutionary adaptions which have significantly impacted the appearance of rams since the time of the Bible's writing.[117] This suggests that the timbre of a ram's horn has remained similarly consistent, meaning that a *shofar* today sounds the same as a *shofar* would have sounded in recent millennia.

In the Bible, *shofarot* are not specified by specific types or species. However, today there are five distinct varieties of animal horn which are used to create *shofarot*. The first is the typical and easily recognizable ram's horn.

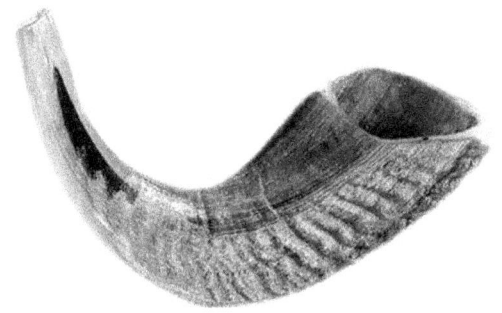

A ram's horn shofar.

A ram.

The second, and largest, is the horn from a kudu, sometimes called a *"Yemenite Shofar,"* though these horns are often seen around the world and are in no way exclusive to Yemen.

A kudu's horn shofar, also called a "Yemenite Shofar."

A kudu.

The third is the straight, black, ribbed horn of the gemsbok (the "g" is pronounced like the "g" in "gum.")

A gemsbok's horn shofar.

A gemsbok.

The fourth and rarely-seen variety is that of the eland (pronounced "yeh-land"). Eland horns are shorter and similar in length to a ram's horn, though they are straight. Despite their twisted appearance, this is their natural shape. An adult male eland can weigh more than 2,000 lbs.

A eland's horn shofar.

A eland.

The fifth and least common of all is the large ibex horn (pronounced like an Apple product: the "iBex"). This horn is large, curved, and ribbed on the outer half. Ibex are among the world's greatest wall and cliff climbers.

An ibex's horn shofar.

An ibex.

All five of these varieties are kosher and available in Israel, though many are native to Africa.

Shofarot in the Bible

The ram's horn is first mentioned as a musical instrument in Exodus 19:13, when God reveals Himself to Moses at Mount Sinai. However, in this first appearance, the less common alternative term *yobel* is used to describe a ram's horn. The term *shofar* is officially used for the first time in Exodus 19:16 and 19:19. With regard to the instruments' construction and appearance, *shofar* and *yobel* are two names for the same instrument. *"Yobel"* refers to the Jubilee Year, the seventh Sabbatical year as described in Leviticus 25, though this term can also imply a *shofar* blast associated with the Jubilee. In this first instance, it simply refers to a *shofar* blast. Moses ascends Mount Sinai and God tells him to prepare the Israelites and have them sanctify themselves, for in three days, God will appear before all of Israel as a cloud. When the day arrives, the Israelites are waiting at the foot of the mountain as the first *shofar* blast announces God's arrival first as a cloud, then as fire. The *shofar* blasts crescendo as Moses ascends Mount Sinai. In Exodus 20, God speaks to Moses and the whole of Israel as He gives the Ten Commandments. After the Decalogue is delivered, a final *shofar* blast sounds. (Exodus 20:18)

The ram's horn is next mentioned in Leviticus 23:24, which describes Rosh Hashanah, the Jewish New Year. The Hebrew term used here is *"teruah."* *"Teruah"* refers to a *shofar* blast. In modern tradition, it specifically implies a quick succession of nine blasts. This often utilizes the double-tonguing technique commonly used in brass instrument performance. Rosh Hashanah is also known as the "Festival of Trumpets" because the *shofar* plays such an important role in this religious observance and in welcoming the new year.

The *shofar's* final reference in the Torah describes its role during Yom Kippur. (Leviticus 25:9) Yom Kippur is the annual

Day of Atonement, which is observed ten days after Rosh Hashanah each year. On this day of prayer and fasting, the *shofar* plays an important part in ritual ceremonies. The *shofar* is to be played in a long, loud blast, today referred to as a *tekiah gedolah*. Together, Rosh Hashanah and Yom Kippur are known collectively as the High Holy Days.

In examining the prophetic books, the ram's horn is mentioned sixteen times in Joshua 6:4-20. The terms *shofar, yobel,* and *tekeu* (the call of a *shofar*) all appear in this passage. When the Israelites journey to the Promised Land, they are required to conquer the city of Jericho, which lies on the far east border of what is today known as the West Bank. The Ark of the Covenant is carried around the perimeter of Jericho for seven days. Seven priests walk in front of the Ark, each holding a *shofar*. On the seventh straight day of circling the city, the priests blast their *shofarot*, ushering in God's destruction of Jericho's city walls and allowing Joshua's army to capture the city.

Shofarot are mentioned once in Judges 6:34 and eight times in Judges 7:8-22. In all nine examples, the *shofar* is an instrument of war. In Judges 6:34, the Israelite judge Gideon blows the *shofar* as a call to arms. In Judges 7:8, it is implied that many, if not all of the Israelite warriors carried their own *shofarot* into battle. This allowed for signaling and communicating across a wide area. The supernatural sound of a *shofar* could also serve as a form of psychological warfare, not unlike the modern-day Māori *haka*, a Polynesian war chant. The Māori *haka* has been appropriated by many sports teams around the world as a means to intimidate and unnerve their opponents. The sound of an army of men all blasting their *shofarot* in the otherwise silent land would have been an unimaginable sonic phenomenon. In one particularly incredible moment, 300 Israelite soldiers do blast each of their own *shofarot* simultaneously! (Judges 7:22) What a magnificent cacophony it must have been. Throughout the rest of Judges 7, the *shofar* is also depicted as Gideon's principle means of communicating with his soldiers.

In 1 Samuel 13:3, King Saul carries on the tradition of using a *shofar* as an instrument of war when its sound signals a call for uprising and revolt against the Philistines. Upon the death of Saul, Israel's first king, his son Ish-bosheth, also a Benjamenite, was crowned king after being proclaimed the rightful heir to the throne by Abner, a captain in Saul's army. (2 Samuel 2:9) However, David, a Judahite, had already been anointed by God (through Samuel) as Israel's next rightful king. People from the southern Tribe of Judah pledged their allegiance to David rather than Ish-bosheth. This led to a power struggle and infighting among the Israelite tribes. During the conflict, Joab, one of David's generals, uses a *shofar* to signal his troops to cease their pursuit of the Israelite army following the death of Joab's brother, Asahel. (2 Samuel 2:28) Shortly after this event, Abner, who had faithfully served both Saul and Ish-bosheth, pledges his loyalty to David. (2 Samuel 3:6) The Judahites emerge victorious over Ish-bosheth, and David is officially recognized as the new King of Israel. David unites the Twelve Tribes of Israel into one United Kingdom of Israel. King David establishes Jerusalem as Israel's capital and the future home of the Holy Temple around the year 957 B.C.E.

To fully invite God's presence into the new capital of Jerusalem, David endeavors to re-capture the Ark of the Covenant, which was stolen by the Philistines before Saul was anointed King of Israel years earlier. When the Ark is successfully captured and delivered to Jerusalem, David dances as a *shofar* is sounded to celebrate its arrival. (2 Samuel 6:15)

Years later, David's son Absalom attempts an insurrection against his father. At the sound of a *shofar,* Absalom's followers are to declare him, Absalom, their new king. (2 Samuel 15:10) Absalom and his rebellion are eventually defeated. (2 Samuel 18:9) Later, in 2 Samuel, David's general, Joab, again sounds a *shofar,* this time as a signal for his soldiers to abandon their chase of the retreating rebels. (2 Samuel 18:16)

Like Absalom before him, a man named Sheba, son of Bikhri, later attempts a coup d'état against King David, which is signaled by a *shofar* blast. (2 Samuel 20:1) Once again, the traitor is captured and killed, and Joab uses a *shofar* to signal his men to cease their pursuit. (2 Samuel 20:22)

After a forty-year reign as the King of Israel, a seventy-year-old David abdicates the throne as his son Solomon is crowned the fourth King of Israel. *Shofar* blasts usher in his coronation both before and after the priest Zadok anoints Solomon's head with oil. (1 Kings 1:34, 39, 41) A *shofar* is also described ushering in the reign of Jehu, the tenth King of the Northern Kingdom of Israel. (2 Kings 9:13)

Numerous musical instruments are described in the Book of Isaiah, with a *shofar* first mentioned in Isaiah 18:3. In this passage, the author uses the *shofar's* war blast as a metaphor. The *shofar* is next mentioned in Isaiah 27:13, where its sound announces the future homecoming of the Jews as they return from the Babylonian Exile. Isaiah's final mention of a *shofar* is once again metaphorical. It describes false worship, and calling out sinners with "a voice like a blast from a ram's horn." (Isaiah 58:1)

The *shofar* is used for several diverse purposes throughout the seven times it appears in the Book of Jeremiah. Jeremiah was a Jewish priest living in Jerusalem in the days leading up to the

Babylonian Exile. By Jeremiah's lifetime, the Kingdoms of Israel and Judah had long since broken their covenant with God through idolatry and injustices. The Northern Kingdom had already fallen to Samaria in 722 B.C.E.[p] In Jeremiah 4:5, the author, perhaps Jeremiah himself or his scribe Baruch, describes God's impending condemnation of the Southern Kingdom of Judah. The *shofar* blast is described like an air raid siren, warning of God's imminent retribution. Jeremiah writes of a *shofar* blast twice in quick succession in 4:19 and 4:21. The first blast is for his heart's pain for the people of Israel and Judah who have strayed from God's teachings. The second time relates Jeremiah's desire to stop hearing the blasts of war. In Jeremiah 6:1, the *shofar* blast signals a final warning for the Jerusalemites to abandon the city posthaste or be captured by Nebuchadnezzar's army. In Jeremiah 6:17, the author writes that the people rejected his *shofar's* warning. In 42:14, a group of Israelites describe a plan to escape Jerusalem's siege and the blasts of war by fleeing to Egypt and taking Jeremiah with them. Jeremiah's final use of the *shofar* is when he describes nations rising up in reaction to Babylon's transgressions against Israel. (Jeremiah 51:27).

---

[p] The people of the ten tribes of the Northern Kingdom of Israel largely assimilated into the culture of the Samarians and were lost to history. These Israelites are known today as the "Lost Tribes of Israel." Since the remaining Israelites were from the Tribes of Judah (originally *Yehudah*) and Levy, they are known today simply as "Yehudim/Jehudim" or "Jews." Today's living descendants from the Tribe of Levi often have the surname of Levy or Levine. Living descendants of men who served as priests, or the Hebrew *cohen,* often have the surname Cohen.

In Ezekiel, the *shofar* is mentioned four times between Ezekiel 33:3-6. Ezekiel was a Jewish priest in Jerusalem, and a contemporary of Jeremiah. When Babylon destroyed Jerusalem in 586 B.C.E., Ezekiel was among the first round of captives taken into exile in Babylon. In 33:3-6, Ezekiel describes himself as a watchman over the Jewish people, and the *shofar* blast serves as a metaphor for Ezekiel speaking out against Israel's transgressions against God.

In the Book of the Twelve, also known as the Minor Prophets due to the short length of each author's contribution, the prophet Hosea describes the war blasts of both the *shofar* and its silver trumpet cousin, the *chatzotzerot*, which will be described in the next section.

Joel mentions the *shofar* twice: once to announce an incoming plague of locusts, (Joel 2:1) and again to signal that Israel should begin its fasting and repentance. (Joel 2:15)

The prophet Amos first cites a *shofar* when describing the war against the nation of Edom. (Amos 2:2) He also mentions a *shofar* metaphorically with regard to Israel's moral and spiritual degradation. (Amos 3:6)

In the writings of Zephaniah, he, too, comments on God's growing anger, and writes that the war blast of a *shofar* will usher in God's impending punishment. (Zephaniah 1:16)

The final minor prophet to mention music is Zechariah, who writes that the sound of a *shofar* will announce the coming of the messiah. (Zechariah 9:14)

Curiously, the *shofar* is only mentioned four times throughout the Psalms, and always in the context of worship: (Psalm 47:6 (or 47:5, depending on the translation), Psalm 81:4

(or 81:3, depending on the translation), Psalm 98:6, and Psalm 150:3. In Psalm 47, the *shofar* underscores God's ascension, while in Psalm 150, the psalmist commands readers to praise God and rejoice with eight different instruments, the *shofar* among them. The *shofar's* appearance in Psalm 81:4 has both a civic and a ritual function. The *shofar* is blasted on the evening of a new moon, signifying the beginning of the month according the lunar Jewish calendar. (Psalm 81:4-17)

The *shofar* is mentioned twice in the same passage in the Book of Job. God, in an attempt to convey the magnitude of His power and responsibilities, describes horses as one of His creations, remarking that this beast of war is unafraid of the war blasts of *shofarot*. (Job 39:24-25)

In the Book of Nehemiah, the titular post-exilic Jewish official is working in Persia under King Artaxerxes, but travels to Jerusalem to oversee the rebuilding of Jerusalem's city walls in approximately 538 B.C.E. Nehemiah describes a *shofar* player within the city walls ready to blast an alarm. (Nehemiah 4:12 [or 4:18, depending on the translation] and Nehemiah 4:14 [or 4:20, depending on the translation]).

The Bible's final references to a *shofar* are found in the Book(s) of Chronicles. One of the most noteworthy differences between these books from a bibliomusicological perspective is the fantastic detail with which David's Temple Orchestra is described. A doublet of 2 Samuel 6:15 and 1 Chronicles 15: 28 recounts *shofarot* sounding to celebrate reclaiming the Ark of the Covenant from the Philistines and bringing it to Jerusalem. It should be noted that in 2 Samuel 16:5, only *shofarot* are listed, while in 1 Chronicles 15:28, a *shofar* is listed alongside *chatzotzerot, metziltayim, nevalim,* and *kinnorot.* Note that only the *shofar* is singular; all other instruments listed in this verse are plural. This is the only instance of a *shofar* in the entire Book of 1 Chronicles.

2 Chronicles 15 takes place during the reign of King Asa, the grandson of Solomon and the third king of the Southern Kingdom of Judah. In recognition of the nation's failure to maintain its covenant with God, Asa launches a series of religious reforms. A *shofar* blasts as the Judahites shout and worship, pledging their renewed allegiance to God. (2 Chronicles 15:4) As in 1 Chronicles, 2 Chronicles only mentions the *shofar* once.

In conclusion, the *shofar* was an extremely versatile instrument and served many religious, civil, ritual, and military functions. With the abundant supply and minimal associated costs of the ram's horn, as well as its loud and powerful sound, it should come as no surprise that the *shofar* is the most frequently-mentioned musical instrument in the Bible. To this day, *shofarot* continue to play a significant role in synagogues, churches, and musical ensembles around the world.

Shofar references in the Bible:

Exodus 19:16, Exodus 19:19, Exodus 20:15 (or 20:18, depending on translation), Leviticus 25:9 (2x), Joshua 6:4 (2x), Joshua 6:5, Joshua 6:6, Joshua 6:8 (2x), Joshua 6:9 (2x), Joshua 6:13 (3x), Joshua 6:16, Joshua 6:20 (2x), Judges 3:27, Judges 6:34, Judges 7:8, Judges 7:16, Judges 7:18 (2x), Judges 7:19, Judges 7:20 (2x), Judges 7:22, 1 Samuel 13:3, 2 Samuel 2:28, 2 Samuel 6:15, 2 Samuel 15:10, 2 Samuel 18:16, 2 Samuel 20:1, 2 Samuel 20:22, 1 Kings 1:34, 1 Kings 1:39, 1 Kings 1:41, 2 Kings 9:13, Isaiah, 18:3, Isaiah 27:13, Isaiah 58:1, Jeremiah 4:5, Jeremiah 4:19, Jeremiah 4:21, Jeremiah 6:1, Jeremiah, 6:17, Jeremiah, 42:14, Jeremiah 51:27, Ezekiel 33:3, Ezekiel 33:4, Ezekiel 33:5, Ezekiel 33:6, Hosea 5:8, Hosea 8:1, Joel 2:1, Joel 2:15, Amos 2:2, Amos 3:6, Zephaniah 1:16, Zechariah, 9:14, Psalm 47:6 (or 47:5, depending on translation), Psalm 81:4 (or 81:3, depending on translation), Psalm 98:6, Psalm 150:3, Job 39:24, Job 39:25, Nehemiah 4:12 (or 4:18, depending on translation), Nehemiah 4:14 (or 4:20, depending on translation), 1 Chronicles 15:28, 2 Chronicles 15:14.

חֲצֹצְרוֹת

CHATZOTZEROT

BACKGROUND, CONSTRUCTION, AND ARCHEOLOGY

Shofarot and *chatzotzerot* are both translated as "trumpets" in many English Bibles, especially older versions. While the *shofar* is actually a ram's horn that has been fashioned into a musical instrument,[118] *chatzotzerot* (or the singular *chatzotzerah*) are valveless metal trumpets made of hammered silver.[119] (Numbers 10:2) *Chatzotzerot* are mentioned thirty times throughout the Hebrew Bible. These ancient antecedents closely resemble their modern European counterparts, which also lacked valves until the early 1800s. *Chatzotzerot* are first mentioned in the Book of Numbers, when God commands Moses to craft them as signaling instruments for "summoning the congregation and breaking down camp." (Numbers 10:1-2) *Chatzotzerot* are mentioned throughout the Bible, with the most prevalent references relating to the Temple Orchestra, as described throughout the Book(s) of Chronicles. These silver trumpets were only played by Levite priests, marking them as sacred instruments to the Israelites.[120] The term *chatzotzerot* is always written in the plural, save for one instance, indicating that these trumpets were almost always played in pairs. The sole exception is Hosea 5:8, when the singular *chatzotzerah* makes its only appearance.

One of the greatest advantages to studying bibliomusicology in Hebrew rather than in English is the specificity of the original diction. Many English Bibles use the terms "horn" and "trumpet" interchangeably throughout Scripture. In contrast, the Hebrew terms of *shofar* and *chatzotzerot* inform the reader whether the instrument in question is a ram's horn or a pair of silver trumpets. These two instruments differ in both timbre and musical context, since the *chatzotzerot* are only used in sacred settings. *Shofarot* are used in civil, ritual, and military settings, as well as sacred contexts.[121]

When *chatzotzerot* are first described in Numbers 10:2, readers may wonder how the Hebrews, recently freed from slavery in Egypt, came into possession of two silver trumpets. In Exodus 3:22, 11:2, and 12:35, the Israelites comply with God's instructions to take the Egyptians' gold, silver, and clothing as spoils and reparations for their enslavement. One might imagine gold and silver coins, bars, or rough pieces of precious metals, but the text more likely refers to jewelry, cutlery, works of art, and yes, musical instruments. Babylon's Lyres of Ur were plated in silver, and Egypt fashioned their trumpets from hammered silver. Evidence that Egypt had similar trumpets from this time period resides in the Museum of Egyptian Antiquities in Cairo.[122] To be clear, the Torah describes that Israelites made their own silver trumpets (Numbers 10:1-2), but the silver used to make them likely came from Egypt, as would their design.

In Exodus, the Egyptian Pharaoh is never mentioned by name, but many scholars suggest that Ramesses II (1303-1213 B.C.E.) is the most likely. Working within this theory, the trumpets played in the Book of Numbers would have been made from or possibly modeled on 13th century B.C.E. Egyptian spoils from the Israelites' escape.

The Pharaoh Tutankhamen, or as he is more famously known, "King Tut," died and was entombed in 1325 B.C.E. Tutankhamen's mummified remains were buried along with a massive treasure of artwork, jewelry, and abundant works of gold and silver. Among these were two trumpets: one silver, the other of bronze and copper. Ramesses II assumed the throne forty-six years later in 1279 B.C.E. This means that

Tutankhamen's trumpets, which were taken from the tomb and reside in the Museum of Egyptian Antiquities in Cairo, may be only forty-six years removed the trumpets of the Exodus narrative. If Ramesses II was indeed the Pharaoh during the historical migration of Semitic people to the land of Canaan, then trumpets from his reign would be no more than 112 years removed from Tutankhamen's. This means that modern scholars have an excellent idea as to what the *chatzotzerot* looked and sounded like.

In addition to the dominant theory that Ramesses II is the most likely candidate for the Pharoah depicted in the Exodus story, a competing theory is that the pharoah's identity could be Thutmoses III, who lived 117 years before Tutankhamen.[123]

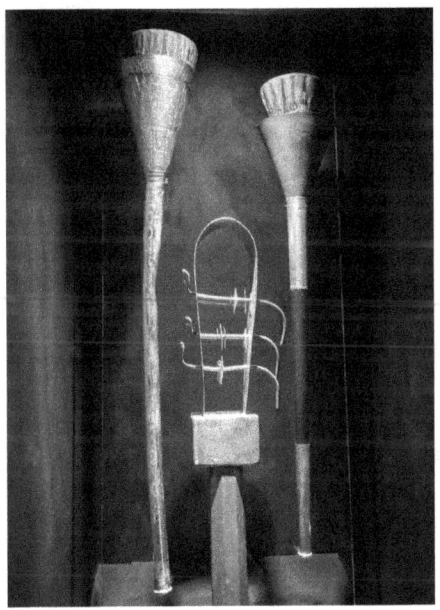

Tutankhamun's Trumpets with their wooden cores inserted, as well as a sistrum in the middle.

*Tutankhamen's silver trumpet (left),
alongside its protective wooden core.*

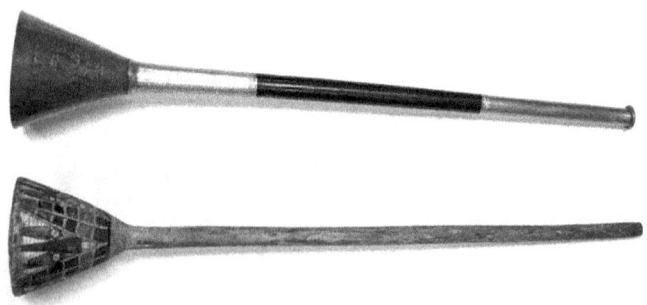

*Tutankhamen's copper trumpet (top),
alongside its protective wooden core.*

Known today as "Tutankhamun's Trumpets," these instruments were re-discovered in 1922 C.E., 3,247 years after being buried. They are widely considered to be the oldest working trumpets in existence from any culture.[124] The silver trumpet is 22½ inches in length, while the copper/bronze trumpet is 19½ inches in length. Both have an internal diameter graduating from ½ inch at the mouthpiece to 1 inch at the base of the flared bell.[125] Each trumpet is made of a sheet of metal that has been rolled into its conical shape.[126] The bronze trumpet features a gold-alloy bell.[127] Both trumpets were found with a protective wooden core insert which preserved the instruments' shape.

Tutankhamun was buried with these instruments in 1325 B.C.E, where they laid silent for 3,247 years. Incredibly, they were played once again in 1939, over the radio airwaves of the BBC.[128] An audio recording of this fantastic performance has thankfully been preserved.[129] The sound is similar to that of modern trumpets to a remarkable degree. The silver trumpet's lowest pitch is B4, while the copper trumpet's lowest pitch is a half-step higher at C5.[130] From there, they follow the same overtone series as all other horns. To hear these magnificent instruments played for the first time in more than three thousand years, please listen to the audiobook version of this book, or visit www.musicinthebible.com.

Tutankhamun's Trumpets' 1939 BBC performance.

There have been claims that the instruments are haunted or have magical properties. This is because each of the three times the trumpets have been blown in the last fifty years, it is always followed by a conflict. A museum staffer blew the trumpets in 1967. Days later, the Six-Day War began between Israel and her neighbors, Jordan, Syria, and Egypt. A different museum staffer also blew the trumpets in 1991. Shortly thereafter, the Gulf War began between a United States-led coalition and Iraq. The last time the trumpets were played was in 2011. One week later, the 2011 Egyptian Revolution began. During the rioting and chaos, the copper trumpet was stolen from the museum. It was anonymously returned to the museum a few days later.

Bar Kokhba Coin Depicting Chatzotzerot, 132-136 C.E.

The trumpets found in Tutankhamun's tomb could very likely be contemporaneous with and built to the same specifications as the earliest *chatzotzerot* of Israel.[131] The coins recovered from the Bar Kokhba Revolt of 132 C.E., noted earlier for their depictions of the *kinnor* and *nevel*, also feature a pair of *chatzotzerot* that closely resemble Tutankhamun's Trumpets.[132]

Chatzotzerot in the Bible

As described above, the *chatzotzerot* are first mentioned in Numbers 10:2 on the first anniversary of the Passover, which reads:

> *The* Lord *spoke to Moses, saying: Have two silver chatzotzerot made; make them of hammered work. They shall serve you to summon the community and to set the divisions in motion.*
>
> Numbers 10:1-2

By this account, the two specific trumpets played in Numbers 10:1-2 were clearly not taken from Egypt as intact musical instruments, as they were hand-hammered by Israelites. Yet considering the complete lack of available resources, they were almost certainly crafted from the Israelites' spoils of Egyptian silver.

The Israelites developed a system of *chatzotzerot* calls, each with a different meaning or direction:

> *When both [chatzotzerot] are blown in long blasts, the whole community shall assemble before you at the entrance of the Tent of Meeting; and if only one is blown, the chieftains, heads of Israel's contingents, shall assemble before you. But when you sound short blasts, the divisions encamped on the east shall move forward; and when you sound short blasts a second time, those encamped on the south shall move forward. Thus short blasts shall be blown for setting them in motion, while to convoke the congregation you shall blow long blasts, not short ones.*
>
> *The chatzotzerot shall be blown by Aaron's sons, the priests; they shall be for you an institution for all time throughout the ages. When you are at war in your land against an aggressor who attacks you, you shall sound short blasts on the chatzotzerot, that you may be remembered before the LORD your God and be delivered from your enemies.*
>
> *And on your joyous occasions—your fixed festivals and new moon days—you shall sound the trumpets over your burnt offerings and your sacrifices of well-being. They shall be a reminder of you before your God: I, the LORD, am your God.*
>
> Numbers 10:3-10

TABLE 7:
CHATZOTZEROT DESCRIPTIONS

- Only Levites are permitted to blow *chatzotzerot.*
- Blow short blasts when Israel is attacked on her own soil.
- *Chatzotzerot* are to be made in pairs and of hammered silver.

CHATZOTZEROT SIGNALS:

Both *chatzotzerot*, long blasts:	Everyone gathers before the Tabernacle.
One *chatzotzerah*, long blasts:	Leaders gather before the Israelites.
One round of short blasts:	Israelites on the eastern side advance.
Two rounds of short blasts:	Israelites on the southern side advance.
Short blasts:	Signal motion.
Long blasts:	Call to assemble.

Chatzotzerot differ from *shofarot* in that there are specific rhythmic patterns for these instruments which are outlined in the Bible. While the modern rhythmic variants of the *shofar* are named in Scripture (*tekiah, shevarim,* and *teruah*), their specific meanings are not described. The modern interpretation and meanings for these three Hebrews terms for *shofar* blasts, pictured below, are seemingly arbitrary inventions by the 4th century C.E. by Rabbi Abbahu of Caesarea.[133] Rabbi Abbahu's system is still practiced today. This system is referred to as "The "Order of Blowing" in the Talmud.[134] A fourth call, *tekiah gedolah,* is an elongated variation of the first call, *tekiah.*

Chatzotzerot are absent from the biblical text between Deuteronomy and 1 Kings.

Chatzotzerot are next mentioned in 2 Kings 11. Athaliah, the daughter of Ahab and Jezebel (from the story of Elijah), learns that her son King Ahaziah of the Southern Kingdom of Judah has been killed. Upon hearing this news, Queen Athalia begins killing every potential heir in an attempt to claim the throne for herself. Ahaziah's infant son Joash, the rightful heir to the throne, is taken and hidden by Athaliah's daughter, Jehosheba. After six years of Queen Athaliah's tyrannical reign, a Temple priest named Jehoiada decides to act. Jehoiada brings the young Joash to the Temple to protect him from Athaliah's forces. When Athaliah confronts King Joash, the child is surrounded by both warriors and *chatzotzerot* players to protect him and celebrate his coronation. (2 Kings 11:14) *Chatzotzerot* are then sounded throughout the land, along with chants of "Long live the King!" (2 Kings 11:14) Athaliah is taken outside and killed by an order from the priests. (2 Kings 11:1-16)

By 2 Kings 12, Joash has become a young man and is a righteous king. Seeing that the Holy Temple is in disarray and in need of repair and restoration, Joash commands that all incoming funds first be used to restore the Temple. This includes temporarily ceasing the creation of *chatzotzerot* so that the silver may instead be used to pay the workers laboring over the Temple's restoration. (2 Kings 12:14)

The only time the singular variant *chatzotzerah* is written in the Bible is found in Hosea 5:8. The prophet Hosea lived about two hundred years after the Northern Kingdom of Israel seceded under the reign of Jeroboam II, arguably one of Israel's worst kings. The *chatzotzerah* is mentioned alongside the *shofar* as Hosea calls for the two to metaphorically "sound the alarm" on Israel's failing leaders. Hosea predicts Israel's fall, which is realized in 722 B.C.E. when the Northern Kingdom is conquered by Assyria. There is no explanation or contextual information which would provide a clue as to this strange singular use of this word rather than the traditional *chatzotzerot*.

Chatzotzerot are next mentioned in Psalm 98:6. The oft cited Psalm 98 urges readers to "Sing to the LORD a new song."

In this musical verse, the anonymous author writes:

> Raise a shout to the LORD, all the earth, break into joyous songs of praise!
> Sing praise to the LORD with the kinnor, with the kinnor and melodious song.
> With chatzotzerot and the blast of the shofar raise a shout before the LORD, the King.
>
> Psalm 98:5-7

In the Book(s) of Ezra-Nehemiah, the Jews are freed from their Babylonian captivity by King Cyrus the Great of Persia. Cyrus permits the Jews to return to their homeland and rebuild the Temple in Jerusalem.⁷ Once the new Temple's foundation is complete, the priests *(Cohanim)* don their linen robes and blast *chatzotzerot,* while the Levites crash *metziltayim* (cymbals). (Ezra 3:10) Later in the narrative, upon the completion of the wall around Jerusalem, the *chatzotzerot* are sounded by priests once again, along with singing and the playing of *metziltayim, nevalim,* and *kinnorot*. (Nehemiah 12:35) These instruments are collectively referred to as the "musical instruments of David." (Nehemiah 12:36) The *chatzotzerot* are later mentioned in the same chapter upon the introduction of the new Temple Orchestra music director, Jezrahiah. (Nehemiah 12:41-42) Some translations write that Jezrahiah was "in charge," while

---

⁷ This reconstructed House for God is known as the "Second Temple." The Second Temple stood in Jerusalem from 516 B.C.E. until the Romans destroyed it in 70 C.E. Prior to its destruction, it was greatly expanded by King Herod the Great, beginning in 19 B.C.E. The Islamic Dome of the Rock was erected in its place between 691-692 C.E., where it still stands today.

others use the term "choir director." The specifics of Jezrahiah's position are unknown, but he may have been a "chironomer," a special variety of music conductor that will be explored in Chapter 9: Biblical Music Notation.

The final seventeen *chatzotzerot* references are found in the Book(s) of Chronicles, and describe the Temple Orchestra. The first of these references describes the musical celebration when David first endeavors to retrieve the Ark of the Covenant and bring it from Philistia to Jerusalem. *Chatzotzerot* are blasted, along with music from an ensemble of singers, *kinnorot, nevalim, tuppim,* and *metziltayim*. (1 Chronicles 15:8) However, this first attempt to move the Ark to Jerusalem failed when an ox that was pulling the Ark stumbled. The Ark was temporarily left in the Philistine city of Gath. After David conquered the Philistines, the Ark was successfully relocated to Jerusalem, with priests Shebania, Joshaphat, Nethanel, Amasai, Zechariah, Benaiah, and Eliezer sounding *chatzotzerot* in front of the Ark on its journey. (1 Chronicles 15:24) Upon its arrival in Jerusalem, David, dressed in priestly garments of fine linen, dances while *chatzotzerot* and *shofarot* are blasted, *metziltayim* are crashed, a choir sings, and *nevalim* and *kinnorot* are loudly played. (1 Chronicles 16:27-28) The Ark is placed within its tent (remember, this is decades before the First Temple was erected) and everyone continued to celebrate with the aforementioned instruments, sans *shofar*. (1 Chronicles 16:6) David then proceeds to offer a song of worship and thanksgiving. (1 Chronicles 16:7-36)

In Chronicles 16, the author describes the worship practices that David established in Jerusalem and Gibeon. David appoints Levite priests named Heman, Jeduthun, and "others chosen by name" to lead worship with familiar refrains of "His faithful love endures forever!," accompanied by *chatzotzerot, metziltayim,* and other instruments. (1 Chronicles 16:42)

In 2 Chronicles 5:12-14, we receive another portrait of David's Temple Orchestra, though by this time, David has since passed away. The Temple—imagined by David and realized by Solomon—is complete, and Solomon orders that the Ark of the Covenant be brought inside.

This passage reads:

> . . . *all the Levite singers, Asaph, Heman, Jeduthun, their sons and their brothers, dressed in fine linen, holding metziltayim, nevalim, and kinnorot, were standing to the east of the altar, and with them were 120 priests who blew chatzotzerot. The chatzotzerim[v] and the singers joined in unison to praise and extol the* LORD; *and as the sound of the chatzotzerot, metziltayim, and other musical instruments, and the praise of the* LORD, *"For He is good, for His steadfast love is eternal," grew louder, the House, the House of the* LORD, *was filled with a cloud. The priests could not stay and perform the service because of the cloud, for the glory of the* LORD *filled the House of God.*
>
> 2 Chronicles 5:12-14

Moving through the end of 2 Chronicles, the stories of the kings from the Northern Kingdom of Israel and the Southern Kingdom of Judah are revisited. In 2 Chronicles 13:12-14, *chatzotzerot* are used in warfare once again when King Abijah of Judah waged war against Jeroboam of Israel around the time of the Northern secession.

When the third king of the Southern Kingdom of

---

[v] Musicians who play *chatzotzerot*.

Judah, Asa, institutes religious reforms in an attempt to return to the terms of their covenant with God, the people celebrate by blasting *chatzotzerot* and *shofarot*. (2 Chronicles 15:14)

Chatzotzerot are next mentioned in 2 Chronicles near the conclusion of the story of the Levite musician Jahaziel. After their victory over the Moabites, Ammonites, and Meunites, the Southern Kingdom of Judah's warrior-musicians enter Jerusalem playing *nevalim, kinnorot,* and *chatzotzerot*. (2 Chronicles 20:28)

The revolt against Queen Athalia is described with the same musical elements in Chronicles as it was in Kings, both with commanders and *chatzotzerim (chatzotzerah-playing* priests) surrounding the young Joash, and with *chatzotzerot* being sounded throughout Judah celebrating the new King Joash. (2 Chronicles 23:13)

After a succession of righteous kings alternating with kings who fell short of God's expectations for them, the Temple had been desecrated and was in need of ritual cleansing. King Hezekiah ordered the Levite priests to carry out a ritual cleansing. Upon the Temple's rededication, the designated Levite musicians took their places around the Temple with the instruments of David (singers, *nevalim, kinnorot, metziltayim,* et cetera) while the priests took their positions with *chatzotzerot*. Hezekiah ordered that a burnt offering be placed on the altar as the instruments were played and the singers recited a song of worship and thanksgiving. (2 Chronicles 29:25-28) This concludes the *chatzotzerot* references in the Hebrew Bible.

Chatzotzerot references in the Bible:

Numbers 10:2, Numbers 10:8, Numbers 10:9, Numbers 10:10,
Numbers 31:6, 2 Kings 11:14 (2x), 2 Kings 12:14, Hosea 5:8,
Psalm 98:6, Ezra 3:10, Nehemiah 12:35, Nehemiah 12:41,
1 Chronicles 13:8, 1 Chronicles 15:24, 1 Chronicles 15:28,
1 Chronicles 16:6, 1 Chronicles 16:42, 2 Chronicles 5:12,
2 Chronicles 5:13 (2x), 2 Chronicles 13:12, 2 Chronicles 13:14,
2 Chronicles 15:14, 2 Chronicles 20:28,
2 Chronicles 23:13 (2x), 2 Chronicles 29:26,
2 Chronicles 29:27, 2 Chronicles 29:28.

עוּגָב

Ugav

The first time music is mentioned in the Bible identifies Jubal as the ancestor of all who play the *kinnor* and *ugav* (pronounced oo-gahv). (Genesis 4:21) It is unclear why he is given this designation. The specific diction used may indicate that Jubal invented or refined the instruments utilized within ancient Israelite culture. Or perhaps he popularized these instruments or was an early virtuoso. The *ugav* is mentioned a mere four times in the Bible.

Modern scholars almost unanimously agree that an *ugav* was a flute, though the King James Version translates *ugav* as an "organ." This has misled and confused English readers around the world.[135] Many readers see the term "organ" and assume that some ancestor of the modern pipe organ is being described. This confusing translation is derived from the Old English word *organe*, which was a general term for a musical instrument.[136] It appears that the KJV translators were unsure as to the identity of an *ugav*, so they chose a general term instead.[137] In modern Hebrew, *ugav* does refer to a pipe organ, which further compounds the mistranslation issue. While modern scholars generally agree that an *ugav* was a flute, historically, musicologists have suggested everything from a flute to a *kithara* or even a bagpipe as its true identity.[138]

Two of the most prominent 20th century scholars in the field of bibliomusicology, Alfred Sendrey and Curt Sachs, agree that, based on contextual clues throughout Scripture combined with etymological analyses, *ugav* is an early ancient term for some specific type of flute.[139] However, they further posit that the word *ugav* later evolved, taking on a new meaning as a general term for flutes.¹⁴⁰ To compare this to a modern example, an electric guitar, acoustic guitar, and nylon string classical guitar are three distinct varieties of instrument, each with their own recognizable tone, timbre, and playing style. At the same time, they are all varieties of guitar, with many shared musical and physical attributes. According to Sendrey's and Sachs's theories, by the time Psalm 150 was composed, *"ugav"* had already evolved into a general term for flutes.¹⁴¹

When searching for a modern descendant of the *ugav*, one might first consider the *ney*, a 5,000-year-old flute that remains a staple of Middle Eastern music to this day.¹⁴² This end-blown flute was originally from Persia (modern-day Iran). There are a few different varieties, but most are between twenty and forty inches long, with six finger holes. Considering how widespread other musical instruments from the biblical era were throughout the Near and Middle East, it is highly probable that the *ney* or a similar flute would have been played by the ancient Israelites.

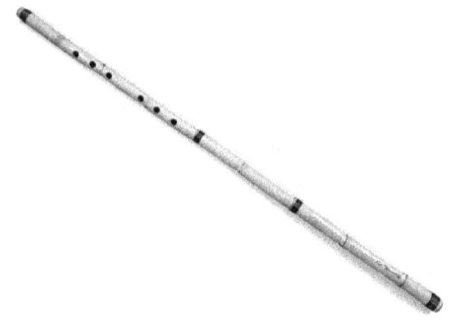

A Persian ney.

Unfortunately, wooden instruments almost never survive over many centuries, even if they are well-preserved.¹⁴³ The Lyres of Ur remained intact for so many years only due to their gold plating and air-tight entombment.[144] However, archeologists have discovered eleven bone flutes in and around Megiddo, Israel.[145] They are all between 2.75 inches and 4.74 inches in length, and are composed of bird or goat bone. They each have a single finger hole in the center, and are highly polished.[146] The earliest of these flutes date back to 3000 B.C.E, two millennia before the Israelite Monarchy, and the latest can be dated to the 6th century B.C.E, around the time of the Southern Kingdom of Judah's fall and the Babylonian Exile.[147] These flutes could produce two pitches, often at an interval of a perfect fourth, and a player could quickly trill between the two notes.[148] While these bone flutes could have been played as a musical instrument, they were also likely used by shepherds like a whistle for herding purposes.[149] The eleven Megiddo Flutes are the only examples of bone instruments that have been found in Israel.[150]

The Megiddo Flute, 3rd Millennium B.C.E.

Ugav references in the Bible:

Genesis 4:21, Psalm 150:4, Job 21:12, Job 30:31.

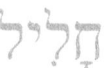

Chalil

The *chalil* is a woodwind instrument mentioned just four times throughout the Bible.[151] Its name is derived from the verb *chalal*, which means "to hollow out, to pierce."[152] This etymology has contributed to a general understanding that the *chalil* was some type of flute or pipe. Based on available resources, as well as the practices of Israel's neighbors, most scholars agree that the *chalil* was likely a reed instrument, and more specifically a double-reed akin to an oboe.[153] Archaeologists have recently found a small bronze figure of a girl playing a woodwind instrument, in much the same way as one would play a clarinet or oboe today.[154] Some argue that this is an additional clue that gives credence to this theory as to the *chalil's* identity. A contemporary instrument which is played the same way and fits the *chalil's* general description is the Armenian *duduk* (pronounced: doo-dóok), a double-reed instrument that appeared as early as 1200 B.C.E. Most *duduks* range from 9 to 31 inches in length and have eleven finger holes. Though double-reed woodwinds are often associated with a shrill timbre, in the hands of a virtuoso, its tone is sweet and mellow like a clarinet's lower register. Similar double-reeds were discovered along with the Lyres of Ur.[155] This ancient traditional instrument may account for the importance of the clarinet in the Eastern European Klezmer music of Ashkenazi Jews.[156]

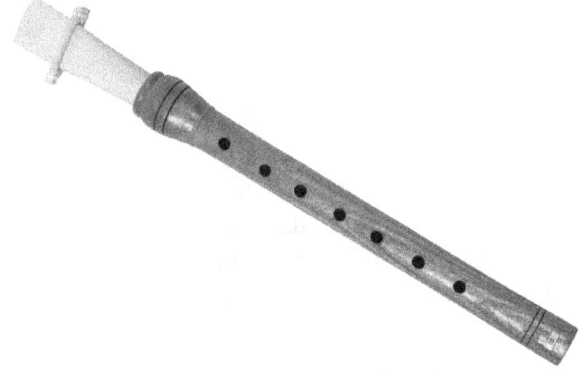

An Armenian duduk.

Chalil references in the Bible:

1 Samuel 10:5, 1 Kings 1:40, Isaiah 5:12, Isaiah 30:29.

Machol

Machol is the only *potential* musical term which is <u>not</u> included in this book's official list of all musical references in the Bible (see Appendix). While the term *machol* is clearly present in ten different verses that relate to music, its identification as a musical instrument is highly contested among most, but not all, scholars, as well as the translators of every major English version of both Jewish and Christian Bibles. The root of *machol* is *hul*, which means "to whirl" or "to dance in a circle."[157] Accepting this translation, every major English Bible translates *machol* as "dance." Numerous biblical scholars, both ancient and modern, agree that *machol* means "dance." However, some scholars disagree, and assert that the *machol* was a woodwind instrument, similar to a *chalil*. The most notable voice of dissension was the famous eleventh century French rabbi and Jewish commentator Rashi.[158] Rabbi <u>Sh</u>lomo <u>Y</u>itzchaki, known more commonly by his acronym nickname "Rashi," posits that if the verses are read with his proposed meaning in mind, they make perfect sense.[159] His observation may have merit.

Take, for example, Psalm 150:

> *Hallelujah.*
> *Praise God in His sanctuary;*
> *praise Him in the sky, His stronghold.*
> *Praise Him for His mighty acts;*
> *praise Him for His exceeding greatness.*
> *Praise Him with blasts of the shofar;*
> *praise Him with nevel and kinnor.*
> *Praise Him with tof and* **machol***;*
> *praise Him with minnim and ugav.*
> *Praise Him with resounding tzitzel;*
> *praise Him with loud-clashing tzitzel.*
> *Let all that breathes praise the LORD.*
> *Hallelujah.*
>
> Psalm 150

Are the translators right to follow the widely-accepted and agreed-upon meaning of "dance," or is another instrument more likely? Does it seem more logical that *machol* means dance, even though it is surrounded by a list of all the major musical instruments? This question has been raised and pondered for centuries, and there is no definitive answer at this time. Rashi believed that the *machol* was a woodwind instrument that was used to accompany dancing, which explains the *hul* root. This book's appendix omits the *machol*, but Rashi's theory is presented here for readers' consideration.

Machol references in the Bible:

Exodus 15:20, Exodus 32:19, Judges 11:34, Judges 21:21, Jeremiah 31:4, Jeremiah 31:13, Psalm 30:12, Psalm 149:3, Psalm 150:4, Lamentations 5:15.

עֲלָמוֹת

Alamot

Not to be confused with the anagram *ma'alot* (a variety of psalm called the "song of degrees"), the term *"alamot"* is one of the most curious music-related terms in all of Scripture. The singular variant, *alemah* (עַלְמָה), is understood to mean a young woman of marriageable age. In fact, *alemah* is the word used in Isaiah 7:14, which describes that a young woman will give birth to a son named Emanuel.

According to Sendrey, *Alamot* appears in a musical context four times.[160] Psalms 9 and 46 both contain "on *alamot"* in the heading. In Psalm 68:26, David describes *alamot toffot*, which is generally understood to mean young women playing drums. Lastly, 1 Chronicles 15:20 describes *nevalim al-alamot*. In this case, the JPS translators opted not to translate *alamot* and simply provided a transliteration. This is interesting, since based on Psalm 68:26, one might assume that women are playing *nevalim* in 1 Chronicles 15:20. The KJV and NRSV both similarly translate Psalm 68:26 as young women playing drums, but transliterate *"alamoth"* in 1 Chronicles 15:20. This suggests that there may be some disagreement and mystery surrounding *alamot's* meaning.

The editors of the JPS Jewish Study Bible and www.Sefaria.org agree that, when used in a musical context, *alamot* simply refers to female musicians or singers. However, Sendrey suggests the strange contexts surrounding *alamot* may mean that it could actually be a Hebrew rendering of a Greek instrument's name, an *elymos,* which itself is a variety of another Greek instrument, the *aulos*.[161] An *elymos aulos* is a double-barreled woodwind that can therefore produce two simultaneous pitches. Most double-barreled woodwinds typically produce a droning pitch with one pipe and a wide range of melodic notes with the other pipe. The *aulos* is an exception to this standard, as both barrels have finger holes, and can therefore both perform melodies. Sendrey seems to suggest that when the term *alamot* is used in conjunction with the name of another instrument, it refers to a double-barreled version of the instrument in question. One aspect of his theory is that the "*-ot*" suffix which denotes a plural noun refers in this case to the fact that there are two barrels on the instrument. The problem with Sendry's theory is that *alamot* only appears alongside *toffot* (drums) and *nevalim*, two instruments which cannot have a double barrel. These are also the two instruments most associated with women in the ancient world. For more information on the *aulos,* see Chapter 2 of the companion piece to this book, *Music in the New Testament* by Charles Jirkovsky.

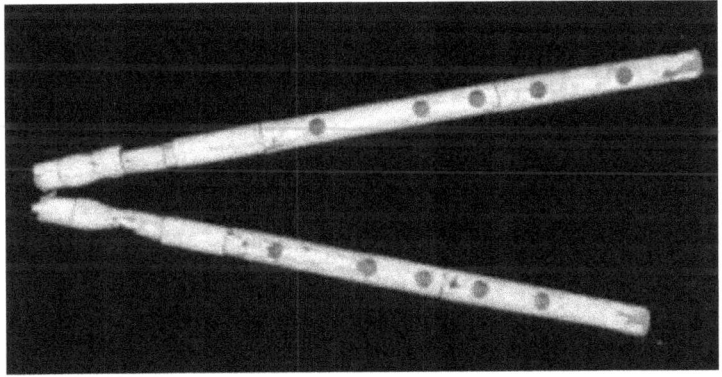

A Greek elymos aulos.

Perhaps, if these biblical passages received final redactions and edits during the Hellenistic period, a Greek *elymos aulos* could theoretically have been a commonplace instrument in Israel. After all, the *kinnor* adopted a noticeably Greek look during the Greco-Roman era. The Book of Daniel also features some Greek-influenced musical instruments that will be described in Chapter 6.

Another possibility is that the Greek name was adapted during the Hellenistic era to fit an ancient, traditional Near Eastern instrument for which the Jews simply did not have a name. In identifying a Near Eastern double-barreled woodwind instrument that might have been played in Israel, the Egyptian *yarghul* is the clear frontrunner. This instrument utilizes a single-reed, but otherwise fits the description of an *alamot* and an *elymos* in every respect. A *yarghul* has a truly unique timbre, sounding somewhat like a bagpipe plugged into an electric guitar distortion pedal.[162]

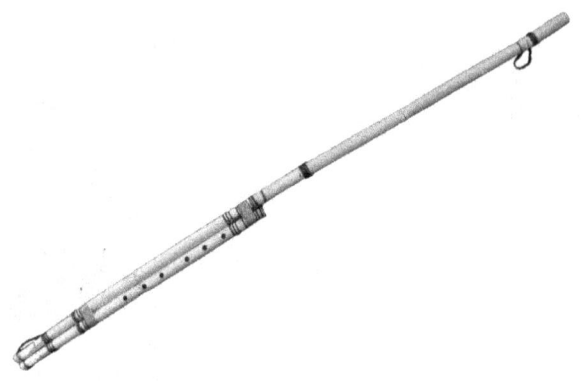

An Egyptian *Yarghul*.

On a typical modern *yarghul*, the longer droning pipe is approximately thirty-six inches in length. *Yarghuls* commonly drone at a D4 pitch. The shorter melodic pipe is approximately twelve inches in length and has six finger holes. Both end-blown pipes are inserted into the player's mouth and blown simultaneously. To maintain a constant drone, circular breathing, a technique which allows a musician to play continuously without stopping to take a breath, is often employed.

Alamot references in the Bible:

Psalm 9:1, Psalm 46:1, Psalm 68:26, 1 Chronicles 15:20.

Chapter 5

Drums and Percussion

תֹף

Tof

Tof is a general term referring to all drums. Ancient drums were made of wood, with a tightly stretched and fastened animal hide serving as the drum head.[163] In Israel, the hide was usually taken from a ram or wild goat.[164] The *tof* holds the distinction of being the only musical instrument in the Bible that is rendered in both the masculine and feminine noun classes across the sixteen biblical references. Psalm 68:26 uses the feminine *"toffot."* The other fifteen instances use the masculine *"tuppim."* The plural of *tof* is *tuppim* as the Hebrew letter פ/ף *(fe/pe)* is equivalent in sound to both the English "F" and "P," distinguished only by a small dot in the center of the letter called a *dagesh*.

Iconographic and archeological evidence within Israel and her neighbors suggests that a variety of drums were used throughout ancient Israel. These include drums with a single head, and others with a drumhead on each side. Additionally, recognizable drums from other cultures, such as the West African *djembe* or the Persian *tombak,* also appeared in Israel. Even Indian *tabla* drums, which must have traveled quite a distance to be used in Israel, are mentioned in rabbinic literature.[165] However, the most common variety of Israelite drum was undeniably the frame drum. Frame drums are medium-to-large hand drums made from a thin strip of wood bent into a circle, with an animal hide drumhead covering one or both sides. Archeologists have discovered nearly sixty terracotta figurines of women playing drums that date from 1200-600 B.C.E.[166]

A modern tof-style frame drum.

*Terracotta figurine of a woman playing a tof,
1200-600 B.C.E.*

Curiously, every English translation, both Jewish and Christian, identifies the *tof* as either a timbrel or a tambourine, two names for basically the same instrument. This is just as true of the older translations, such as the King James Version, as it is for the newer, scholarly translations, including the Jewish Publication Society and New Revised Standard Version. Scholars generally agree that tambourines did not exist in ancient Israel, yet centuries of translators have called the *tof* a tambourine or a timbrel. The Bible does name two metallic rattles, the *mena'anim* and the *shalishim,* but the consensus is that the *tof* was simply a frame drum.

If *tof* is a general term encompassing all drums, and *mena'anim* and *shalishim* are both varieties of rattle, this begs the question: how did the *tof's* association with a tambourine or a timbrel begin? Three years after initially beginning research for this book, I was reading about the music of ancient Persia (modern-day Iran) and learned of a large frame drum called a *daf* (Persian: دف). The linguistic resemblance between the *"daf"* and *"tof"* is only the beginning of their similarities. The *daf* is a large frame drum which varies in its specific size, though a diameter of more than twenty inches is common. The *daf's* defining characteristic is the numerous rings attached to the interior of the drum frame, which jingle as it is played. The rings are approximately one inch in diameter, which are fixed to the wooden drum frame, and are each linked to two other rings. The rings are side-by-side, and the three layers resemble a fishing net.

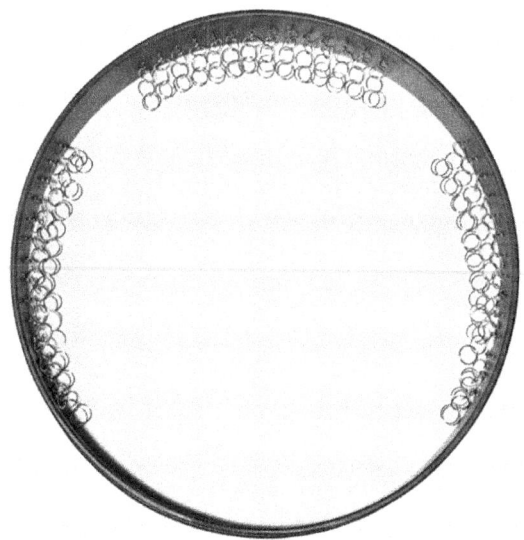

A modern Persian daf.

The *daf* is doubtless the Middle Eastern instrument which most closely resembles the modern-day tambourine, but did the *daf* and the *tof* overlap historically? Though the *daf* originated in ancient Persia, it has been used in music across the Middle East and Near East for more than 3,000 years. This includes the historical setting for the stories of Esther, Ezra, and Nehemiah, which are set in Persia. Some sources estimate that the *daf* is still many millennia older than that.[167] The *daf* appears in art from ancient Assyria and India, and is even the modern-day national instrument of Pakistan. In short, yes—the *daf* and the *tof* were contemporary instruments. Archeological evidence confirms that the *daf* was an integral part of Assyrian music, and scholars agree that there are doubtless Assyrian influences on Israelite music, as well as widespread trade between these two cultures.[168]

One of the most noteworthy aspects of the *tof* is its biblical association with women. When Moses and the Israelites cross the Sea of Reeds, Moses's sister Miriam and a group of women lead a song and dance of worship and thanksgiving accompanied by *tuppim*. (Exodus 15:20) As can be observed by the nearly sixty terra-cotta figurines unearthed in Israel, Israelite women were frequently described and depicted playing drums.

Tof references in the Bible:

Genesis 31:27, Exodus 15:20 (2x), Judges 11:34, 1 Samuel 10:5,
1 Samuel 18:6, 2 Samuel 6:5, Isaiah 5:12, Isaiah 24:8,
Isaiah 30:29 (or 30:32, depending on the translation),
Psalm 68:26, Psalm 81:3, Psalm 149:3, Psalm 150:4, Job 21:12,
1 Chronicles 13:8.

צְלָצְלִים מְצִלְתַּיִם

METZILTAYIM AND TZELTZELIM

Metziltayim and *tzeltzelim* are two varieties of bronze cymbals.[169] Both terms come from the root *tzalal*, which means "to ring," "to cling," or "to chime."[170] *Metziltayim* are mentioned ten times in the Bible and *tzeltzelim* are mentioned three times. The difference between them is not definitively known, but may be based on size. Twenty-eight cymbals that date back to the biblical era have been discovered throughout Israel in two distinct size ranges: the smaller from 1 to 2.25 inches and the larger between 2.75 to 4.75 inches.[171] These two ranges may be examples of *metziltayim* and *tzeltzelim*. If this theory is correct, that would suggest that *tzeltzelim* are the earlier, smaller variety, since this term only appears in the Books of Samuel and Psalms and the *metziltayim* are the later, larger variety, since this term only appears in the Books of Ezra-Nehemiah and Chronicles.

The earliest cymbals in the region date back to the 10th century B.C.E. These small cymbals are called finger cymbals and are played in pairs by fastening each cymbal to a different finger and bringing them together with a pinching motion. Conversely, Josephus describes the bronze cymbals as "broad and large."[172] This may suggest that as metalworking techniques improved over the centuries, cymbals became increasingly larger. Of the twenty-eight early cymbals that have been discovered, many of them are still playable and produce a clear, ringing tone.[173]

Finger cymbals discovered outside of Jerusalem, circa 1000-500 B.C.E.[174]

Metziltayim references in the Bible:

Ezra 3:10, Nehemiah 12:27, 1 Chronicles 13:8, 1 Chronicles 15:16, 1 Chronicles 15:19, 1 Chronicles 15:28, 1 Chronicles 16:5, 1 Chronicles 16:42, 1 Chronicles 25:1, 2 Chronicles 5:13.

Tzeltzelim references in the Bible:

2 Samuel 6:5, Psalm 150:5 (2x).

שְׁלִשִׁים   מְנַעַנְעִים

Shalishim and Mena'anim

Shalishim and *mena'anim* are both generally understood today as a handheld metal or clay rattle, widely known as a *sistrum* (or *sistra*, plural).[175] Each instrument appears only once in the Bible: *shalishim* in 1 Samuel 18:6, and *mena'anim* in 2 Samuel 6:5. While the *"-im"* suffix normally denotes plurality, *shalishim* and *mena'anim* are terms which describe singular instruments. Instead, the confusing *"-im"* suffix may reflect the multiple moving metallic pieces that give these instruments their signature sound, which is similar to a tambourine. The root *"shal"* comes from *"shalosh,"* meaning three. This suggests that there are three primary moving pieces. The Egyptian example on the next page also happens to feature three pieces.

Sistra are used in many Near Eastern cultures, but are primarily associated with Egypt. Numerous sistra have been collected in Israeli archeological excavations.[176] Keeping with the theory that the *shalishim* is one instrument that is named for its three moving parts, many of the recovered examples do indeed have three rattles, or three bars on which smaller, distinct pieces move freely.[177]

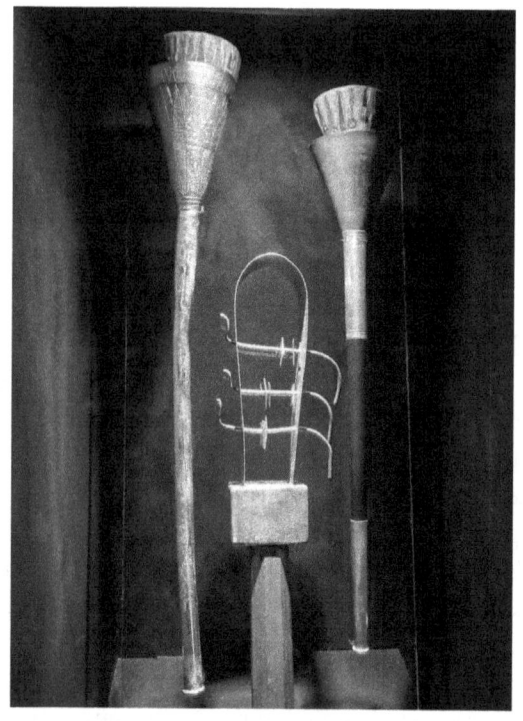

An Egyptian sistrum between Tutankhamen's trumpets.

Shalishim references in the Bible:

1 Samuel 18:6.

Mena'anim references in the Bible:

2 Samuel 6:5.

מְצִלּוֹת   פַּעֲמֹנִים

PA'AMONIM AND METZILOT

Pa'amonim are the golden bells that Israelite priests attached to their robes so that the bells jingled as they walked.[178] They are mentioned four times in Exodus 39:25-26. Similar to *pa'amonim*, *metzilot*, mentioned only once in the text, were bells attached to horses used when riding to Jerusalem to worship the LORD.[179] Zechariah 14:20 describes these bells as having a special inscription: "Holy to the LORD." In the relative silence of the ancient Holy Land, the pleasant, whimsical peals of chiming bells as someone walked would have surely set them apart as priests. *Metzilot* share the same *"tzalal"* root as *meltziltayim* and *tzeltzelim*, the two names for cymbals.[180] Archeologists have discovered more than 165 bells throughout Israel dating back to the biblical period. These are yet another example of archaeological evidence which confirms the descriptions of music which are found in the Bible.[181] All of these excavated bells are made of bronze and possess an iron clapper (the moving piece inside that strikes the bell). They range in size from 0.4 to 2.3 inches, with the earliest examples being the largest.[182]

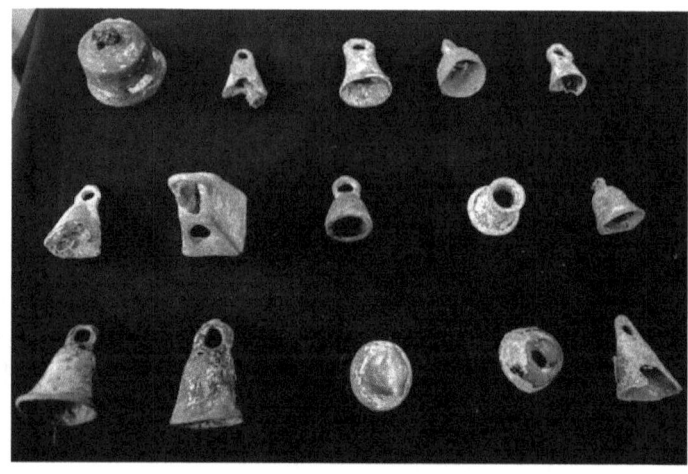

Israelite bells.

Pa'amonim references in the Bible:

Exodus 39:25 (2x), Exodus 39:26 (2x).

Metzilot references in the Bible:

Zechariah 14:20.

CHAPTER 6

THE INSTRUMENTS OF KING NEBUCHADNEZZAR'S COURT

The Book of Daniel is set in Babylon during the Babylonian Exile in the 6th century B.C.E. The armies of King Nebuchadnezzar sacked Jerusalem, destroyed the Temple, and took many Jews into captivity. Daniel 3 describes King Nebuchadnezzar's court musicians, and offers a glimpse into an interesting cultural intersection of music. Daniel is a Jewish text, and therefore written in Hebrew, but because it is the latest canonical entry in the Hebrew Bible, it features a significant portion written in Aramaic.ⁿ However, since Daniel is set in Babylon, the instruments described in the text should be understood as Babylonian. This is easy, since none of these

---

ⁿ Aramaic is a Semitic language closely related to Hebrew. Like Yiddish, which would emerge more than 1,000 years later, Aramaic uses the Hebrew alphabet. During the Second Temple era, Aramaic was more common than classical Hebrew among many Jews.

instruments are mentioned anywhere else throughout the Bible. Interestingly, half of the instruments in the Babylonian court orchestra have Greek-inspired names.

In the Book of Daniel, a set of six instruments which comprise King Nebuchadnezzar's court orchestra are listed four consecutive times. They are the *karnah, mashrokita, kateros, sebbekha, pesantarin,* and *sumponya,* as well as "and all types of instruments." These instruments are listed the same way in Daniel 3:5, 3:7, 3:10, and 3:15, with the exception of the *sumponya,* which will be described in further detail later. It should be noted that the phrase *v'kol zen z'marah* does literally translate as "and all other instruments," and is not an untranslated placeholder for other unknown or unidentified instrument names. It is curious, however, that the author wrote "musical instruments" using *"zamer"* for "musical" instead of *"shir"* (as is the case in 2 Chronicles 23:13) because *shir* is a general term for music, while *zamer* implies a religious or sacred aspect to the music.

Karnah

The *karnah* is consistently translated as "horn" across both Jewish and Christian English translations. This may be due to its linguistic similarity to the Hebrew word, *keren,* which is the anatomical name for "horn."[183] Based on its apparent etymology, as well as standard musical practices at the time, the *karnah* was likely quite similar to a *shofar,* but could have been crafted from the horn of any animal, including those that are not kosher.[184]

מַשְׁרוֹקִיתָא

MASHROKITA

Throughout the 20th century, scholars were not able to agree on the identity of the *mashrokita*.¹⁸⁵ There is a general consensus that, etymologically, its root suggests a whistling quality, leading many to conclude that it was almost certainly a woodwind. However, the agreement ends there.¹⁸⁶ Double-reeds were widely used in ancient Middle Eastern music, but based on the "whistling" timbre of this instrument, some variety of flute seems more likely. *Mashrokita* is most commonly translated as "pipe" in English Bibles.

KATEROS

Scholars generally agree that *kateros* is an Aramaic/Hebrew rendering of a Greek instrument called the *kithara*.¹⁸⁷ There is some debate over the composition date of the Book of Daniel, or at least chapters 8-12. Most scholars date the final redaction to around the time of the Maccabean Revolt in 167-164 B.C.E.¹⁸⁸ This late date explains how a Grecian musical instrument could appear in Near Eastern literature, since it was canonized more than 150 years after the conquests of Alexander the Great and the Hellenization of the ancient world.

The *kithara* is a lyre, traditionally strung with seven strings.¹⁸⁹ By the turn of the first millennium, centuries of Greek influence on Judea resulted in the *kinnorot* more closely resembling a *kithara* than a Near Eastern box lyre. The *kithara* is the namesake of the guitar.

First Century C.E. kithara-inspired kinnor depicted on a Judean coin.

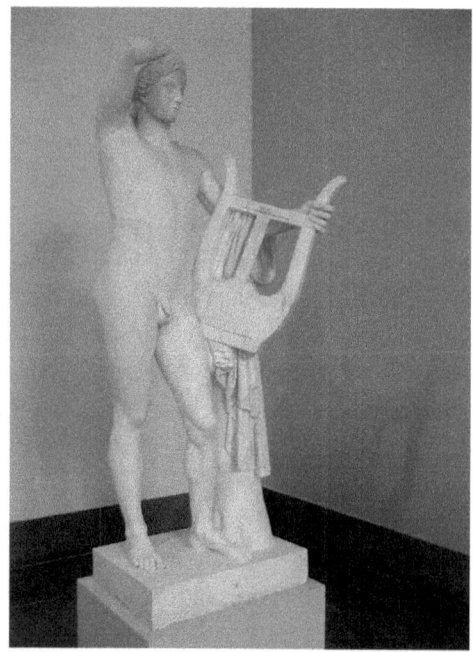

"Apollo Kitharodidos," circa 320 B.C.E., Greece.

Sebbekha

The *sebbekha* is the second instrument of King Nebuchadnezzar's court that is of seemingly Greek origin. The King James Version (KJV) translates this word as a *sackbut*, a Renaissance-era European trombone contemporaneous with the 1611 KJV translation.[190]

A sackbut, for reference.[191]

Bibliomusicologist Alfred Sendrey posits that the Babylonian *sebbekha* is "identical with" the Greek *sambyke* (also called a *sambuca*) and the Phoenician *sabecha*.[192] The *sambyke* first appeared in Greece in the 6th century B.C.E., during the time of the Babylonia Exile, so Sendrey's assertion is possible.[193] Assuming this is correct, the *sebbekha* resembles a West African *kora*, or a cross between a modern harp and banjo. The Greek *sambyke* is an instrument with seven strings that are positioned perpendicular to the neck, rather than parallel to the neck like a guitar. The strings are attached to cubical tuning heads atop the significantly bowed neck. The body/resonating chamber of the instrument is composed of a large turtle shell with animal hide suspended tightly over the exposed portion. Like a banjo, this animal hide holds the bridge. Yet unlike a banjo or guitar, the bowing of the neck is so severe that the strings could never be pressed to the neck. Instead, the strings are played like a harp or a lyre.

A modern sambyke recreation.[194] Image used with permission by Nikolaos Koumartzis of Lutherios Musical Instruments. www.luthieros.com

In Greece, *sambykes* were associated with exuberant banquets, and were often played by prostitutes.[195] Curiously, throughout the ancient world, prostitutes were often musicians, too. In particular, many prostitutes were also harpists. Even the prostitute described in Isaiah 23:16 plays the *kinnor*. However, female musicians should not be offended. Remember that David himself played and mastered the *kinnor*, one of the few musical instruments that has been viewed as acceptable for worship, even on the Sabbath, throughout the millennia. In the ancient world, prostitution was legal and did not carry the same social stigma it garners today. These women sought to offer pleasure and entertainment, so they were trained to play a beautiful musical instrument, as were kings and the aristocracy. It is worth noting that, until very recently, musical training was considered part of most young women of noble birth's education. Every aristocratic woman was expected to be proficient on a musical instrument. Harps were a particular favorite amongst the nobility and royalty.

Mandinkan Kora, ca. 1960.
Courtesy of the Metropolitan Museum, NY, USA

פְּסַנְתֵּרִין

Pesanterin

The fourth instrument mentioned in Daniel, and the third possibly Greek instrument in the Babylonian court, is the *pesanterin*. Sendrey suggests that this name is adapted from the Greek *psaltery*.[196] A *psaltery* is a lap harp with many strings running parallel against a flat body.[197] The King James Version translates several instruments as "psaltery," but the only actual use of these Hebrew/Aramaic words are in Daniel 3.

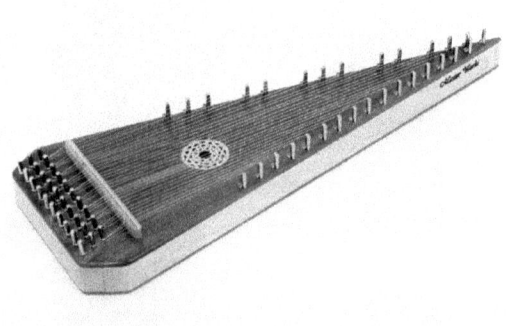

A modern psaltery.

Sumponya

The *sumponyah* is doubtless the most inconsistent musical instrument in the Bible, as it is never spelled the same way twice in the original Hebrew.¹⁹⁸ It is first spelled "סוּמְפֹּנְיָא" (*sumponya*) with a *samekh* ס (a letter with an "s" sound) and a *mem* מ (a letter with an "m" sound) in Daniel 3:5. It is curiously absent from Daniel 3:7, but then reappears in Daniel 3:10 as "סוּפֹּנְיָה," (*suponyah*,) without the *mem* and with the final consonant changed from an *aleph* א to a *heh* ה. Finally, in Daniel 3:15, it is written as "סוּמְפֹּנְיָה" (*sumponyah*). This time, the *mem* is reintroduced, but the final consonant remains as a *heh*. The *sumponyah*'s absence from Daniel 3:7 is the only such omission in the four descriptions of Nebuchadnezzar's court instruments.

Readers of Christian translations will typically see that the English translation of *sumponyah* (usually as "bagpipe" or "harp") is included in Daniel 3:7 despite its absence from the Masoretic Hebrew text. Jewish English translations tend to follow the Hebrew and omit the *sumponyah* in Daniel 3:7.

The word *sumponyah* is suspiciously similar to the Greek instrument *symphonia*. The fact that other Greek or Greek-inspired instruments are present in the Babylonian ensemble is also a compelling reason to suspect that the *sumponyah* is indeed a product of Greek influence.¹⁹⁹ However, scholars are less inclined to concede that this is another Greek instrument. A Greek *symphonia* is a variety of bagpipe, and has survived to the present day. The problem with labeling a *sumponyah* as a *symphonia* is that during the relevant historical time period, the term *symphonia* was not yet associated with any specific musical instrument in Greece, much less a bagpipe.[200] The *sumponyah* has also been associated with a drum, a clavichord (a European keyboard instrument from the Renaissance, Baroque, and Classical eras), a dulcimer (an American Appalachian fretted-string instrument and cousin of the acoustic guitar), and even the hurdy-gurdy, which is a hand-cranked, bowed string instrument, also called a "wheel fiddle." Obviously, all of these suggestions fall short of being the Babylonian *sumponyah* upon closer examination.

The Greek word *symphonia* literally means "sounding together." Therefore, it could refer to another polyphonic instrument, such as a *yarghul*-like double-barrel woodwind instrument capable of sounding two simultaneous pitches.[201] The polyphonic implications of the instrument's name are the reason that the bagpipe has been suggested as the *sumponyah's* identity, though there is no evidence to suggest that ancient Babylonians played anything resembling a bagpipe. In the Book of Daniel, the *sumponyah* is described as accompanying dance, For this reason, Polybius, the 2nd century Greek historian, posits that the *sumponyah* may even have been a percussion instrument such as castanets or a sistrum.[202] The translators of the New Revised Standard Version appear to agree with Polybius's logic, as their translation uses the word "drum." Based on all of this evidence, scholars can say with certainty that…they have no definitive idea what the *sumponyah* was. However, it was likely a polyphonic instrument.

Another theory to explain the Greek influence on these instruments' names is that traditional Babylonian names were originally used, but were replaced in the following centuries with the names of their Greek counterparts. This would have been in keeping with the *lingua franca* so that readers could more easily recognize the instruments.[203]

Musical Instruments in the Bible

Now that all musical instruments in the Bible have been discussed, the following tables show how often each instrument is mentioned in the Bible.

Table 8 measures the frequency of each instrument's appearance in the Bible. However, the Babylonian instruments of King Nebuchadnezzar's Court are not included, as they are not Israelite or Jewish instruments. The unconfirmed instruments *(machol* and *alamot)* are similarly not included, as there is significant disagreement as to whether they were indeed musical instruments. Table 9 then includes the Babylonian instruments, while Table 10 includes both the Babylonian instruments, as well as those that are unconfirmed (the *machol* and *alamot*).

(See next page)

TABLE 8:
CONFIRMED ISRAELITE MUSICAL INSTRUMENTS

	Instruments	Occurrences	Percentage
1.	Shofar	72	31.5%
2.	Kinnor	42	19.8%
3.	Chatzotzerot	30	13.5%
4.	Nevel	23	11.3%
5.	Tof	16	7.2%
6.	Metziltayim	10	4.1%
7.	Ugav	4	1.8%
8.	Chalil	4	1.8%
9.	Pa'amonim	4	1.8%
10.	Asor	3	1.4%
11.	Gittit	3	1.4%
12.	Tzeltzelim	3	1.4%
13.	Minnim	2	0.9%
14.	Shalishim	1	0.5%
15.	Mena'anim	1	0.5%
16.	Metzilot	1	0.5%
	Total	219	100%

The other remaining 42 musical references to instrumental music are *nagen* (8), yisu, (1), *neginot* (6), *kle* (9), *sharim* (1), *yobel* (6), *teruah* (7), *tekiah* (4).

TABLE 9:
ALL CONFIRMED MUSICAL INSTRUMENTS IN THE BIBLE (INCLUDING BABYLONIAN INSTRUMENTS)

	Instruments	Occurrences	Percentage
1.	Shofar	72	30.13%
2.	Kinnor	42	17.57%
3.	Chatzotzerot	30	12.55%
4.	Nevel	23	9.62%
5.	Tof	16	6.69%
6.	Metziltayim	10	4.18%
7.	Ugav	4	1.67%
8.	Chalil	4	1.67%
9.	Pa'amonim	4	1.67%
10.	Karnah	4	1.67%
11.	Mashrokita	4	1.67%
12.	Kateros	4	1.67%
13.	Sebbekha	4	1.67%
14.	Pesanterin	4	1.67%
15.	Sumponyah	3	1.26%
16.	Asor	3	1.26%
17.	Gittit	3	1.26%
18.	Tzeltzelim	3	1.26%
19.	Minnim	2	0.84%
20.	Shalishim	1	0.42%
21.	Mena'anim	1	0.42%
22.	Metzilot	1	0.42%
	Total	239	100%

TABLE 10:
ALL POSSIBLE MUSICAL INSTRUMENTS IN THE BIBLE (INCLUDING BABYLONIAN AND UNCONFIRMED)

	Instruments	Occurrences	Percentage
1.	Shofar	72	28.46%
2.	Kinnor	42	16.60%
3.	Chatzotzerot	30	11.89%
4.	Nevel	23	9.09%
5.	Tof	16	6.32%
6.	Machol	10	3.95%
7.	Metziltayim	10	3.95%
8.	Ugav	4	1.58%
9.	Chalil	4	1.58%
10.	Pa'amonim	4	1.58%
11.	Alamot	4	1.58%
12.	Karnah	4	1.58%
13.	Mashrokita	4	1.58%
14.	Kateros	4	1.58%
15.	Sebbekha	4	1.58%
16.	Pesanterin	4	1.58%
17.	Sumponyah	3	1.19%
18.	Asor	3	1.19%
19.	Gittit	3	1.19%
20.	Tzeltzelim	3	1.19%
21.	Minnim	2	0.79%
22.	Shalishim	1	0.40%
23.	Mena'anim	1	0.40%
24.	Metzilot	1	0.40%
	Total	253	100%

CHAPTER 7

FUNCTIONAL MUSIC IN THE BIBLE

When a musicologist or an ethnomusicologist observes and documents the music of a cultural group, one of the most important aspects they study is the role or roles that music plays in a society. These roles can be classified into two varieties: "use" and "function." To articulate the importance of identifying these two roles, renowned ethnomusicologist Alan P. Merriam writes, "We wish to know not only what a thing is, but, more significantly, what it does for people and how it does it."[204] In further outlining this distinction, Merriam goes on to write, "In observing *uses* of music, the student attempts to increase his factual knowledge *directly*; in assessing *functions* he attempts to increase his factual knowledge *indirectly* through the deeper comprehension of the significance of the phenomenon he studies."[205] As explained by Merriam, functional music can be analyzed and categorized into "use" and "function." "Use" is literally how the song is used. "Function" is the role this song plays in society. Merriam's distinctions are helpful, but many musicians and laymen alike still find these concepts abstract.

Any music that serves a specific societal role or fulfills a function is called "functional music" (not to be confused with the unrelated music theory term "functional harmony"). Interestingly, nearly every documented culture on earth utilizes functional music. In many cultures, music *only* exists as functional music. Some examples of functional music include work songs, as well as ritual music associated with anything from a wedding to a prayer for a good rain season. "Work songs" are *used* by singing aloud while working alone or in groups, often in an agricultural or manual labor setting. "Work songs" *function* by focusing one's mind on the task at hand, building comradery, establishing a cadence and rhythm for a repeated task, and staving off boredom. Functional music has extrinsic value to society.

A culture with comparatively little functional music is that of modern-day America. Most music heard in America today lacks a formal societal function. "Recreational music," which is music with intrinsic value, is music that exists solely for music's sake or for people's enjoyment.

One of the best ways to determine whether a piece of music is *functional* or *recreational* is to imagine the piece in an unfamiliar context. For example, Garth Brooks' 1990 classic, "Friends in Low Places," is an example of *recreational* music, which does not play a specific role in American society. It can be played practically anywhere, at any time, and no one will think it sounds out of place: on the radio, in a supermarket or department store, in a hair salon, at a party, in a restaurant, or at a concert. Conversely, some examples of America's few *functional* songs include "Happy Birthday to You," "We Wish You a Merry Christmas," "Auld Lang Syne," "The Star-Spangled Banner," Wagner's processional "Bridal Chorus," Mendelssohn's recessional "Wedding March," and Chopin's "Funeral March." These examples would all sound woefully out of place in any context other than that to which Americans have already become accustomed. If you are listening to the radio while driving and "Happy Birthday to You" comes on, you may likely wonder whose birthday is being celebrated. If "We Wish You a Merry Christmas" begins to play inside of Target in the middle of summer, you might complain that holiday music is played earlier and earlier every year.

Religious liturgical calendars incorporate many examples of functional music. If a church leader wants to lead the congregation in "Silent Night" in April, that will most likely generate a few confused looks. If a cantor were to lead their congregation in singing "Mi Chamocha" using the High Holy Days nusach melody in March, the rabbi will assume that the cantor does not know what he or she is doing. In short, there is an appropriate time and place for functional music because it plays a very specific role in society. In contrast, recreational music exists simply to be enjoyed, often anywhere and anytime.

Throughout the world's cultures, a music's "use" can be thought of as objective, but its "function," or at least how one describes, labels, and categorizes its function, can be subjective. One such example is Psalm 23. This psalm is labeled as a *mizmor*, a sub-category of worship defined as a "sacred song with stringed accompaniment." Psalm 23 fits perfectly within the function of "worship," especially since the lyrics are clearly an expression of worship for God.

Alas, not all examples of music in the Bible are as easy to categorize by function. For example, in Exodus 19:13, Moses is told by God that He, God, will deliver His commandments to all of the people of Israel. The Israelites are not to ascend or even touch Mount Sinai until they are instructed to do so, which will be signaled by a *shofar* blast. This was one of the more challenging musical instances to categorize. Its *use* is crystal clear: when the people hear the *shofar*, they approach the mountain. But what is the *function* of this *shofar* being sounded? In the most general sense, it could be described as "worship." Through observing the expectations associated with this *shofar* blast, the Israelites are obeying the Will of God. Their obedience can be taken as an expression of worship. Another interpretation of the *shofar's* function in Exodus 19:13 is in a "civil" capacity. After all, using a *shofar* call to instruct people to move or do something specific is not unique to this verse. There are twelve other instances in which music in the Bible has a civil function. The *shofar* signal can even change its function based on context. An example of a civic signal changing function based on context is the London church bells during World War II. The English stopped striking church bells on the hour and quarter hour to signal the time, and instead reserved their ringing to signal an incoming Nazi attack from the air. Similarly, the *shofar's* call is used during wartime in the Bible; most famously, *shofarot* were blown in warning before the Battle of Jericho described in Joshua 6:1-27.

Within the Bible, music functions in twenty-eight unique ways. The most common function, worship, can be further divided into sixteen sub-categories. When the categories and sub-categories are all counted together, there are a total of forty-seven different functions of biblical music.

Note: The following tables refer to the total number of musical references, not the sum of the music-related verses. Some musical passages function in more than one way, with both functions accounted for. See the Appendix for a complete list of all musical verses.

TABLE 11-A:
ANALYSIS OF FUNCTIONAL MUSIC IN THE BIBLE

Function		Occurrences	Percentage
1. Worship		375	68.56%
	a. General Worship	140	25.59%
	b. Temple Orchestra	72	13.16%
	c. Mizmor	57	10.42%
	d. Thanksgiving	33	6.03%
	e. Ma'alot	15	2.74%
	f. Maskil	14	2.56%
	g. Lament	12	2.19%
	h. Shabbat	8	1.46%
	i. Michtam	6	1.10%
	j. Shushan	4	0.73%
	k. Mercy Plea	4	0.73%
	l. Ritual	2	0.37%
	m. Covenant	2	0.37%
	n. Lehazkir	2	0.37%
	o. Personal Worship	1	0.18%
	p. Corporate Worship	1	0.18%
2. Warfare		55	10.05%
3. Metaphor/Simile		39	7.13%
4. Babylonian Court		27	4.94%
5. Victory		14	2.56%
6. Civil		12	2.19%
7. Historical		10	1.83%

8.	Celebration	8	1.46%
9.	Coronation	7	1.28%
10.	Dedication	7	1.28%
11.	Construction	7	1.28%
12.	Prophetic	6	1.10%
13.	Music Therapy	6	1.10%
14.	Wedding/Love Song	6	1.10%
15.	Fanfare	5	0.91%
16.	Priestly Attire	4	0.73%
17.	Mnemonic	4	0.73%
18.	Recreation	4	0.73%
19.	Send-off	3	0.55%
20.	Rosh Hashanah	2	0.37%
21.	Yom Kippur	2	0.37%
22.	Homecoming	2	0.37%
23.	Insurrection	2	0.37%
24.	General Signal	2	0.37%
25.	Messianic	2	0.37%
	Total		100%

TABLE 11-B:
ANALYSIS OF FUNCTIONAL MUSIC IN THE BIBLE
(WITH EACH SUB-CATEGORY OF WORSHIP CONSIDERED SEPARATELY)

Function	Occurrences	Percentage
1. General Worship	140	25.59%
2. Temple Orchestra	72	13.16%
3. Mizmor	57	10.42%
4. Warfare	55	10.05%
5. Metaphor/Simile	39	7.13%
6. Thanksgiving	33	6.03%
7. Babylonian Court	27	4.94%
8. Ma'alot	15	2.74%
9. Maskil	14	2.56%
10. Victory	14	2.56%
11. Civil	12	2.19%
12. Lament	12	2.19%
13. Historical	10	1.83%
14. Celebration	8	1.46%
15. Shabbat	8	1.46%
16. Coronation	7	1.28%
17. Dedication	7	1.28%
18. Construction	7	1.28%
19. Prophetic	6	1.10%
20. Music Therapy	6	1.10%
21. Michtam	6	1.10%
22. Wedding/Love Song	6	1.10%

23.	Fanfare	5	0.91%
24.	Shushan	4	0.73%
25.	Priestly Attire	4	0.73%
26.	Mnemonic	4	0.73%
27.	Recreation	4	0.73%
28.	Mercy Plea	4	0.73%
29.	Send-off	3	0.55%
30.	Ritual	2	0.55%
31.	Rosh Hashanah	2	0.37%
32.	Yom Kippur	2	0.37%
33.	Homecoming	2	0.37%
34.	Insurrection	2	0.37%
35.	Remembrance	2	0.37%
36.	Covenant	2	0.37%
37.	Lehazkir	2	0.37%
38.	General Signal	2	0.37%
39.	Messianic	2	0.37%
40.	Personal Worship	1	0.18%
41.	Corporate Worship	1	0.18%
	Total		100%

MUSICAL FUNCTIONS IN THE BIBLE

WORSHIP

"Worship" is by far the most common function of biblical music, with 375 examples of music-based worship. These account for 68.56% of all bibliomusical functions. Even when worship is subdivided into more specific sub-categories, the top three (general worship, Temple Orchestra, and *mizmorim*) each outnumber "warfare," the second most common musical function in the Bible, which only occurs fifty-five times.

Over the following pages, worship, or more specifically, musical worship, will be divided into fifteen sub-categories: General Worship, Temple Orchestra, *Mizmor*, Thanksgiving, *Maskil*, Lament, *Michtam*, *Shushan*, Mercy Plea, Ritual, Covenant, *Lehazkir*, Personal Worship, and Corporate Worship.

As many people of faith and/or religious scholars will attest, defining "worship" can *and has* filled many books. For the purposes of this topic, the definition of worship will be defined as "any expression of reverence to a deity." Of course, in this case, "deity" refers to the God of Abraham, Isaac, and Jacob. Notice the lack of *music* in this definition. There are innumerable non-musical ways that one may worship, including private and public displays, both personal and in groups. Living a "lifestyle of worship" can be as broad as trying to live one's life in accordance with God's commandments and expectations.[206] Many people assume that worship refers exclusively to the music played and sung during a religious ceremony, but that is just one expression of worship. Music is the facet that most applies to the topic at hand, but there are hundreds of non-musical examples of worship in the Hebrew Bible.

General Worship

Of the 375 examples of music that function as an expression of worship in the Bible, 138 of those fit nicely into one of the sixteen sub-categories of worship. The remaining 140 examples are clearly musical expressions of worship as well, but are without a more specific defining characteristic that would result in categorization into one of the other sixteen sub-categories. For the purposes of this book, therefore, these references will be classified under "general worship." One such example is Isaiah 30:29, which reads:

> *For you, there shall be singing, as on a night when a festival is hallowed; there shall be rejoicing as when they march, with chalil, with tuppim, and with kinnorot, to the Rock of Israel on the Mountain of the* LORD.
>
> Isaiah 30:29

Much can be gleaned about biblical worship from this passage alone. The verse mentions a hallowed festival, or holy day ("holiday"), suggesting that worship should be expressed with the same passion and enthusiasm on a normal day as during the most reverent religious ritual. The *chalil, tof,* and *kinnor* are clearly presented as instruments of worship, which affirms that instrumental music played alongside or accompanying singing was suitable for worship. One could argue that this example should be categorized as "holiday worship." Yet it has been categorized as general worship here because it does not refer to any specific holiday, unlike most cases in the Bible. Rather, Isaiah teaches that God should always be worshiped *as though* it were a festive hallowed day. This notion is the essence of "general worship."

Number of verses with a general worship function: 137 (25.18%)

Judges 5:3 (2x), Isaiah 30:29 (4x), Isaiah 42:10 (2x), Jeremiah 4:5, Jeremiah 51:27, Psalm 4:1, Psalm 7:1, Psalm 18(17), Psalm 8:1, Psalm 33:1, Palm 33:2 (3x), Psalm 33:3 (2x), Psalm 46:1, Psalm 47:2, Psalm 47:6, Psalm 47:7 (4x), Psalm 47:8, Psalm 48:1, psalm 49:1 Psalm 54:1, Psalm 55:1, Psalm 57:9 (2x), Psalm 57:10(9), Psalm 66:1, Psalm 67:1 (2x), Psalm 68:1, Psalm 71:22 (3x), Psalm 71:23, Psalm 76:1, Psalm 81:1, Psalm 81:2, Psalm 81:3 (4x), Psalm 81:4, Psalm 83:1, Psalm 84:1, Psalm 84:2, Psalm 87:1, Psalm 88:1, Psalm 96:1 (3x), Psalm 96:2, Psalm 98:1 (2x), Psalm 98:4, Psalm 98:5 (4x), Psalm 98:6 (2x), Psalm 101:1 (2x), Psalm 105:2 (2x), Psalm 108:1, Psalm 108:2 (2x), Psalm 108:3 (2x), Psalm 120:1 (2x), Psalm 121:1 (2x), Psalm 122:1 (2x), Psalm 123;1 (2x), Psalm 124:1 (2x), Psalm 125:1 (2x), Psalm 126:1 (2x), Psalm 127:1 (2x), Psalm 128:1 (2x), Psalm 129:1 (2x), Psalm 132:1 (2x), Psalm 133:1 (2x), Psalm 134:1 (2x), Psalm 144:9 (4x), Psalm 145:1, Psalm 146:2, Psalm 147:1 (2x), Psalm 147:7 (2x), Psalm 149:1 (2x), Psalm 149:3 (2x), Psalm 150:3 (3x), Psalm 150:4 (3x), Psalm 150:5 (3x), Ezra 3:10 (2x), 2 Chronicles 20:21, 2 Chronicles 20:28 (3x).

The Temple Orchestra

The Temple Orchestra is one of the most intriguing musical aspects of all of Scripture. This music ministry of the Holy Temple is mentioned seventy-two times, accounting for 13.24% of all musical references in the Bible, and 19.30% of the 373 examples of musical worship in the Bible. The term "Temple Orchestra" may refer to any musical ensemble that leads or accompanies worship within the First or Second Temple in Jerusalem. This institution was established by King David in the later years of his life once his son, Solomon, completed the First Temple. The establishment of the Temple Orchestra was a natural extension of David's lifelong passion for music and worship philosophy. Throughout the Bible, David often included instrumental music in acts of worship. This is evident from his many *mizmor* psalms, as well as the musical celebration that erupted following his stewardship of the Ark of the Covenant's entry into Jerusalem. (2 Samuel 6:5, 1 Chronicles 16:28). 1 Chronicles 6:31-32 explains that the musicians appointed by David to perform during the Ark's arrival in Jerusalem continued their music ministry through the completion of the First Temple, when they became the inaugural members of the Temple Orchestra.

The Temple Orchestra performed during the dedication of the First Temple sometime around 957 B.C.E. The Temple Orchestra was disbanded when the First Temple was destroyed in 586 B.C.E. by Nebuchadnezzar's Babylonian army. When the Second Temple was erected in about 515 B.C.E., the Temple Orchestra was reestablished even before the new Temple was completed. (Ezra 3:10) The Second Temple was later destroyed by the Romans in 70 C.E. The Temple Orchestra was once again disbanded and has never resumed its sacred duty.

The most detailed account of the Temple Orchestra comes from the Book of Chronicles. Despite David's Judahite lineage, he decreed that the Temple Orchestra members must be Levites, or priests from the Tribe of Levi. Further, they must be at least thirty years old. (1 Chronicles 23:2) The author of Chronicles writes that at the time of appointment, there were 38,000 qualified Levite priests. Of the 38,000, 24,000 (~63%) were to serve in the Temple, 6,000 (~16%) were to serve as officials and judges, 4,000 (~10.5%) were to serve as gatekeepers, and 4,000 (~10.5%) were to serve in the Temple Orchestra and "...praise the LORD with the 'instruments that [David] made.'" (1 Chronicles 23:4-5) The "instruments of David" are listed differently in various scriptural passages, but the complete list, in alphabetical order, is:

- *Chatzotzerot*
- *Kinnorot*
- *Metziltayim*
- *Nevalim*
- Singers
- *Tuppim*
- The phrase *u'vi' khelim ha' shir*, which is translated as "and with other musical instruments." Its literal translation is simply, "and with musical instruments." These "other instruments" likely include, but are not limited to, the *shofar*, which was prominently used with the Temple. (1 Chronicles 15:28) Other instruments may include the *ugav* and *minnim* since they are mentioned in Psalm 150.

David appoints Asaph, Heman, Jeduthun, and their families/descendants to play *kinnorot, nevalim*, and *metziltayim* in the Temple Orchestra. Although 1 Chronicles 23:5 describes a total of 4,000 musicians, the Levite musicians from the lines of Asaph, Heman, and Jeduthun are listed at just 288. (1 Chronicles 25:7) Later, in 2 Chronicles 5:12-14, Solomon brings the Ark of the Covenant to the Temple once the Temple is completed. In this passage, the Levite musicians of the families of Asaph, Heman, and Jeduthun are joined by 120 priests who played *chatzotzerot*. Together, this ensemble played *metziltayim, kinnorot, nevalim, chatzotzerot*, "other instruments," and also included singers as they worshiped together.[הא]

Further requirements for Temple Orchestra members include that they are highly-skilled and accomplished musicians. (1 Chronicles 25:7) Appointment as a member of the Temple Orchestra was determined by "sacred lots," with no deference based on years of experience, as long as the musician was able

---

[הא] Many translations of 2 Chronicles 5:13 use the English word "unison." There are two Hebrew terms used in this sentence which the translators have combined to mean "unison." The first is *khe'echad*, which means "as one," and the second is *kol-echad*, which means "all as one." Literally, these phrases mean that the musicians are performing simultaneously and contributing to one sound, but not necessarily playing the exact same notes. Among musicians, the word "unison" has a very specific meaning, implying that everyone is performing the same monophonic melody on the same exact pitches at the same time. Reading this passage literally, it only describes the trumpeters and singers playing together, without comment regarding the pitches being played. However, based on other examples of non-Western vocal music from around the world, it is likely that they were also singing either in unison or with "perfect" intervals, such as a fourth or fifth. In summary, the actual language here is inconclusive.

to perform at the required level. (1 Chronicles 25:8) The Temple Orchestra was somewhat of an "equal opportunity employer," and did not discriminate on the basis of age or years of musical experience. Ability was paramount. While it is true that musicians were required to be at least thirty years old, this was likely to ensure a certain level of experience and maturity.

In summary, a member of the Temple Orchestra must:
- Be of the Tribe of Levi. (1 Chronicles 23:2)
- Be a highly-skilled and trained musician. (1 Chronicles 25:7)
- Be at least thirty years old. (1 Chronicles 23:2)
- Wear fine linen robes during worship services. (2 Chronicles 5:12)
- Play *chatzotzerot, kinnor, metziltayim, neval, tof* or sing. (1 Chronicles 25:1, 2 Chronicles 5:13)
- Be appointed by merit, not age or experience. (1 Chronicles 25:7)

1 Chronicles 15:28 describes the "loud music" offered as worship by the Temple Orchestra. Don Wyrtzen, a composer and professor of church music at Southwestern Baptist Theological Seminary, asserts that, historically, many Americans have held the theological position that slow and quiet religious music is "holier" than loud, raucous worship, but that this position is actually contrary to scriptural precedent. With as many as 4,000 musicians playing joyously together, it is not difficult to imagine just how loud and exuberant the worship music of the Temple Orchestra must have sounded. While the official ensemble ceased when the Second Temple was destroyed, the practices and traditions of the Temple Orchestra continue to echo in worship ceremonies today.

Number of verses with a Temple Orchestra function:
72 (13.24%)
1 Chronicles 6:16, 1 Chronicles 6:17, 1 Chronicles 13:8 (6x),
1 Chronicles 15:16 (5x), 1 Chronicles 15:20, 1 Chronicles 15:21,
1 Chronicles 15:24, 1 Chronicles 15:27 (2x),
1 Chronicles 15:28 (5x), 1 Chronicles 16:5 (3x),
1 Chronicles 16:6, 1 Chronicles 16:42 (5x),
1 Chronicles 23:5 (2x), 1 Chronicles 25:1 (3x),
1 Chronicles 25:6 (4x), 1 Chronicles 25:7,
2 Chronicles 5:12 (5x), 2 Chronicles 5:13 (5x),
2 Chronicles 7:6 (3x), 2 Chronicles 9:11 (3x),
2 Chronicles 29:25 (3x), 2 Chronicles 29:26 (2x),
2 Chronicles 29:27 (3x), 2 Chronicles 29:28 (3x),
2 Chronicles 31:2.

MIZMOR

The term *mizmor*, which was discussed in Chapter Two, appears in the heading of fifty-seven of the 150 psalms. Sendrey writes that a *mizmor* is a sacred song accompanied by stringed instruments.[207] In the Bible, those stringed instruments were primarily (if not exclusively) the *kinnor* and *nevel*. Not surprisingly, many of the psalms designated as *mizmorim* are attributed to David, history's most famous *kinnorist*. *Mizmor* comes from the root word *zamer*, leading many scholars, including Sendrey, to the conclusion that a *mizmor* is a sacred song with string accompaniment.[208] The translators of the JPS Bible, as well as many other biblical scholars, differentiate between *shir* and *zamer,* in that a *shir* is defined as any kind of song, sacred or secular, but a *zamer* is specifically a sacred song. The Talmud corroborates the definition that a *mizmor* is a piece accompanied by strings, but further specifies that when the terms *shir* and *mizmor* are placed together as *"shir mizmor,"* as in the cases of Psalms 66, 83, and 88, it instead means "recited with choral accompaniment."[209] By this definition, the terms *shir, mizmor,* and *shir mizmor* must be thought of as three unique song types.

Six psalms include the phrase *b'neginot,* or "with stringed instruments," in their headings. While these are not specifically designated as *mizmorim,* they are still accompanied with stringed instruments, and their inclusion amongst the Psalms certainly indicates that they are sacred in nature. One could argue that the function of these psalms (Psalms 4, 54, 55, 61, 67, 76) could, or even *should,* categorize them as *mizmor.* This would then bring the total *mizmor* count up to sixty-six. However, in this book, psalms have only been categorized as *mizmorim* when the term is actually present in each psalm's title.

Number of verses that function as a *mizmor:* 57 (10.48%)
Psalm 3, Psalm 4, Psalm 5, Psalm 6, Psalm 8, Psalm 9,
Psalm 12, Psalm 13, Psalm 15, Psalm 19, Psalm 20, Psalm 21,
Psalm 22, Psalm 23, Psalm 24, Psalm 29, Psalm 30, Psalm 31,
Psalm 38, Psalm 39, Psalm 40, Psalm 41, Psalm 47, Psalm 48,
Psalm 49, Psalm 50, Psalm 51, Psalm 62, Psalm 63, Psalm 64,
Psalm 65, Psalm 66, Psalm 67, Psalm 68, Psalm 73, Psalm 75,
Psalm 76, Psalm 77, Psalm 79, Psalm 80, Psalm 82, Psalm 83,
Psalm 84, Psalm 85, Psalm 87, Psalm 88, Psalm 92, Psalm 98,
Psalm 100, Psalm 101, Psalm 108, Psalm 109, Psalm 110,
Psalm 139, Psalm 140, Psalm 141, Psalm 143.

Thanksgiving

Songs that give thanks to God are another expression of worship. The subject of these songs may be something specific, such as Moses' and Miriam's songs of the sea following the parting of the Reed Sea.ים סוף (Exodus 15:1-18, Exodus 15:20-21) The subject matter may also be a general expression of gratitude for the many gifts God has bestowed upon His people, as described in Psalm 26:7. There are thirty-five instances of music functioning as an expression of thanksgiving to God.

Number of verses with a thanksgiving function: 33 (6.07%)
Exodus 15:1 (2x), Exodus 15:20 (2x), Exodus 15:21 (2x),
Judges 5:1, 2 Samuel 22:1, 2 Samuel 22:50 (2x), Isaiah 51:3,
Psalm 18:1, Psalm 26:7, Psalm 40:1, Psalm 42:5, Psalm 64:1,
Psalm 65:1, Psalm 75:1 (2x), Psalm 100:1, Ezra 3:11,
Nehemiah 12:8, Nehemiah 12:46 (2x), 1 Chronicles 16:9 (2x),
1 Chronicles 16:23, 1 Chronicles 25:3, 2 Chronicles 5:13 (2x),
2 Chronicles 31:2.

ים סוף The Hebrew name *Yam Suf* literally translates to "Reed Sea" or "Sea of Reeds." However, it is commonly mistranslated as "Red Sea."

MA'ALOT

As described on page fifty-eight, there have been many theories suggested as to the nature of the *ma'alot,* the psalms of ascent or songs of degrees. One Jewish tradition teaches that these songs of worship were reserved for ascending the stairs to the Temple entrance.

Number of verses that function as a *ma'alot:* 15 (2.76%)
Psalm 120, Psalm 121, Psalm 122, Psalm 123, Psalm 124, Psalm 125, Psalm 126, Psalm 127, Psalm 128, Psalm 129, Psalm 130, Psalm 131, Psalm 132, Psalm 133, Psalm 134.

MASKIL

As described in the section about the Psalms found in Chapter Two, *maskilim* are didactic songs intended to teach a particular lesson or message. As an exercise, try reading Psalms 32, 42, 44, 45, 47, 52, 53, 54, 55, 74, 78, 88, and 142 and see if you can identify the intended lesson of each psalm.

Number of verses that function as a *maskil:* 14 (2.57%)
Psalm 32, Psalm 42, Psalm 44, Psalm 45, Psalm 47, Psalm 52, Psalm 53, Psalm 54, Psalm 55, Psalm 74, Psalm 78, Psalm 88, Psalm 142.

LAMENT

The Oxford English Dictionary defines a "lament" as "a passionate expression of grief or sorrow."[210] The most well-known example of lament, biblical or otherwise, is possibly The Book of Lamentations, traditionally attributed to the prophet Jeremiah. Throughout the five chapters of Lamentations, the author grieves the fall of Jerusalem and the destruction of the First Temple at the hands of Nebuchadnezzar's Babylonian army. Surprisingly, Lamentations is one of the five books of Scripture without a single reference to music. However, there are twelve other examples of music functioning as an expression of lamentation. One well-known example is the tragic Psalm 137, written by another author who is grieving the fall of Jerusalem.

Psalm 137 reads:

> *By the rivers of Babylon, there we sat, sat and wept, as we thought of Zion.*[הנ] *There on the poplars we hung up our kinnorot, for our captors asked us there for songs, our tormentors, for amusement: "Sing us one of the songs of Zion." How can we sing a song of the* LORD *on alien soil? If I forget you, O Jerusalem, let my right hand wither; let my tongue stick to my palate if I cease to think of you, if I do not keep Jerusalem in memory even at my happiest hour. Remember, O* LORD, *against the Edomites the day of Jerusalem's fall; how they cried, "Strip her, strip her to her very foundations!" Fair Babylon, you predator, a blessing on him who repays you in kind what you have inflicted on us; a blessing on him who seizes your babies and dashes them against the rocks!*
>
> Psalm 137

Number of verses that function as a lament: 12 (2.21%)
Psalm 51:1, Psalm 131:1 (2x), Psalm 137:2, Psalm 137:3 (3x), Psalm 137:4 (2x), Psalm 142:1, Job 30:31 (2x).

[הנ] Zion is the name of the mountain upon which Jerusalem rests.

Shabbat

Literally meaning "Saturday," Shabbat, or "Sabbath," is the seventh day of the week, which commemorates when God rested in the Creation narrative. (Genesis 2:3) So, too, do Jews reserve Shabbat for rest and worship. The Ten Commandments include the requirement to:

> *Remember the Sabbath day and keep it holy. Six days you shall labor and do all your work, but the seventh day is a sabbath of the LORD your God: you shall not do any work—you, your son or daughter, your male or female slave, or your cattle, or the stranger who is within your settlements.*
> Exodus 20:8-10

There are eight musical passages related to playing music on Shabbat in the Bible. It is written in the Talmud that even music is prohibited on this day of rest, *unless* that music is used as worship.[211] Instrumental worship is so important that despite the prohibition of work and medial tasks, *kinnor* players were permitted to change a broken string on Shabbat so that worship might continue. (Eruvin 102b:14, 103b:6, 105a:10)

Number of verses with a Shabbat function: 8, 1.47%
Psalm 92:1 (2x), Psalm 92:2, Psalm 92:4 (3x), Psalm 92:5 (2x).

Michtam

A *michtam* is a song variety which contains a hidden or concealed meaning.[212] These songs occur six times in the Book of Psalms. Though they can be thought of as musical riddles, in the Bible they are always expressions of worship.

Number of verses that function as a *michtam*: 6 (1.10%)
Psalm 16, Psalm 56, Psalm 57, Psalm 58, Psalm 59, Psalm 60.

Shushan

Sendrey writes that a *shushan* is a song in which a sacred text is set to a secular melody.[213] Ethnomusicologists and anthropologists refer to this practice as syncretism. This is very much still a practice today among both Jews and Christians. Four of the psalms contain headings identifying them as a *shushan*. Unrelatedly, "Shushan" is the name of the city setting for the Book Esther. The name also means "lily."

Number of verses that function as a *shushan*: 4 (0.75%)
Psalm 45, Psalm 60, Psalm 69, Psalm 80.

Mercy Plea

There are four musical passages in the Bible in which the author begs for God's mercy through song. These are classified as a sub-category of worship because the mercy pleas simultaneously extol God.

Number of verses that function as a mercy plea: 4 (0.74%)
Psalm 130:1 (2x), Psalm 140:1, Psalm 142:1.

Ritual

Throughout history, religious rituals have played an important role in cultures across the globe; the Israelites are no exception. There are countless examples of biblical music that can be classified as rituals, but Numbers 10:10 and Joel 2:15 can *only* be described as part of a *worship* ritual. Numbers 10:10 describes the Israelite tradition of blowing *chatzotzerot* in times of gladness and during annual feasts. Joel 2:15 commands that a *shofar* be sounded in Jerusalem to announcing the beginning of a fast.

Number of verses with a ritual function: 2 (0.37%)
Numbers 10:10, Joel 2:15.

Lehazkir (Remembrance)

Meaning "remembrance," the two examples of this variety of psalms are both attributed to David. These utilize the text of a song to call upon the people of Israel to remember something of importance.

Number of verses that function as a *lehazkir:* 2 (0.37%)
Psalm 38:1, Psalm 70:1.

Covenant

There is one musical verse that describes worship based on God's covenant with humanity. This verse, 2 Chronicles 15:14, mentions both *chatzotzerot* and *shofarot*, which are blasted to seal God's covenant oath with the Jews.

Number of verses with a covenant function: 2 (0.37%)
2 Chronicles 15:14 (2x).

Personal Worship

Personal worship is an expression of worship by one individual, rather than a group of people. It may be spoken, sung, or consist of silent prayer, or it may be musical worship without a congregation or fellow worshipers. The author of Psalm 43:4 writes of praising God with his *kinnor*. The singular verb conjugation confirms that the author is performing this worship music alone.

Number of verses with a personal worship function: 1 (0.18%)
Psalm 43:4.

Corporate Worship

Unlike personal worship, which only occurs between the worshiper and God, corporate worship happens when an entire congregation worships together. The Sabbath worship ceremony today is an example of corporate worship. Nehemiah 12:36 describes Levite priests coming from across the land to worship at the dedication of Jerusalem's new wall, not just the members of the Temple Orchestra. In Leviticus 22:32, God commands that a "minyan", or quorum of ten adult men, is required to pray and worship together in corporate worship.

Number of verses with a corporate worship function: 1 (0.18%) Nehemiah 12:36.

This concludes the sixteen sub–categories of worship.

Warfare

The fifty-five examples of music which function within the context of "warfare" account for 10.11% of all musical references in the Bible. This makes warfare the second-largest category of musical function after worship. Within the spectrum of "warfare," music generally has two functions: *signals* and *intimidation*.

The *shofar* was the loudest readily-available instrument in ancient Israel. *Chatzotzerot* were just as loud, if not louder, but required a significant amount of silver to create them, as well as a silversmith with all of the necessary resources, knowledge, and tools. A *shofar* merely required an adult male sheep or some other qualifying kosher ovine. In the relative quiet of the ancient world, the sound of a *shofar* blast carries through the air like no other. A specific pattern of blasts could instruct troops to move in a variety of formations and directions. See page 141 for a complete list of trumpet blasts.

The loud, almost supernatural sound of the *shofar* could also strike fear into the hearts of an enemy in this quiet world, especially when a cacophony of dissonant pitches all blasted together, produced by many *shofarot* with different fundamental pitches. When the priests circling the city of Jericho blasted their *shofarot* for seven days, it surely terrified the Jerichoites within the city walls. (Joshua 6:1-27) A terrorized enemy lacks focus, a fact that the Israelites are able to take advantage of throughout Scripture.

Number of verses with a warfare function: 55 (10.11%)
Numbers 10:9 (2x), Numbers 31:6 (2x), Joshua 6:4 (2x),
Joshua 6:5 (3x), Joshua 6:6, Joshua 6:8 (2x), Joshua 6:9 (2x),
Joshua 6:13 (3x), Joshua 6:16, Joshua 6:20 (2x), Judges 3:27,
Judges 6:34, Judges 7:8, Judges 7:16, Judges 7:18 (2x),
Judges 7:19, Judges 7:20 (2x), Judges 7:22, 2 Samuel 20:22,
Jeremiah 4:19, Jeremiah 6:1, Jeremiah 42:14, Ezekiel 26:13 (3x),
Ezekiel 33:3, Ezekiel 33:4, Ezekiel 33:5, Ezekiel 33:6,
Hosea 5:8 (2x), Hosea 8:1, Amos 2:2, Zephaniah 1:16, Job 39:24,
Job 39:25, Nehemiah 12:41, 2 Chronicles 20:21,
2 Chronicles 20:28 (3x).

METAPHOR/SIMILE

Forty examples of music in the Bible involve the use of metaphors and similes. The prophets Isaiah, Jeremiah, Ezekiel, Hosea, Amos, and Job, as well as the psalmists, often employ music-related metaphors. One example is when the Jews hang their *kinnorot* on tree branches while mourning the fall of Jerusalem. The message is that after the destruction of the Temple, joyous music shall be played no more. (Psalm 137)

Number of verses with a metaphor/simile function: 39 (7.17%)
2 Samuel 19:36(35), Isaiah 5:1 (2x), Isaiah 5:12 (4x), Isaiah 6:11, Isaiah 18:3, Isaiah 23:15, Isaiah 23:16 (3x), Isaiah 24:8 (2x), Isaiah 24:9, Isaiah 30:29 (4x), Isaiah 51:3, Isaiah 58:1, Jeremiah 4:21, Jeremiah 6:17, Ezekiel 26:13 (3x), Ezekiel 33:3, Ezekiel 33:4, Ezekiel 33:5, Ezekiel 33:6, Hosea 5:8 (2x), Joel 2:1, Joel 2:15, Amos 3:6, 1 Chronicles 16:33, 2 Chronicles 13:12,
2 Chronicles 13:14.

BABYLONIAN COURT

Like many kings, Nebuchadnezzar fancied an ensemble of court musicians to perform at his pleasure. (Daniel 3) Many of history's most notable musicians served as a court musician or composer for a monarch.

Number of verses with a Babylonian court function: 27 (4.96%)
Daniel 3:5 (7x), Daniel 3:7 (6x), Daniel 3:10 (7x),
Daniel 3:15 (7x).

Victory

On various occasions, the Israelites signaled and celebrated a military victory with musical performance.

Number of verses with a victorious function: 14 (2.57%)
1 Samuel 18:6 (3x), 2 Samuel 6:5 (6x), 2 Chronicles 23:13 (5x), 2 Chronicles 23:18.

Civil

Civil functions include when the *shofar* or *chatzotzerot* are blasted to convey something unrelated to religion or military endeavors, such as the beginning of a new month. (Numbers 3:10, Psalm 81:4-17)

Number of verses with a civil function: 12 (2.21%)
2 Samuel 20:1, Nehemiah 4:12, Nehemiah 4:14, Numbers 10:2, Numbers 10:3, Numbers 10:4, Numbers 10:5, Numbers 10:6 (2x), Numbers 10:7, Numbers 10:8 (2x).

Historical

Biblical verses with a historical function describe the history of an instrument, such as Genesis 4:21, which describes that Jubal was the father of all who play the *kinnor* and *ugav*.

Number of verses with a historical function: 10 (1.84%)
Genesis 4:21 (2x), Psalm 30:1 (2x), Psalm 82:1, Deuteronomy 31:19 (2x), Deuteronomy 31:21, Deuteronomy 31:22.

CELEBRATION

Verses with a celebratory function are those that use music to celebrate anything that does not already have its own subcategory. One such example is the *shofar* blasts which celebrate the Ark's entrance into Jerusalem. (2 Samuel 6:5)

Number of verses with a celebratory function: 8 (1.47%)
2 Samuel 6:15, Job 21:12 (5x), Ezra 3:10 (2x).

CORONATION

This category refers to music that accompanies the coronation of a new king. Examples include 2 Kings 9:13 and 2 Kings 11:14, which describe the coronation ceremonies of Kings Jehu and Joash, respectively.

Number of verses with a coronation function: 7 (1.29%)
1 Kings 1:34, 1 Kings 1:39, 1 Kings 1:40, 1 Kings 1:41, 2 Kings 9:13, 2 Kings 11:14 (2x),

DEDICATION

This describes music used during a dedication ceremony, such as when the foundation was laid for the Second Temple in Nehemiah 12:27.

Number of verses with a dedicatory function: 7 (1.29%)
Nehemiah 12:27 (4x), Nehemiah 12:28, Nehemiah 12:29, Nehemiah 12:35.

INSTRUMENT CONSTRUCTION

This usage describes how instruments were made and the materials used. 1 Kings 10:12 and 2 Chronicles 9:11 both describe that algum wood was used to build *kinnorot* and *nevalim*.

Number of verses with a construction function: 7 (1.29%)
1 Kings 10:12 (3x), 2 Kings, 12:14, 2 Chronicles 9:11 (3x).

PROPHETIC

Verses with a prophetic function use music as part of a prophecy. One such example is 1 Samuel 10:5, during which a band of prophets prophesize while playing the *nevel, tof, chalil,* and *kinnor*. The verses designated as "prophetic function" describe the act of prophesizing itself. These verses specifically describe the use of music, rather than a general description of music within the prophecy.

Number of verses with a prophetic function: 6 (1.10%)
1 Samuel 10:5 (4x), 2 Kings 3:15 (2x).

Music Therapy

By no means unique to biblical music, the Cleveland Clinic defines "music therapy" as:

> The clinical use of music to accomplish individualized goals such as reducing stress, improving mood and self-expression. It is an evidence-based therapy well-established in the health community. Music therapy experiences may include listening, singing, playing instruments, or composing music. Musical skills or talents are not required to participate. Music therapy may help you psychologically, emotionally, physically, spiritually, cognitively and socially.[214]

David playing his *kinnor* when Saul was tormented by his inner demons is one of history's most famous examples of music therapy. (1 Samuel 16:14-23)

Number of verses with a therapeutic function: 6 (1.10%)
1 Samuel 16:17(16) (2x), 1 Samuel 16:18(17), 1 Samuel 16:23, 1 Samuel 18:10, 1 Samuel 19:9.

Wedding/Love Song

Biblical songs of love range from Psalm 45, which is often recited at wedding ceremonies; to the metaphorical prose of Isaiah 5:1, to Solomon's Song of Songs, which is an entire book of the Bible that is itself one epic love song. The purpose of these songs is simply to celebrate love, which is arguably the most important aspect of the human experience.

Number of verses that function as love songs: 6 (1.10%)
Psalm 45:1 (2x), Psalm 45:9, Song of Songs, Isaiah 5:1 (2x).

Fanfare

The Oxford English Dictionary defines "fanfare" as "a short ceremonial tune or flourish played on brass instruments, typically to introduce something or someone important."[215] Though fanfares are most often associated with monarchs and national leaders, in the Bible, fanfares are played for God (Exodus 19:16-19, Exodus 20:15(18), Joel 2:1) and the Ark of the Covenant. (1 Chronicles 15:24)

Number of verses that function as a fanfare: 5 (0.92%)
Exodus 19:16, Exodus 19:19, Exodus 20:15(18), Joel 2:1, 1 Chronicles 15:24.

Priestly Attire

In Exodus 39:25-26, priests are commanded to adorn the bottom of their fine linen robes with golden bells that jingle as they walk.

Number of verses that relate to priestly attire: 4 (0.74%)
Exodus 39:25 (2x), Exodus 29:26 (2x).

Mnemonic

The Oxford English Dictionary defines a mnemonic as "a device such as a pattern of letters, ideas, or associations that assists in remembering something." In Deuteronomy 31, God gives a dying Moses a song to teach to the Israelites so that they may remember the Torah after Moses's passing.

Number of verses which feature a mnemonic function: 4 (0.74%)
Deuteronomy 31:19 (2x), Deuteronomy 31:21, Deuteronomy 31:22.

Recreation

In the United States, songs of recreation are by far the most-commonly performed song, as American culture has very little proper functional music. Songs of recreation are played and listened to only for their own inherent enjoyment factor. All contemporary popular styles of American music are recreational. A fact which may surprise modern readers is that the Bible describes very little recreational music. The only example of recreational music referenced in the Bible is in Amos 6:5, where the author describes people who leisurely play music.

However, this does not mean that ancient Jews did not enjoy public performances of recreational music. In 2017, a Second Temple-era, Roman-style public amphitheater was discovered by archeologists in Jerusalem.[216] This led musicologists to conclude that public music performances in spaces devoted to the performing arts may have been a source of enjoyment in Jerusalem, at least from the time of the Roman occupation beginning in 63 B.C.E., and lasting through to the Romans' sackings of Jerusalem in 70 C.E. and 135 C.E.

Number of verses that function as recreation: 4 (0.74%)
Amos 6:5 (4x)

SEND-OFF

In Genesis 31:27, Laban wishes to give Jacob, Leah, and Rachel a proper send-off with the playing of a *tof* and a *kinnor* before they moved away to a distant land.

Number of verses that function as a send-off: 3 (0.55%)
Genesis 31:27 (3x).

ROSH HASHANAH

Rosh Hashanah is the beginning of the Jewish New Year and a day of remembrance. Interestingly, every other instance in the Bible explicitly describes what should be remembered, but this is not the case with Rosh Hashanah. One Jewish tradition teaches that the *shofar* is blasted repeatedly on Rosh Hashanah to attract God's attention so that He will not forget His people. On Rosh Hashanah, the *shofar* is blasted several times during the day's worship services. The *shofar's* role in worship during Rosh Hashanah lead to this holiday's nickname: "The Feast of Trumpets." See the section on the *shofar* in Chapter Four for a detailed description of the *shofar's* various calls.

Number of verses that function as part of Rosh Hashanah: 2 (0.37%)
Leviticus 23:24, Numbers 29:1.

Yom Kippur

Yom Kippur is the Jewish Day of Atonement, which was first described in Leviticus 25:9. The *shofar* is used both during the worship service and as part of the general observance of Yom Kippur.

Number of verses that function as part of Yom Kippur: 2 (0.37%)
Leviticus 25:9 (2x).

Homecoming

The opposite of a send-off, homecoming music is played to welcome someone's return, such as when Jephthah's daughter dances to the sound of *tuppim* to welcome her father home in Judges 11:34.

Number of verses with a homecoming function: 2 (0.37%)
Judges 11:34, Isaiah 27:13.

Insurrection

2 Samuel 15 and 18 each describe an insurrection and attempted coup against David by his son, Absalom. In both verses, a *shofar* blast signals the revolt.

Number of verses with an insurrection function: 2 (0.37%)
2 Samuel 15:10, 2 Samuel 18:16.

GENERAL SIGNAL

The blasting of signals is the primary function of both the *shofar* and *chatzotzerot*. Many of the verses categorized as having warfare, civil, and insurrection functions, among others, could just as easily be categorized as signals. The two verses listed here are more general, and simply did not align with any of those more specific functions listed above.

Number of verses with a general signal function: 2 (0.37%)
Exodus 19:13, Nehemiah 4:12(18).

MESSIANIC

Zechariah 9:14 describes that a *shofar* blast will usher in the arrival of the Messiah. Zechariah 14:20 tells that in the time of the Messiah, the horses of the Temple will be adorned with bells inscribed with the words "Holy to the LORD."

Number of verses with a messianic function: 2 (0.37%)
Zechariah 9:14, Zechariah 14:20.

CHAPTER 8

THEORETICAL MUSIC TONALITY

What can be said of a culture's music that existed thousands of years before audio recording? There are plenty of people, learned musicians and scholars alike, who argue that practically nothing can be definitively determined with regard to the actual sound of any ancient culture's music. I not only reject this position with regard to the music of biblical-era Israel, but I posit that the tonality of this ancient culture can be determined with a high degree of certainty based on surviving instruments, the known capabilities and limitations of wind instruments, the fundamentals of music based on the principles of physics, and modern musical trends that are rooted in ancient practice.

Before discussing the music of Israel during the biblical era, it must be established that there are and have been numerous "tonal systems" throughout history. The modern twelve-note chromatic scale is simply the most familiar to many Western musicians. For the purposes of this book, I will define two aspects of a tonal system. The first is how the octave is divided. Any two pitches of the same name, for example, the "A" above

Middle C (A4) and the "A" one octave above that (A5), vibrate at frequencies with a 1:2 ratio. On a modern piano, the pitch "A4" produces sound waves that vibrate at a frequency of 440 Hz (Hertz), or 440 sound wave cycles per second. The "A" an octave lower (A3) vibrates at 220 Hz, while the "A" an octave higher (A5) vibrates at 880 Hz. From the starting point of "A4," one can determine the frequency in hertz of each subsequent "A" by either multiplying by two as the player ascends each octave or or dividing by two as one descends by an octave. On an 88-key piano, the "A's" vibrate at the following frequencies, from left to right:

A0	A1	A2	A3	A4	A5	A6	A7
27.5	55	110	220	440	880	1,760	3,520

Every pitch or "note" also adheres to the same 2:1 ratio by octave. When two pitches or frequencies sound together, one is double (or quadruple, etc.) the vibrations per second of the other. The notes are perceived to harmonize perfectly because the sound waves of the higher pitch fit perfectly within the sound waves of the lower pitch.

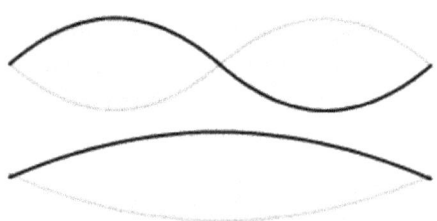

The top waveform signal represents sound that is vibrating at twice the speed or "frequency" of the bottom waveform signal. Notice the exact 2:1 ratio.

Because of this sonic phenomenon, every culture in the world recognizes the octave as a fundamental interval‎יד of music. In most cultures, if men and women sing together, the men will naturally sing one octave lower than the women without anyone necessarily realizing that there is difference.

Once the two notes of an octave have been identified, how do cultures divide the octave? Another way of asking this question is "What are the musical notes in a given culture?" In Western music, the octave is divided into twelve equidistant notes. When all twelve notes are played in order, this sequence is called the chromatic scale. American, British, German, Swedish, and Dutch musicians (amongst others) call these notes:

1	2	3	4	5	6	7	8	9	10	11	12
	C#/D♭		D#/E♭			F#/G♭		G#/A♭		A#/B♭	
C		D		E	F		G		A		B

Musicians from the majority of other Western and Near Eastern countries call these notes:

1	2	3	4	5	6	7	8	9	10	11	12
	Do#/Re♭	Re#/Mi♭				Fa#/Sol♭		Sol#/La♭		La#/Si♭	
Do		Re		Mi	Fa		Sol		La		Si‎חח

This twelve-way division is only one way that the cultures

יד The distance between to notes.

חח Note: This neo-Latin system uses "Si" as the leading tone, not the American "Ti." Also, unlike the "Fixed Do," the note above C is called Do #, not "Di."

of the world have divided the octave. In some varieties of traditional Chinese music, the octave is divided not into twelve even parts, but into five uneven parts that modern Westerners would recognize as a Major Pentatonic Scale.[217] Several composers, such as the Hungarian Franz Liszt, experimented with dividing the octave into six equal parts, called a "Whole Tone Scale." Moving the opposite direction, some Indonesian and Middle Eastern music divides the octave into more than twelve parts, utilizing what Western musicians call "microtones." An example is a pitch that is between C and C#. A Western musician who was unfamiliar with microtonal music might simply perceive these microtones to be out of tune, but in these cultures, they are a normal and important aspect of the musical vernacular.

Joey Weisenberg, author of *The Torah of Music* (2017), explains that Western music emphasizes harmony, homophony and polyphony. He cites the grandiose German music of the early 19th century, such as Salomon Sulzer's (1804-1890) setting of the *"Sh'ma"* from Deuteronomy 6:4, as an excellent example of these concepts.[218] Weisenberg describes that the further east one travels, the emphasis on harmony diminishes in favor monophony, as well as modal music played over one chord or even over a single droning note.[219] Because Israel has historically been influenced by both the Western and Eastern worlds, Jewish music often features qualities of both. When examining biblical music, it is reasonable to assume that the earliest Israelite music was more in line with monophonic, single chord, and drone-based practices, and an emphasis on harmony increased as Greek and Roman culture slowly began to influence the region.

In describing the harmony-focused music of the West, one of the most important aspects to discuss is "functional harmony" (not to be confused with "functional music" described in the previous chapter). Functional harmony can be defined as the principles and theories applied in music composition and analysis. In Western music, the V-I (written and read as Roman numerals, but pronounced as "five-one"), dominant-tonic relationship has been the primary basis of music for hundreds of years. The rules of functional harmony and proper voice leading are unique to Western music and would have been completely foreign to musicians in the ancient Near East. Chords and chord progressions as we know them were not recognized in Israel millennia ago. Based on surviving practices from Israel's neighbors, it seems that a drone from a *yarghul* or droning open intervals of fifths and fourths played on a *nevel* (as one would on an Indian *tambura*) would have been far more common.

So what *was* the tonal system of ancient Israel? The instrument that offers the most clues is the *shofar*. While no surviving *shofarot* from the period have been recovered, or likely ever will be due the decomposing organic nature of the instrument, the animals from which *shofar* are crafted have changed little in the last three millennia since the biblical era. This can be observed by examining the remains of sheep discovered in 2016, which date back more than 10,000 years, and whose horns are incredibly similar to modern sheep throughout Asia, including the Middle East.[220] Since rams' horns have remained unchanged, scholars have concluded that the notes of the *shofar* were part of the ancient Jews' musical vocabulary. Similarly, Tutankhamen's Trumpets, the closest surviving contemporaries to the Israelites' trumpets, also provide sonic clues as to the playable pitches and timbre of *chatzotzerot*.

As described in Chapter Four, a layperson can usually play one or two notes on a *shofar*. A skilled player can often play four different notes. Each note requires a significantly greater volume of air and air velocity to achieve, which is why skilled players can produce more notes. The playable notes on a *shofar* are based on the overtone series, which means there is 100% consistency in the playable notes on every *shofar* of a given fundamental pitch (lowest playable note) throughout history. For example, one *shofar* might produce a fundamental pitch of E3. The first note in the overtone series at which most players can produce sound is E4. E4 is the second partial (a note in the overtone sequence). The next notes of this particular *shofar*, in order, are B4, E5, and G#5. This can also be thought of as ascending from the lowest playable pitch by a Perfect Fifth, a Perfect Fourth, and then a Major Third. A true master of the instrument might even be able to play the sixth partial, and produce an additional Minor Third (of D6) on the *shofar* previously described. If another *shofar* has a lowest playable note of C4, then without even playing the instrument, one can determine that the other playable notes are G4, C5, E5, and perhaps B♭6. The longer the *shofar,* the more likely it is that players can reach these higher partials. Since the spiral *shofar* of the kudu is typically the longest variety, kudu *shofarot* typically have the greatest range and are the easiest on which to produce a wide range of notes.

A kudu shofar.

Relating the *shofar's* notes to the Major Scale, with a given *shofar's* most playable note functioning as the tonic, a *shofar* can play the first, third, fifth, and lowered seventh notes. In other words, the notes of a *shofar* (the Perfect First, Major Third, Perfect Fifth, and Minor Seventh degrees of a Major Scale) were doubtless a critical aspect of Israelite music, and there is absolute certainty that these intervals were part of the ancient Israelite musical vocabulary. By transposing these intervals to the key of C, an inventory of Israelite notes can be created. The playable notes of a *shofar* allow us to fill in the notes of a major triad. Further, assuming that the Temple Orchestra had its fair share of virtuosos who could access the sixth partial on their *shofarot,* the minor seventh can be included, as well. Therefore, the following notes provide the foundation for the Israelite tonal system:

C   E   G   B♭   C

Tutankhamen's Trumpets, the closest surviving relative to the Bibles' *chatzotzerot,* adhere to the same principle.

One of the most important archeological finds from Israel is the Megiddo Flute described earlier. You will recall that this bone flute is still playable, and can produce two pitches: A and D, which are a Perfect Fourth apart.[221] Through this surviving example, it can also be proven that the interval of a Perfect Fourth was part of Israel's musical vocabulary. Transposed to C, the addition of a Perfect Fourth brings the scale degree interval to:

C   E   F   G   B♭   C

This is the culmination of the physical evidence for the Israelite's tonal system, but further speculation can be supported by examining ancient cultural musical practices that continue today. Suzanne Haïk-Vantoura writes that the combination of notes and intervals that modern Western musicians call the Major Scale was a prominent musical feature of ancient Sumer-Akkadian music.[222] As the Sumer-Akkadian influence on Israelite life is undeniable, it is indeed feasible to consider that the Major Scale may not have been out of place in the music of ancient Israel.

The suggestion that the Major Scale may have been familiar within Israelite music might be considered Eurocentric, anachronistic, and irresponsible from a scholarly perspective. On the contrary, I am suggesting that the musical language of the Middle East and Near East may have migrated to Europe, where it was then adopted by the West. There is already ample circumstantial evidence to support such a claim. One example is that the violin, the quintessential instrument of the European classical orchestra, actually originated in the Middle East as the *rebab* and was brought to Europe centuries later. Another important European instrument, the lute, began as the Middle Eastern *oud*. Since these instruments migrated to Europe, it is reasonable to consider that modes and tonal systems may have been adopted by the West, as well.

*(Left) A rebab, the Middle Eastern ancestor of the violin.
(Right) A kamancha, a modern descendant of the rebab.*

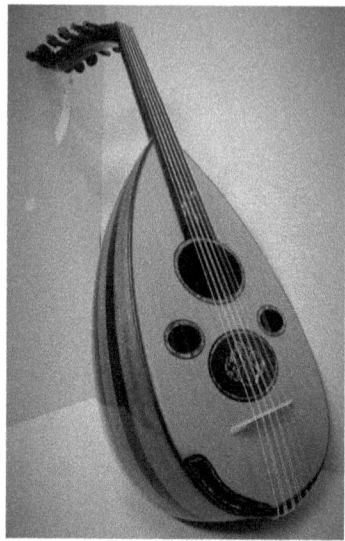

An oud, the Middle Eastern ancestor of the lute.

If this hypothesis is correct, then the Jewish Diaspora may also have contributed to the spread of Major tonality to the West. The story of Judaism after the Diaspora in the year 70 C.E. is a tale of a people who fiercely held on to their traditions for nearly two thousand years. The Jews who were forcibly removed from their ancestral homeland and relocated across Europe and Asia Minor likely brought their musical traditions with them. Similarly, many Arabs were displaced from their homeland, and relocated to Spain and the rest of the Iberian Peninsula beginning in the 8th century C.E. Today's Sephardic Jews are also descendants of Jews who relocated to Spain. The forced migrations of these two people groups helps to explain the spread of Near Eastern musical traditions to Europe in the first through eighth centuries C.E.

Ancient Sumer-Akkadian music is not the only culture to suggest evidence of the sequence of pitches we today refer to as the "Major Scale." Haïk-Vantoura writes that the Major Scale, alternatively known as the Ionian Mode, was also a staple of Greek music in antiquity.[223] The spread of Christianity in the first four centuries of the Common Era are further evidence of both Jewish and Greek ideas spreading through Asia Minor and Europe.

The Major Scale may have had a place in ancient Israel, but it is not the iconic sound associated with Jewish or Near Eastern music today. That distinction goes to a scale that classical musicians call the "fifth mode of the Harmonic Minor scale," or what jazz musicians call "Phrygian Dominant." Since a scale's nomenclature denotes or implies its function, this scale will henceforth be referred to as the "Hebraic Scale." This new name has been adopted because "Harmonic Minor" and "Phrygian Dominant" both relate to European functional harmony, which leads musicians to expect the scale to behave as it would in functional harmony. The name "Hebraic Scale" better allows musicians to remove their preconceived notions as to the harmonic and functional nature of this scale. The Hebraic Scale is still prominently used in performance and composition throughout the Middle East and Near East, notably in Israel.

In order to understand the Hebraic scale, it is helpful to review it in relation to the more familiar Harmonic Minor scale. The Harmonic Minor scale, in the key of E, is as follows:

E – F# – G – A – B – C – D# – E

To play the "fifth mode" of this scale means to play the same series of notes, but starting on the fifth note rather than the first. As the fifth note is "B," the fifth mode of the Harmonic Minor scale is played:

B – C – D# - E – F# - G – A – B

This is one way that Western musicians can understand the Hebraic Scale. Another way to think of the Hebraic Scale is a dominant chord juxtaposed against a major triad that is one half-step higher. For example, the notes of a a B7 chord, combined with a C chord, also produce the Hebraic Scale.

```
B7:              B       D#      F#     A   B
C Major:             C        E       G
Hebraic Scale:   B – C – D# - E – F# - G – A – B
```

The note sequence that makes up the Hebraic Scale is not used in many cultures in recent history, but it is foundational within Near Eastern music. It is also fundamental to the music of Eastern European Ashkenazi Jews and Spanish Sephardic Jews, not to mention the music of Spain in general. One example of Eastern European Jewish music that utilizes the Hebraic Scale is Klezmer music. In fact, the song "Hava Nagila" was composed exclusively using the Hebraic Scale, as every note of the melody and harmony is diatonic to the Hebraic Scale. Additionally, the worship song "Avinu Malkeinu" (folk) was almost exclusively composed using the Hebraic Scale. The singular exception is one chord near the end of the bridge. The song "Tradition!" from *Fiddler on the Roof* draws heavily on the Hebraic Scale, with its alternating chords of C Major and D♭ Major. Flamenco music of Spain does not specifically use the Hebraic Scale, but it prominently utilizes the Harmonic Minor Scale, which is comprised of the same pitches. This wide use around the world in places where Jewish people have significant populations suggests that the Hebraic Scale was widely in practice prior to the Diaspora and spread throughout the Jewish communities of Europe and Asia Minor following the forced exile and relocation at the hands of the Romans. The Hebraic Scale also remained in use in the Near East and Middle East.

It should also be noted that most modern *kinnorot* are tuned to:

```
                    Low ←              →High
String No.:   10 – 9 – 8 – 7 – 6 – 5 – 4 – 3 – 2 – 1
Note:         E – F# – G – A – B – C – D# – E – F# – G
```

This is a curious tuning system, until one realizes that these notes make up the Hebraic Scale in the key of B, and features the tonic (starting note and tonal center) in the middle of the instrument's range, with the Perfect Fifth on either side.

Let's next examine how the notes of the Hebraic Scale align with the playable notes of the *shofar, chatzotzerot,* and the Megiddo Flute, whose sounds scholars know with absolute certainty were heard in antiquity.

The Hebraic Scale in B is:

$$B - C - D\# - E - F\# - G - A - B$$

The Hebraic Scale transposed to C becomes:

$$C - D\flat - E - F - G - A\flat - B\flat - C$$

The inventory of known Israelite notes (from page 228) in C is:

$$C \quad E \quad F \quad G \quad B\flat \quad C$$

As can be observed above, the known Israelite notes perfectly fit within the Hebraic Scale and have no contradictions. The only difference between the known Israelite notes and the Hebraic Scale is that the Hebraic Scale features the addition of a D♭ and an A♭. Notice that these two notes would each be a half step above the tonic and dominant (the first and fifth notes of the scale, respectively). In Middle Eastern and Near Eastern music, it is common to play *metziltayim* finger cymbals that are tuned a half-step apart. If today, one were to purchase a brand-new pair of Middle Eastern finger cymbals from Zildjian (which people seldom realize is a 400-year-old company originally based in Istanbul), they would be sold as two cymbals, the first tuned to E, and the second tuned to F. The dissonant ringing offers a whimsical flare that is iconic within music from this region. If this half-step dissonance was used in ancient Israel, it could have been played using *shofarot*, as well. If two *shofarot* were played by a pair of musicians, with one *shofar*'s fundamental pitch a half-step higher than the other, the combined partials of the two *shofarot* would together create the notes of the Hebraic Scale:

Low *Shofar* (Key of C):   C   E   G   B♭
High *Shofar* (Key of D♭):   D♭   F   A♭

The Hebraic Scale beginning on C:

C   D♭   E   F   G   A♭   B♭   C

It cannot be definitively proven that the Hebraic Scale was used by the ancient Israelites. While many scholars agree that the Major Scale was an important aspect of Sumer-Akkadian music, this does not necessarily mean that it was adopted by Israel, as well. However, the notes that make up the Hebraic

Scale were playable on ancient Israelite musical instruments such as the *shofar* and *chatzotzerot,* as well as the Megiddo Flute and any tunable stringed instrument (such as the *kinnor* and *nevel*). Further, Jewish populations of Israel, the Iberian Peninsula, and Eastern Europe all employed the use of the Hebraic Scale in their music, despite the Diaspora, which forcibly displaced the Jews by thousands of miles and for thousands of years. It appears that, like the keeping of the Torah, the Jewish people held on to and maintained their musical traditions throughout the millennia, wherever they settled.

Chapter 9

BIBLICAL MUSIC NOTATION

Each facet of music in the Bible described thus far has presented unique challenges in understanding and reconstructing music as it would have sounded in ancient Israel. In the case of musical instruments, there are biblical descriptions in varying degrees of detail, but few surviving examples have been excavated from Israeli soil. Most of the surviving instruments are bronze bells and bone flutes. When considering music tonality and tonal systems, scholars have been able to make confident inferences and drawn educated conclusions. Yet when it comes to biblical music notation, the ancient equivalent of modern sheet music, few people realize that a complete library of written notation accompanies every line of text in the Hebrew Bible.

That last sentence may surprise many readers, but *yes,* you read that correctly. Millions of people around the world have a copy of the notated music for every verse in the Bible sitting on their bookshelves at home. This is because practically every copy of the Hebrew Bible printed in Hebrew rather than in

English actually contains the music notation embedded within its text. For those who do not own a physical copy, digital copies are available for free from a variety on online resources, such as www.Sefaria.org, or numerous free smart phone apps.

Take for example:

בְּרֵאשִׁית בָּרָא אֱלֹהִים אֵת הַשָּׁמַיִם וְאֵת הָאָרֶץ׃

The Hebrew sentence above is the first line of text from the Bible: *"B'reshit barah Elohim et ha'shmayim v'et ha'aretz...,"* which means "In the beginning, God created the heavens and the earth..." By now, anyone reading this book will recognize that the text above is Hebrew language script. Some readers may not realize that even though many of the symbols above and within the text are vowel markers, some of these symbols are a form of music notation.

Most people would recognize the following example as music notation,

but this is merely the most recent Western European iteration of musical notation prevalent during the last millennium. In reality, there are numerous varieties of written notation among the world's cultures. The notation styles of the Medieval-era Jewish scribes and rabbis in Galilee, Israel (the music notation found in the Bible) and the contemporaneous Christian monks of Europe (the antecedent of the above example of modern music notation) developed almost simultaneously, roughly a 2,400-mile journey apart from one another in the 9th century C.E. Despite how differently they appear today, their beginnings were surprisingly similar. However, Western music notation continued to evolve significantly over the centuries, whereas biblical notation has remained unchanged since its completion no later than 1000 C.E.

The challenge that a modern bibliomusicologist faces is that while there exists a complete set of the music notation of the Bible, painstakingly created by a group of rabbis and scribes over multiple generations, they did not provide a written record describing how to interpret their musical system. This is not unlike the plethora of Egyptian hieroglyphs that adorn the pyramids, but which were indecipherable without the Rosetta Stone. The story of the *te'amim* (טעמים)(tay-ah-meem), the music notation of the Bible, is very similar.

This chapter is not intended to teach readers how to read the *te'amim*, also known as "trope." Indeed, it would be absurd to suggest that any person, even a trained and highly skilled musician, could learn to read, understand, and perform biblical music notation based on a single chapter from just one book. It takes cantors and rabbis many years to develop a sense of proficiency in the art of cantillation. And even then, many people rely on rote memorization when chanting/singing from the Torah. This chapter does not aim to serve as a method for learning to read biblical notation, nor as a primer for learning, but as an explanation and history of biblical notation, as well as a foundation for how the written musical system works. However, for those who are interested in learning to read the *te'amim*, I would suggest the books *Chanting the Hebrew Bible* by Joshua R. Jacobson, specifically his "student edition" (2005), *The Art of Cantillation* by Marshall Portnoy and Josee Wolff (2000), or Arianne Brown's YouTube series "Tricks of the Trope."

THE MASORETIC TEXT

In the Jewish tradition, the Hebrew Bible has always been sung, but a written representation and record of the melodies did not appear within the Hebrew text of the Bible as a complete musical notation until the 9th and 10th centuries C.E. From approximately 500 C.E. to 1000 C.E., a group of Jewish scribes known as the "Masoretes" (mă-sor-eets), or the more biblical-sounding variant, "Mesorites," (mess-or-ites) lived primarily in the city of Tiberias on the western shore of the Sea of Galilee in Israel, though their tradition also had a presence in both Jerusalem and Babylon. These rabbinic scribes are sometimes known collectively as the "Masoretic School" or the "Tiberian School." The city of Tiberias was erected around 20 C.E. on the site of what was previously the Jewish village of *Rakkat*, first mentioned in Joshua 19:35. (Megillah 6a) The city was renamed for then-Roman Emperor Tiberias. The Masoretes produced a complete manuscript of the Tanakh. This version became the Hebrew Bible or Old Testament as we know it today.

These rabbis and scribes are also known as the Scribes of ben-Asher. "Ben" means "son of" or sometimes "progeny of" in Hebrew. If one were to write "*Yitzchak ben-Avraham*," that would mean "Isaac, son of Abraham." However, when some of the psalms are attributed to "*ben-Korah*," meaning in English "Sons of Korah" or the "Korahites," this could literally refer to his sons, but more likely his lineage, perhaps removed by multiple generations. The term may even more loosely mean "in the tradition of," and refer to those trained and taught by Korah or his descendants. In the case of the "Scribes of ben-Asher," this term likely encompasses all of those possible meanings. Producing the Masoretic Text was a massive undertaking that extended over centuries and must have involved many people. However, there was an actual Asher family. Two well-known men involved in the Masoretic project were Moses ben-Asher and his son, Aaron ben-Moses ben-Asher. These men were descendants in a long line of Masoretes, and their name implies that one person earlier in the lineage was simply named "Asher." Those who specialize in specific areas of biblical scholarship will use the terms that are prominent in their fields, but the terms "Masoretes," the "Tiberian School," and the "Scribes of ben-Asher" all refer to the same group of people.

There were two critical contributions added by the Masoretes. The first is the *niqqud* (נִקּוּד)(nee-kood), which is a system of dots and lines that indicate vowel markings and consonant modifiers. The Hebrew alphabet, or *aleph-bet,* is comprised exclusively of consonants. The language does have vowels and always has, but they were originally pronounced from memory, and were not a component of the written language. A similar English practice can be observed with the word "bicycle." The two Cs are pronounced differently, but there is no clue in the letters to indicate this difference. It is simply learned as part of the language as a special observance for that word. So too, the learned and literate Israelites may not have read notated vowels, but they learned pronunciation as part of reading and writing. The second critical contribution of the Masoretes, and that with which this book is most concerned, is the *te'amim*. These are the Bible's own form of music notation, which have been present in Hebrew editions of the Bible for more than one thousand years. The word *te'amim* comes from the word *te'am,* which means "delicious," and which originally simply meant "sense." On a personal note, the notion that music can be "delicious" is one of my favorite aspects of the Hebrew language.

The niqqud and *te'amim* are represented with dots and lines above, below, to the side of, and within the Hebrew letters.

Before the work of the Masoretes, the opening line of the Bible would have looked like this:

בראשית ברא אלהים את השמים ואת הארץ

With the Masoretic additions of the *niqqud* and *te'amim,* it looks like this:

בְּרֵאשִׁית בָּרָא אֱלֹהִים אֵת הַשָּׁמַיִם וְאֵת הָאָרֶץ׃

The latter is how the Hebrew text appears in nearly every home and study edition of the Hebrew Bible today.

Around the time of the destruction of the Second Temple in Jerusalem in 70 C.E., a group of rabbis recognized that the Jewish people could lose their culture and religion as a product of the Diaspora, an all too recent echo of sentiments felt during the Babylonian Exile. These rabbis began the lengthy process of producing a written record of the Mishnah: the oral law to accompany the Torah, and the written law given to Moses and all of Israel at Mount Sinai, which previously only existed as an oral tradition. Fast-forward to the ninth and tenth centuries C.E., when the Masoretes also feared that the Jewish people would lose the Hebrew language as it was displaced by the local languages of areas to which Jews were forced to relocate. One of the greatest challenges of reading Hebrew is that, as previously mentioned, there are no vowels. Only learned men, mostly rabbis and scribes, were able to read and write Hebrew. As centuries passed, many lay people in Judea[th] were more likely

---

[th] When the Romans occupied Judah, its name was Romanized to the "Province of Judea." Following the Bar Kokhba Revolt, the Romans changed the name again, this time to "Palestine" in an attempt to diminish its Jewish identity. In 1948, the Jews

to speak Greek or Aramaic, a closely related linguistic cousin of Hebrew that uses the same alphabet. Following the Diaspora, many exiled Jews adopted the language of their new country of residence.

As Jews began to forget their native tongue, critical language elements required definitive clarification to ensure not only that the Hebrew language would survive, but also so that God's commandments could be faithfully observed. Two examples that required clarification from the Masoretes are the Hebrew words for "milk" and "fat," which are *chalev* and *chelev*. Both spelled the same way in the Torah: חלב. When reading Exodus 23:19, this is an important distinction.

> *You shall not boil a kid in its mother's* חלב.
> *(milk or fat?)*
>
> Exodus 23:19

This example is particularly confusing because context alone does not offer an answer, as both words make sense. To remedy this issue, and to make reading Hebrew more accessible to everyone, not just those trained in the ancient language, the Masoretes developed the *niqqud* system of vowels and consonant modifiers, which included fifteen symbols comprised of dots and lines. These symbols are placed either below, above, to the left of, or within a consonant letter, and indicate how it should be pronounced. Because of the Masoretes and their *niqqud* vowel system, modern readers know that Exodus 23:19 commands the

---

returned to their ancestral homeland. It has since been officially recognized as the "State of Israel." Despite the numerous name changes, all of these terms generally refer to the same physical region.

Israelites not to boil a kid in its mother's *chalev,* or milk.

While developing the *niqqud,* the Masoretes also developed the *te'amim,* a musical notation system for reciting the melodies that, as tradition goes, are *"Mi'Sinai,"* or have always been associated with each line of text in the Bible. The beautiful melodies of the Bible complement and even enhance the meaning of the text itself. It must be noted that while every modern printed book or codex of the Hebrew Bible includes both the *niqqud* and the *te'amim,* Torah scrolls found in a synagogue will not contain either. This is because a Torah scroll read in synagogue must present the text "as it was given by Moses," or in its original form. Since the Masoretic additions are only about 1,000 years old, they certainly do not make the cut. However, Torah is still recited with the same Masoretic melodies that are notated in all codices. Remember, the Masoretes did not claim to *compose* the melodies of the *te'amim,* nor the pronunciations of the *niqqud.* Rather, they sought to provide a written reminder of how the words of the Bible have always sounded in order to ensure that they would not be forgotten by future generations. Even Rashi, an 11th century French rabbi and perhaps the most celebrated Jewish mind of the last millennium, wrote of Exodus 21:15, "Had I not seen the punctuation of the *te'amim,* I would have not known how to interpret this verse correctly."[224]

The Masoretes are the enduring and most well-known group to incorporate music notation into the Bible, but they are not the only ones to do so, nor were they the first. Two other groups, one known as the Babylonian School, the other known as the Jerusalem School (sometimes called the Palestinian School), also produced a notation system that functioned in a similar fashion. The Tiberian School even uses many of the same music notation symbols as the others, notably the *Sof Pasuk, Munach, Etnachta,* and *Mercha.* The notation of the Tiberian

School may also have been derived from symbols found in Byzantine music called "ekphonetic" notation.[225] The Byzantine ekphonetic notation is similar to both the *te'amim* and European neumes (described in the following pages).

While the three schools could have borrowed from one another, it is more likely that they all pulled from an earlier music tradition. One theory is that the *te'amim* are pictographical representations of hand shapes used for conducting called chironomy (kai-rah-nuh-mee). If this is the case, that would mean that while the Tiberian, Babylonian, and Jerusalem Schools initiated the practice of producing a written representation of the biblical melodies in the mid-to-late first millennium C.E., the tradition could plausibly go back many centuries further, possibly to biblical times.[226]

Another aspect that raises questions regarding the age of the *te'amim* is that the oldest document referring to *te'amim* is the 895 C.E. *Codex of the Prophets* by Moses ben-Asher. This is curious because the release of *Codex of the Prophets* should have been a revolutionary breakthrough and discovery, prompting commentary and spawning more writing on the subject. Haïk-Vantoura posits that the blasé manner in which the *te'amim* are mentioned in the *Codex of the Prophets* indicates that even in 895 C.E., they were nothing new, exciting, or extraordinary.[227] This may mean that the practices are far older than previously thought. Further supporting this notion, the *te'amim* are seemingly referred to in the Talmud as early as the 6th century C.E.[228] While the written record of the Masoretes' *te'amim* system dates to the 9th and 10th centuries, the practice of singing the ancient cantillations, the melodies themselves, and even the symbols used in the notation are likely a far older tradition.

A Brief History of Western European Music Notation

The biblical notation system may seem strange and foreign to today's musicians who are accustomed to the notation of modern sheet music from the Western European classical tradition (pictured above). Yet 1,100 years ago, when the ink of the *te'amim* was still drying, this Jewish style of written representation of music was surprisingly similar to its contemporary European counterpart. Through examining the history of modern music notation, one can see the similarities between the neumes of Europe and the *te'amim* of Jerusalem, as well as how their paths diverged.

The origins of modern music notation, or "sheet music," date back to the 9th century, when Europeans first began to create a written form of music. Before written "notes" were indicated by an oval with an attached vertical line, such as a "quarter note" ("crotchet"), scribes used written symbols called "neumes." Neumes (shown below) are squiggled lines drawn above printed lyrics. The directional and spatial relationships between the neumes above each piece of text provides a general sense of melodic contour and ornamentation. Imagine the note heads of a melody in modern music notation, but without a staff, stems, or beams. At the time, there was not yet a system in place to indicate rhythm. Melodies were simply sung based on the natural flow and cadence of the words. The same is true of biblical music notation.

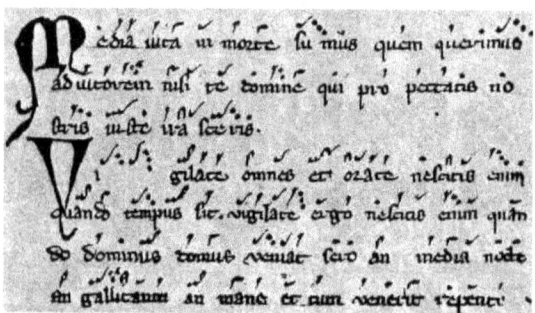

Another aspect shared by the European neumes and the biblical *te'amim* is that neither system was intended to *teach* new melodies. Rather, they offered a short-hand *reminder* of melodies which had been previously learned by rote via oral tradition. Further, both systems lacked an indication of absolute pitches, so melodies were recited arbitrarily in keys that fit the vocal range of the singers.

Eventually, music theorists began to move toward a more specific indication of pitch. The earliest musical staff had only one line, but it allowed for a sense of pitch relative to the line. The line usually (but not always) represented the tonic pitch, most often either "C" or "F." If the line represented "C" it was yellow, and if the line represented "F" it was red.

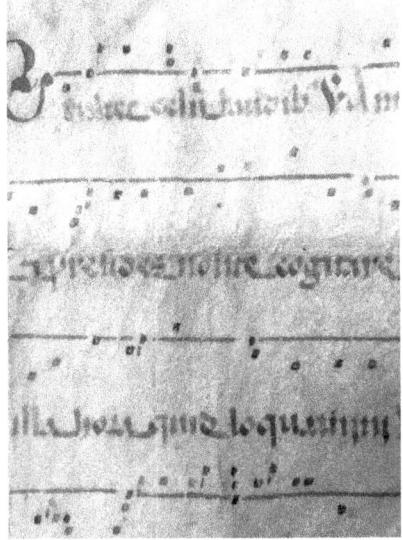

Text with a single "C" line.

Around the year 1013 C.E., a medieval monk and music theorist named Guido d'Arezzo developed the first musical staff. Though it had four lines instead of the modern five, it provided a significant leap forward in terms of indicating specific pitches. Guido d'Arezzo also developed the Solfège singing system, yet another European innovation which closely resembles Jewish musical practices of the same era in that both utilize a "Moveable Do." With Guido's staff, for the first time in history, European musicians were able to learn a piece from sheet music alone, rather than relying on learning by ear.

Guido d'Arezzo's four-line staff.

Despite Guido's advancements with written music, Europeans were still without a systematic way to indicate rhythm. That addition would come more than one hundred years later in the 12th century, thanks to the work of French composers Léonin (1135-1201 C.E.) and Pérotin (1160-1230 C.E.) of the Notre Dame School. Their system relied on a knowledge of preexisting rhythmic patterns. During the same time period, an alternative written musical system in which note heads of different shapes, usually squares, indicated different melodic ornamentations, was emerging simultaneously. In the 13th century, German music theorist Franco of Cologne (1215 – 1270 C.E.) was the first composer to utilize various note head shapes to indicate a note's rhythmic length. During the Renaissance (1400-1600), a movement called "Arz Nova," Latin for "New Art," introduced numerous new note values, which allowed for the transcription of more specific music representation.

By the Baroque period of music (1600-1750 C.E.), European music notation came to resemble that of today. The note heads switched from squares to ovals, and the introduction of new rhythmic symbols of dots and additional beams allowed for increased rhythmic precision. Additionally, accidentals, clefs, and a five-line staff facilitated a written representation of specific pitches. By this point, music notation was able to convey an incredible level of detail regarding specific pitches and precise rhythms.

While this system of written music was practiced throughout Europe, the expressive text within a piece of music was always written in the native language of the country from which it came. This began to change around 1600 C.E., when the popularity of Italian opera spread throughout Europe, and Europeans of all nationalities became familiar with Italian music terminology from reading and performing imported Italian operas. Terms like *forte, decrescendo, pianissimo, accelerando,* and *fermata* became standard musical terms used by all composers, regardless of the composer's nationality or native language. Today, modern European music notation is as ubiquitous around the world as the English language.

THE BIBLICAL TE'AMIM
AND HOW THEY ARE INTERPRETED TODAY

It must first be clearly stated that the modern understanding and interpretation of *te'amim* is itself an oral tradition. Prior to the invention of audio recording technology near the turn of the 20th century, cantillation was based solely on living memory from one generation to the next. Jewish communities from different traditions, denominations, or regions often read the same text and *te'amim,* yet recited the melodies with subtle differences. Joshua R. Jacobson shows the following seven communal variations on *tevir,* a melodic phrase repeated numerous times throughout the Bible.[229]

As can be observed in the preceding examples, these melodies are not the same, but they are quite similar. There are differences in the note-to-note intervals, but importantly, the melodic contours are nearly identical. The main difference is that the Syrian and French variations include a mordant-like turn (a quick trill of upper and lower neighboring tones, such as those found in the introduction to Mozart's "Rondo alla Turca").

Unlike modern music notation, the *te'amim* do not use absolute pitch. In other words, in modern music notation, the pitch "A" within the second space of the treble clef staff should sound at a frequency of 440 Hz. In contrast, the modern concept most similar to the biblical music tradition is the Solfège concept of "Moveable Do," wherein the melody and melodic intervals stay constant, but the starting pitch is arbitrary.

Throughout the Bible, every word contains one of thirty-three different musical symbols, called a *te'am*. Each word of the Bible has a *te'am* attached to it, placed on the letter or syllable to be stressed. The *te'am* indicates a specific, short melodic phrase or motif. Think of the *te'amim* as short melodies or modular formulas that can be rearranged to produce more complex, longer melodic phrases. To relate this concept to Major Scale degrees, one modular formula may be 5-3-5. Another may be 3-2-1. When the two are combined, it creates a longer melody of 5-3-5-3-2-1. In the key of C Major, this looks like:

There is no indication of rhythm or time because, like neumes, the *te'amim* have no indication of rhythm or time. Melodies are recited based on the natural rhythmic flow of the text.

(See next page)

The thirty-three *te'amim* are:

Mercha	בְ	(Zakef) Katon	בֹּ
Tip'cha	בֽ	V'azla	בֿ
Munach	בֻ	Geresh	בֿ
Etnachta	בֽ	R'vii	בֹ
Sof Pasuk	׃ב	Darga	בֽ
Kadma	בֿ	Tevir	בֽ
Mapach	בֽ	Yetiv	בֽ
Pashta	בֿ	Zakef Gadol	בֽ

Gershayim	בּׄ	Karne Farah	בֿ֟
(Telisha) Ketana	בֿ֩	Munach Legarme	ב׀
(Telisha) Gedola	בֿ֠	Mercha Kefula	בֿ֦
Pazer	בֿ֡	Yerach ben Yomo*	בֿ֪
Segol	בֿ֒	Atnach Hafukh*	בֿ֢
Zarka	בֿ֮	Ole	בֿ֥
Shalshelet	בֿ֓	Illu	בֿ֙
Shene Pashtin	בּ֛בּ	Dehi	בֿ֭
		Tsinnorit	בֿ֘

These *te'amim* were used exclusively to convey sacred melodies for worship, and are not found in other contemporary documents notating secular songs. These melodies were also not intended to be sight read, per se. Cantors or worship leaders learn these melodies, often by rote, and then these combinations of symbols function similarly to the neumes of European music, simply offering the worship leader a shorthand reminder of the melody with which they are already familiar.

Adding to the complexity of this musical notation system, the *te'amim* are interpreted differently based on the book of the Bible in which they appear, the time of year, and the specific combination of *te'amim* in any given verse. The most common way of interpreting the *te'amim* is as they appear in the Torah (Genesis, Exodus, Leviticus, Numbers, or Deuteronomy) during most of the year. However, during the High Holy Days of *Rosh Hashanah* and *Yom Kippur*, some melodies are altered to express reverence for these two holiest days of the year. Important narratives, such as Abraham's binding of Isaac (Genesis 22), have their standard melodies, as well as a heightened melody for recitation on *Rosh Hashanah*.

In the *haftarah* excerpts from the books of the Prophets, the melodies are interpreted differently still.[ה] Three books: Psalms, Proverbs, and (most of) Job, are known as the "psalmodic" books because they have unique *te'am* elements not found in the "prosodic" books (everything else in the Hebrew Bible). Lastly, the *Megillah* (plural: *Megillot*), or the five books of Esther, Lamentations, Ruth, Ecclesiastes, and Song of Songs, has its own unique melodies associated with the same te'amim symbols that are found throughout the Bible.

[ה] The tradition of reading *haftarah* emerged in response to the tyranny of King Antiochus IV, also known as "Epiphanes." Antiochus IV is the same ruler under whose reign the Maccabean Revolt of 164 B.C.E. led to the tradition of Chanukah. Each Shabbat, Jews would gather and read aloud from the Torah. Once Antiochus banned the practice of public Torah recitation and made it punishable by death, the Jewish leaders instead identified passages from the Books of the Prophets which aligned with the message, story, or teaching of that week's Torah portion. Although the reading of Torah has long since resumed, most synagogues read the week's Torah portion along with the week's corresponding *haftarah* as both a reminder of their past and to better contextualize the Torah portion itself.

Considering the many unique ways in which each *te'am* may function melodically dependent upon the time of year when it is recited, which book of the Bible a passage comes from, and other details, transcribing the melodies associated with each *te'am* is an endeavor outside the scope of this chapter. Multiply those variables by each country, region, and community's subtle variations, and the results easily fill a separate book. However, to demonstrate one prominent recitation method, I have transcribed a few common passages to show how the *te'amim* fit together to create a melody.

Throughout Scripture, there are many recurring musical phrases which are formed by combining the short *te'am* musical motifs together in the same or similar way each time. These phrases are named for their final *te'am* in the sequence. One of the most common is called an "Etnachta Phrase."[230]

An "Etnachta" phrase:

Mercha > Tip'cha > Munach > Etnachta[חח]

In the following example, the Middle C is the tonal center of the melody. The rhythms presented are merely an estimation. Remember that in biblical music, the rhythm is always secondary to the text and should follow the natural flow of the sentence. For this reason, no time signature is indicated.

[חח] Note that with any of these phrases, some *te'am* may be eliminated to accommodate sentence length. By following along with the *te'amim* musical notation, the cantor will always know the appropriate structure for a given passage of Scripture.

These *te'amim* combine together to create:

One of the many *Etnachta* phrases in the Torah is found in Deuteronomy 6:10. It reads:

When the LORD *your God brings you into the land that He swore to your fathers, Abraham, Isaac, and Jacob, to assign to you—great and flourishing cities that you did not build . . .*

The phrase that features the *Etnachta* is ". . . Isaac, and Jacob, to assign to you..." or "...*l'Yitzchak u'l'Ya'akov latet lach...*"

Which is transcribed as:

Notice that the number of notes for each *te'am* is adjusted to accommodate the number of syllables in the word to which it is assigned. Through this short example, one can observe the logic and fundamental practice by which modern worship leaders recite the melodies of Scripture.

In addition to their musical meaning, *te'amim* also offer information regarding sentence structure and pronunciation. For example, the Etnachta will always indicate the middle of a phrase, while the Sof Pasuk will always indicate the end of a phrase. In this way, the Etnachta is akin to a comma or semicolon, while the Sof Pasuk functions like a period. This means that a Sof Pasuk not only marks the end of a musical phrase, but the end of a sentence as well. *Te'amim* also help readers with pronunciation because the letter to which the *te'am* is attached indicates the stressed or emphasized syllable within a word.

Next, let's examine an alternate theory which has captivated (and divided) audiences for more than forty years, developed by an accomplished musician and biblical scholar by the name of Suzanne Haïk-Vantoura.

Suzanne Haïk-Vantoura
La Musique de la Bible Révelée

In 1976, Suzanne Haïk-Vantoura published a book in which she claimed to have deciphered the "original" interpretation of the *te'amim* musical notation symbols. Haïk-Vantoura posits that each subscript *te'am* represents a different scale degree.[231] According to her theory, a cantor or worship leader would recite the biblical text on the associated pitch of the most recent *te'am*, then change to the next pitch once a new *te'am* appears. Haïk-Vantoura's theory also teaches that superscript *te'amim* indicate specific melodic ornamentations or flourishes. Haïk-Vantoura's method for deciphering the *te'amim* results in a melody in which notes are always repeated in succession multiple times. (See example on page 267) This is markedly different from the widely accepted method of Torah cantillation based on melodic motifs described earlier.

Suzanne Haïk-Vantoura's (1912-2000) book *La Musique de la Bible Révelée* (1976), or as its English translation is titled, *The Music of the Bible Revealed* (1991), is one of the most enigmatic and polarizing treatises of modern bibliomusicology. Haïk-Vantoura was a Parisian Jew, as well as an award-winning organist, teacher, composer, music theorist, and biblical scholar. During World War II, she and her family fled from Paris to southern France to evade the Nazis at the height of the Holocaust. While in hiding, Haïk-Vantoura, a recent graduate of the Conservatoire National Supérieur de Musique et de Danse de Paris (The Paris Conservatory), began researching and studying the *te'amim* of the Bible.

While most scholars hold the position that the modern practice of interpreting and reciting the *te'amim* is rooted in ancient tradition, and to some extent, resembles how these melodies would have originally sounded, Haïk-Vantoura posits that the contemporary recitation practices are far too modern, and are rooted in European musical tradition. Armed with a fluency in biblical Hebrew and a degree from the prestigious Paris Conservatory, Haïk-Vantoura believed she had the skillset to decipher the "original" music of the *te'amim*. And so, she spent the years hiding from the Nazis devoted to this task. When the war ended and she and her family returned to Paris, Haïk-Vantoura resumed her music career, while her *te'amim* studies became a hobby. However, when she retired as a music professor and organist in 1970, deciphering the *te'amim* once again became her primary focus.

In 1976, Haïk-Vantoura published the original French first edition of *La Musique de la Bible Révelée,* along with a full LP album featuring recordings of the melodies in Hebrew as she had deciphered them. These recordings are complete with instrumental accompaniment, intended to recreate the sound and timbre of ancient Israel. This record features some of the most popular biblical passages, such as Psalm 23 ("The LORD is my shepherd, I shall not want..."), Moses and the Burning Bush, the *Sh'ma* ("Hear, O Israel! The LORD is our God, the LORD alone"), and Psalm 150, to name a few.

In 1978, she published an updated second edition, which would later be the basis for the 1991 English edition. She also published the sheet music for her first record, as well as two more volumes of sheet music for other popular Bible verses. Perhaps her most grandiose achievement was deciphering the entire biblical book of Song of Songs. This epic work was recorded by a male and a female singer, as well as biblically-inspired instrumental accompaniment. Haïk-Vantoura then published the sheet music for her deciphered arrangements. The 1986 concert debut of Song of Songs was credited as the "first performance of the original melody in more than three thousand years."[232]

In 2000, Suzanne Haïk-Vantoura passed away in Switzerland, but two decades later, her work is still widely discussed. Her book still incites interest, inspiration, and sometimes indignation, depending on the reader.

Haïk-Vantoura's proposed methodology for deciphering *te'amim* has four primary components: (1) the names of the *te'amim* offer clues to their melodic function, (2) the Masoretes who penned the *te'amim* were stewards of the ancient melodies, not the melodies' creators, (3) each *te'am* represents a pitch, or more specifically, a scale degree, rather than a melodic motif, and (4), the *te'amim* symbols are rooted in chironomy (the practice of using hand shapes to convey musical ideas). Her theory on the meaning of the *te'amim* parallels the standard practice of interpreting and reciting *te'amim* in many respects. She agrees that the *te'amim* penned by the Scribes of ben-Asher documented melodies as they had sounded for generations, perhaps dating back to the First Temple or even earlier.[233] Haïk-Vantoura writes that these melodies may date to the pre-monarchal era.[234] She vehemently rejects any notion that the Tiberian School were recording their own original ideas. The notation system may have been of their invention, but *what* the notation represented musically dates back to the earliest events in Israelite history. However, her theory differs from the conventional interpretation in that she believes each *te'am* represents a pitch, not a musical motif or melodic phrases. Another difference is that Haïk-Vantoura uses the same terminology for the individual *te'amim*, such as *Mercha, Tipecha, Munach,* etc., but she sometimes changes which name represents which term.

Haïk-Vantoura provides the following key, which translates the names of some of the most frequently used *te'amim* as follows:

TABLE 12:
HAÏK-VANTOURA'S SCALE DEGREES

Hebrew Name	English Meaning	Scale Degree[חט]
Sof Pasuk	End	I
Mercha	Extension	II
Tipecha	Palm	III
Etnachta	Resting	IV
Munach	Placed	V
Darga	Ladder	VI
Tevir	Broken	VII

Through trial and error, Haïk-Vantoura discovered that, when aligned with the notes of a scale, the *te'amim* create pleasing melodies. While there is nothing illogical about this position, almost every musical phrase in the Bible features an *Etnachta* in the middle of the phrase and a *Sof Pasuk* at the end of the phrase. If every phrase ends with the same symbol, and that symbol is taken to represent the tonic, then it is not

---

[חט] Lowercase Roman Numerals are not used because biblical music does not adhere to the rules of modern functional harmony.

surprising that it sounds melodically pleasing.

Haïk-Vantoura writes that there are two variations of *te'mim* within the Bible: the prosodic system and the psalmodic system.[235] The prosodic system may be found in the Torah and most other books of the Bible, yet the psalmodic system is unique to the Psalms, Proverbs, and certain sections of the Book of Job. She suggests that the prosodic system borrows the major tonality from the Sumer-Akkadian culture yet starts on the third scale degree.[236]

Written in the key of C Major, the notes are:

C   D   E   F   G   A   B   C

Yet by beginning on the third scale degree, the actual order of notes aligns with a Phrygian Mode as:

E   F   G   A   B   C   D   E

Within the prosodic system, Haïk-Vantoura maintains the root note of E, yet uses the Hebraic Scale[ח]:

E   F#   G   A   B   C   D#   E

[ח] Haïk-Vantoura never uses the term "Hebraic Scale," but she does use the same notes as this scale, described earlier.

Let's examine the differences between the widely accepted method of Torah cantillation and Haïk-Vantoura's method using one of the most often read and recited passages of Scripture:

וְאָהַבְתָּ֗ אֵ֚ת יְהֹוָ֣ה אֱלֹהֶ֔יךָ בְּכָל־לְבָבְךָ֥ וּבְכָל־נַפְשְׁךָ֖ וּבְכָל־מְאֹדֶֽךָ׃

You shall love the LORD *your God with all your heart and with all your soul and with all your might.*

Deuteronomy 6:5

Remember that both approaches read from the exact same *te'amim* notated within Scripture by the Scribes of ben-Asher one thousand years ago. They simply interpret this notation differently. "C" is the tonal center in both of the following examples.

Traditional Torah Cantillation

Suzanne Haïk-Vantoura's Method

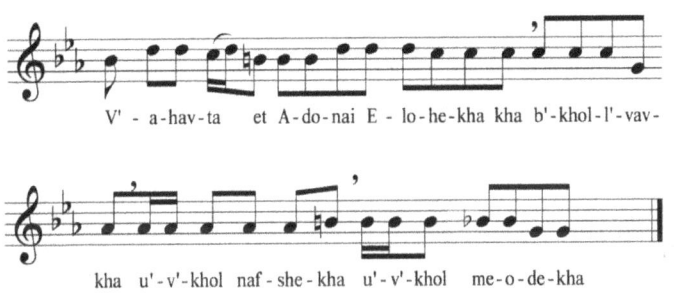

Noteworthy Differences

- Haïk-Vantoura's melody features many repeated notes, while the traditional method has only occasional repeated notes.
- The traditional Torah cantillation melody is rooted in what modern Western musicians would recognize as the Major Pentatonic Scale, while Haïk-Vantoura's melody pulls from both the Harmonic Minor and Natural Minor, despite her assertion that she uses the notes of the Hebraic Scale.

- The traditional method is melismatic (featuring more than one pitch on a single syllable), while Haïk-Vantoura only occasionally introduces melisma during flourishes.

CHIRONOMY

Chironomy (kai-rah-nuh-mee, or occasionally, ker-ah-nuh-mee), sometimes spelled "cheironomy," is the ancient practice of conducting musicians with hand gestures which convey musical melodies. Chironomy has been documented in cultures across Asia (including the Near East, Middle East, India, and China), and extending to Egypt, Asian Minor, and Europe.[237] In each of these cultures, a musical specialist called a "chironomer" dedicates his or her professional and/or religious life to memorizing innumerable musical melodies to conduct musicians through live performance.[238] Since chironomy was practiced in many regions that lacked a written music notation system and in which populations were highly illiterate, chironomy was often (though not exclusively) taught via oral tradition and rote instruction.[239] One exception is Greece, where chironomy was practiced alongside a system for written music notation around 600 B.C.E.[240]

Memorizing hundreds or even thousands of songs and melodies in an illiterate world was an unreasonable and unrealistic expectation of ancient musicians. Instead, musicians and chironomers were familiar with an intricate system of hand shapes and motions that conveyed different musical ideas, notes, melodies, and motifs. The chironomer memorized short melodies which fit together to create larger musical works, and would conduct those melodies for the musicians. The musicians did not memorize the melodies, but they did know how to interpret the hand signs they received. In this way, a single chironomer could conduct a large group of musicians. In Egypt, there are hieroglyphs of chironomers conducting two separate melodies simultaneously (one on each hand) to two different harpists, resulting in a harmonious, polyphonic, or polyrhythmic music.²⁴¹ There are a few possible ways that this Egyptian practice could have made its way to Israel. First, Israel's ancient culture was doubtless influenced by Egypt because the countries are neighbors. Second, the biblical narrative asserts that the Israelites spent 430 years as slaves in Egypt prior to the Exodus, and thus may have adopted Egyptian practices as their own. Extrabiblical sources document the Hyksos, a Semitic Canaanite people in Egypt, who may have brought the Egyptian musical practice of chironomy to Israel, as well as other music elements, such as the silver trumpets, sistrum, and box lyre.

Egyptian hieroglyph of a chironomer conducting a flautist.

Though Haïk-Vantoura famously promoted the notion that chironomy was an important aspect of biblical music, she was not the first to make this assertion. Eight years before *Le Musique de la Bible Révélée* was published, Saul Levin, a professor at the State University of New York at Binghamton, published an article titled "The Traditional Chironomy of the Hebrew Scriptures" (1968). In this article, Levin defines chironomy as "the art of moving the hand to regulate the voice."[242] Levin states that while chironomy never played a significant role in worship for European and American Jews, chironomy has remained in practice since the time of the Masoretes for Asian and African Jews.[243] Professor Levin even video-recorded men in Israel demonstrating chironomy, which proves this practice was still in use as recently as 1966.[244]

Rabbi Akiba (40 C.E.–135 C.E.),[245] Rabbi Nahman bar-Isaac (d. 356 C.E.) (Berakot 62a),[246] and Rashi (1040–1105 C.E.)[247] all wrote about conveying tonal, musical ideas with one's dominant hand while reciting Torah. Rashi wrote in 1105 C.E. that chironomy was a common sight in Israel, but was not widely practiced by Jews in Europe, with the exception of Rome.[248] It should be noted that chironomy was a common fixture of Christian worship services in the Middle Ages in both the Catholic Church and the Greek Orthodox Church.[249] Levin created a video in 1966 which documented chironomy being practiced while chanting Torah in Israel by Jerusalemites who were originally from Jeruba, Tunisia, and Egypt. Levin's point was that chironomy was already unfamiliar to native Israelis, and rarely taught to Israeli children.[250] The chironomers from Levin's video were from other countries where chironomy was still practiced. Thankfully, Levin had the foresight to record video of these men demonstrating chironomy, a link to which is included in the end notes of this book or at www.MusicInTheBible.com.[251]

Chironomy may no longer be the primary method for conducting the music of the Bible, but the use of hand shapes that resemble the symbols of the *te'amim* remains a common pedagogical tool for teaching Torah cantillation. For a superb example, see Cantor Arianne Brown's demonstration in "Tricks of the Trope."[252] Modern chironomy practices are not limited to sacred music. Many K-12 classroom music teachers who lead their students using Kodály handshapes to represent Solfège syllables and scale degrees are essentially chironomers.[253]

REACTIONS TO *THE MUSIC OF THE BIBLE REVEALED*

From its initial release, *La Musique de la Bible Révelée* was immediately polarizing. Though the book won the Institut de France's prestigious 1978 Prix Bernier award, it was also harshly panned in a 1980 review by the Washington Post's musicologist Herman Berlinski.[254]

Berlinski calls Haïk-Vantoura's book "fantasy and speculation," adding that:

> Haïk-Vantoura has not and could not have produced a single document that could have served as a Rosetta Stone for deciphering the Hebrew marks in the Masoretic Bible, which she claims to have done. Such documents simply do not exist, which she acknowledges in her book. Vantoura has done a great deal of research, but it is not accidental that in her book she has studiously avoided the work of all the great accentologists and works of Jewish scholars such as: Alfred Sendrey's "Music [in Ancient] Israel," Eric Werner's "The Sacred Bridge," and Solomon Rosowsky's "The Cantillation of the Bible." Vantoura approaches the problem at hand in a typically Western fashion... Her key is purely the product of her own imagination. But even within the system she has developed, there are some inconsistencies.[255]

Berlinski's review is scathing. Some of his criticisms are valid, such as pointing out that there are inconsistencies within Haïk-Vantoura's theory. However, other aspects of his assessment offer evidence that Berlinski is not an expert on ancient musical notation. For example, he criticizes Haïk-Vantoura because her method does not produce a "full-fledged, exact musical notation."[256] Berlinski does not elaborate on the point, but one could take his comment as a reference to the absence of representation of absolute pitch, indicated rhythms, dynamics, and articulation. If this inference is correct, then his comments are misplaced, as no ancient culture produced written music with that level of detail. The "full-fledged, exact music" of Europe may have developed from Medieval neumes, but only reached its current iteration within the last few centuries.

The Music of the Bible Revealed has a reputation as an extremely difficult read, prompting too many readers to quickly give up reading the book. Not only is its terminology quite dense, but it is also a translation from French into English. Furthermore, Haïk-Vantoura assumes a great deal of both musical and biblical knowledge of the reader. One Amazon reviewer who goes simply be the name "truthwriter," writes "A difficult read that needed more explanations in some areas. I had to consciously chew over every sentence, so would recommend only for most earnest reader." Another reviewer, "ntimeman," writes that "The book is written for someone who has a doctorate in music." Further compounding the inaccessibility of this text, it was only printed in English during its initial publication run in 1991. Copies are thus exceedingly difficult to procure. I was "lucky" in that I "only" had to pay $130 USD for my used copy in 2018. At the time of this writing, some copies are selling online for as much $1,000, though the typical price range remains between $150 and $750. The fact that buyers continue to pay these exorbitant prices is an indication of how curious people remain about music in the Bible.

The purpose of including a section devoted to Suzanne Haïk-Vantoura's *La Musique de la Bible Révélée* in this book was neither to endorse nor repudiate her hypotheses. It is merely offered for your consideration. If you, the reader, believe that there is some merit to her logic, you are not alone, and I encourage you to read her book in its entirety to learn more. If you object to her theory based on her inferences, logic, or any other basis, you too are not alone.

After considering Haïk-Vantoura's theory, I cannot say definitively that her theory is the most likely cipher for understanding and recreating music as it would have sounded thousands of years ago. That level of certainty has, unfortunately, been forever lost to history, based on all available evidence and resources. But who knows? The Dead Sea Scrolls were discovered less than a century ago, and perhaps one day archeologists will uncover an original deciphering key of the Tiberian Scribes of ben-Asher, unlocking the true and original meaning of the *te'amim*.

However, there are aspects of *La Musique de la Bible Révélée* which I believe hold merit. The first is that there is an inherit logic to her suggested method. She suggests that the names of the *te'amim* are related to the way that they function musically. When the notes of the scale are arranged based on her proposed translations, the result is both logical and melodically-pleasing. The melodic end result of her recordings, as well as the melodic emphasis and contour do seem to align perfectly with the content of the text.[257] However, a reasonable criticism of her method is that she uses a combination of the Major Scale, Minor Scales, and the Hebraic Scale. Critics argue that this is simply an anachronistic and Eurocentric interpretation, and that modern Western tonality has no place in ancient Israelite music. While I agree that her interchangeable use of various tonalities does seem somewhat arbitrary, I would still direct critics to the numerous arguments that the Western conception of the "Major Scale" was in fact originally a product of ancient Assyrian music, and also appeared in the music of Classical Greece. Additionally, many European classical instruments have Middle Eastern roots. Like innumerable aspects of human civilization, Major tonality may have originated in the Middle East and Near East long before being shared with the West.

The other area in which I give Haïk-Vantoura tremendous credit is in her insistence that the *te'amim* originated as a written representation of chironomy. Evidence in the form of hieroglyphs, paintings, and written testimony proves that chironomy was an important aspect of numerous ancient cultures, including India and China, as well as Israel's neighbor Egypt.[258] Chironomy is also still widely practiced today in both Torah schools and public schools,[259] though for pedagogical reasons rather than to conduct musicians without a written musical manuscript. Haïk-Vantoura's claims regarding the relationship between chironomy and the *te'amim*, are, perhaps, the most plausible of all her assertions.

CONCLUSIONS

More so than the contents of any preceding chapter, scholarship on the *te'amim* is largely based on speculation and conjecture. However, there are some definitive truths which can be identified. The first is that the Masoretes first incorporated the *niqqud* and *te'amim* in the final centuries of the first millennium C.E. The Masoretes were not and never claimed to be the first to use music notation to accompany the biblical text, and even openly borrowed some symbols from the earlier Babylonian School, Jerusalem School, and Byzantine ekphonetic notations. This cultural sharing may suggest that all four groups were drawing upon an earlier tradition of chironomy, which used pictographical representations of widely used hand shapes for conducting. Regardless of these notation's origins, for more than one thousand years, the *te'amim* have allowed Jews to unite as a worldwide community which uses the notation to facilitate both personal and corporate worship. Though each community of Jews often has subtle distinctions in its interpretation of each *te'am*, there are far more similarities than differences between them. As Jacobson argues, the melodies associated with the *te'amim* did not develop in a bubble.[260] The melodies are likely all rooted in one shared, ancient tradition: the sound of music in ancient Israel prior to the Jewish Diaspora.[261]

CHAPTER 10

ECHOES OF THE PAST IN MUSIC TODAY

The chronological end of the Hebrew Bible recounts the Jews' return to Judah from captivity in Babylon in approximately 538 B.C.E, followed by the rebuilding of the Holy Temple in Jerusalem. Scholars generally agree that the last contribution to the Tanakh was the Book of Daniel, which was added around 167-164 B.C.E.[262] Despite these events dating back more than two millennia, the musical traditions and descriptions within the Bible continue to influence musical practices today. This is particularly true of Jewish and Christian worship music.

Music in the Bible was separated into the secular and the sacred by the terms *shir* and *zamer*, respectively. A *shir* can be used in a secular or sacred context, but the term *zamer* specifically denotes a religious connotation. This distinction can still be found today. Some religious communities abstain from listening to secular music, believing that music should only be used as worship. To them, any other use of music is blasphemy.

The influence of other varieties and genres of music found in the Bible, such as the *mizmor, maskil, michtam,* and *shushan,* can all be observed in contemporary music, as well. Didactic songs that teach lessons, like a *maskil;* songs with hidden meaning, like a *michtam;* and the practice of setting scriptural or liturgical text or religious-themed lyrics to popular, secular songs are all common occurrences today.

MUSICAL INSTRUMENTS AND STYLES

In contemporary religious and worship music, most artists record and write for modern instruments, such as piano, guitar, bass, and drums. However, some Jewish musicians, like Elana Arian, Noam Katz, and the Yamma Ensemble use a combination of ancient and modern instrumentation to evoke Near Eastern sounds and influences. There are other Jewish artists, like Beri Weber, who opt for the opposite approach, exclusively using modern, synth-based, popular, and hip-hop-inspired music.

Within American Christian music, the divide is not between *biblical* and *modern,* but between *American traditional* and *modern.* Gospel music often relies on a piano or an organ with a choir. Some Christian denominations even refrain from instrumental accompaniment altogether in favor of *a cappella* music. Yet ever since the "Jesus Movement" of the 1970s, there has been a growing trend toward using popular and contemporary genres for worship and praise music.[263] Chris Tomlin's pop-rock-inspired worship music of the early-2000s used the same musical palette as the day's most popular secular artists. Some of the most played artists in Contemporary Christian Music (CCM), including Elevation, Hillsong, and Passion, sound like music some would expect to hear at a rave or a rock concert rather than a church on Sunday morning.

Below is a list of the artists described above, along with some song examples to illustrate the various ways that biblically influenced music is played today:

Elana Arian, "Hineh Mah Tov"
Noam Katz, "Bar'chu/Roll into Dark"
Yamma Ensemble, "King David"
Beri Weber, "Yachad"
Chris Tomlin, "Holy is the LORD"
Elevation, "Unstoppable God"
Hillsong, "Oceans"
Passion, "Glorious Day"

STRINGED INSTRUMENTS

Today, the *kinnor* and *nevel* may seem relegated to the realm of "specialty instruments" that only paleomusicologists study. Yet the guitar and bass guitar, staples of almost every modern, popular genre of music among both Jewish and Christian artists, are both descended from these biblical instruments. While the construction, design, and playing style has evolved dramatically over the millennia, the musical art of plucking strings of high tension against a resonant wooden box has persisted. Modern electric guitars, amplifiers, and effects pedals allow for wild sounds that were inconceivable to the ancient Israelites. However, many cantors and worship leaders still favor the humble acoustic guitar. Further, numerous congregations around the world even feature mid-sized orchestras, complete with violin, viola, cello, and bass sections. The word *kinnor* may mean "violin" to a modern Israeli Hebrew speaker, but based on all available artistic depictions and written testimonies, a *kinnor* is far more similar to a guitar in both tone and timbre. The *rebab* and later the *kamancha* (pictured on page 229) were Middle

Eastern biblical contemporaries from which the violin descended.

Wind Instruments

The *shofar* and other animal horn trumpets were the inspiration for later metal trumpets. As is evident from the description of two silver *chatzotzerot* trumpets in Numbers 10:2, metal trumpets were already in use by the era of the Exodus. In addition to these lip-buzzed antecedents of modern brass instruments, the Bible also describes instruments that bibliomusicologists assert were transverse and end-blown flutes, as well as both single- and double-reed woodwinds. These instruments and others like them eventually made their way to Europe, where they were developed into the modern concert flute, clarinet, oboe, et cetera.

Though the *shofar* is played like a brass instrument, it is organic, and therefore not classed with the brass family of instruments. Nor is the *shofar* made of wood, which means it is also not part of the woodwind family of instruments. Hence this book's use of the more general term "wind instruments," meaning that sound is produced via vibrations caused by a person blowing air against a surface or through an opening.

Most modern worship ensembles feature singing, stringed instruments, and drum and percussion instruments more than wind instruments. Yet some congregations do feature wind instruments, such as flutes, saxophones, or an entire brass and woodwind section within an orchestra.

The one biblical instrument that is still widely used in worship and religious rituals today is the *shofar*, and not just during High Holy Days! The *shofar* has even found a place in secular music whenever composers want to capture an ancient or primitive sound. In *Return of the Jedi* (1983), the Ewoks of the forest moon of Endor even blast *shofarot* as battle signals against the Empire, just as Joshua's army did when conquering Canaan.

Drums and Percussion Instruments

The primary drum and percussion instrument most used in synagogues and churches today is one which may not have been played at all in biblical Israel: the tambourine. Remember that the term *tof* is a general term for a drum. In practically every major English Bible translation, *"tof"* is translated as "tambourine" or as a "timbrel," which is essentially also a tambourine. The problem is that there is no evidence to suggest that the Israelites used tambourines. The only possible Israelite use of a tambourine-like instrument would be if the Persian *daf* was used in Second Temple-era Jewish music, likely coming into use following the return from the Babylonian exile. However, various types of drums and cymbals do play an important role in worship ensembles across the globe, though they often take the form of a drum set.

Digital Instruments

In the most modern styles of worship music, digital instruments and software play an important role in music performance and production. Many sounds are either sampled or digitally created on computers. Technicians behind sound boards and mixing consoles send one audio mix to the musicians' in-ear monitors, complete with pre-recorded spoken musical cues, as well as live instruction from the music director. Another audio mix that omits the spoken cues and direction is sent to the house speakers. Synthesizers and piano keyboard MIDI controllers running MainStage are as common among many congregations today as a lone piano or organ was one hundred years ago. Computer keyboard "space bars" trigger songs to begin in Ableton Live and through the use of pedal boards, digital modeling amps, and amp effects processors like the Line 6 Helix or Fender Tone Master Pro, guitarists have literally hundreds of thousands of sounds and tones at their disposal.

Yet in the modern digital age, most musical sounds produced today are still rooted in the real world. Synthesizer pads often sound like a combination of brass and stringed instruments: the modern *chatzotzerot*. Cantors and worship leaders pluck the strings on their guitars like Jubal, David, and Jeduthun plucked their *kinnorot*. *Tuppim* now come mounted on a rack with *metziltaylim* suspended on high-hat and boom stands, but the timbre of drums and cymbals is a spectrum which has changed little since the time of Miriam. Digital instruments have not replaced the instruments of the past; rather, they are an evolution and extension of those instruments.

Many of the musical instrument names or meanings in the Bible have undergone changes since biblical times, and some have even been forgotten. Reading through the King James Version of the Bible, one can observe the mystery that surrounds some instruments, as evidenced by the fact that a Babylonian *sebbekha* was translated as a "sackbut" and the *karnah* was called a "cornet." (Daniel 3:5) The 20th century scholarship of Alfred Sendrey, Curtis Sachs, and Joachim Braun, and especially their use of multicultural etymology, provided modern readers with a far more thorough understanding of these ancient instruments. Yet as instruments evolved over the centuries, many biblical terms have remained in use, even as the instruments themselves have changed. The biblical Hebrew words for "trumpet," "dance," "harp," "ram's horn," "drum," and "cymbal" have not changed, but a *kinnor* is now understood to be a violin, an *ugav* is now a pipe organ, and *pesanter,* a variation on *pesanterin,* now means piano.

The modern Hebrew language spoken in Israel today is a direct descendant of biblical Hebrew, but it was revitalized and reintroduced as the contemporary language of the Jewish people by various European Jewish writers in the 19th century. When these writers sought to express new ideas in Hebrew using biblical and liturgical Hebrew language as their primary resource, they repurposed infrequently-used or unknown biblical words and assigned a new, contemporary meaning to them. The *kinnor* may have been the stringed instrument of choice in the days of David and the Temple Orchestra, but to the Jews of Europe, the violin was the leading string instrument. Therefore, the word *kinnor* was repurposed to mean "violin." The same occurred with other instruments.

In the last one hundred years, the common practice has changed, with a movement toward transliterating English musical terms and instruments into Hebrew, such as *musica* (מוּסִיקָה), *gitara* (גִיטָרָה), and *clarnit* (קלָרנִית), meaning "music," "guitar," and "clarinet," respectively.

(See next page)

TABLE 13:
CONTEMPORARY MEANINGS OF BIBLICAL INSTRUMENT NAMES (In alphabetical order)

Name	Biblical Meaning	Modern Meaning
Alamot	Young Women/ Double-barreled woodwind*	Young Women
Asor	Ten-stringed	Decade
Chatzotzerot	Trumpets	Trumpets, (but it is now spelled: "חצוצרות" instead of "חֲצֹצְרוֹת")
Gittit	Stringed Instrument*	N/A
Karnah	Animal Horn*	N/A
Kateros	Stringed Instrument*	Lute
Kinnor	Lyre	Violin
Machol	Dance/Flute*	Dance
Mashrokita	Woodwind*	N/A
Minnim	Lute*	N/A
Mena'anim	Shaker/Rattle	N/A

Metzilot	Bells	N/A
Metziltayim	Cymbals	Cymbals
Nevel	Harp	Harp
Pa'amonim	Bells	N/A
Pesanterin	Psaltery*	Piano
Sebbekha	Stringed Instrument*	N/A
Shalishim	Sistrum/Rattle	N/A
Shofar	Ram's Horn	Ram's Horn
Sumponyah	Polyphonic Instrument	N/A
Tof	Drum	Drum
Ugav	Flute	Pipe Organ

*Instruments whose meaning is unknown or disputed.

While *shir* still means "music" or "song," the Hebrew word *"musica"* (מוּסִיקָה) has also been adopted.

Functional Music

America may have less functional music than many other cultures, but religious settings are indeed home to a plethora of functional music. In fact, most functional religious music practices today are rooted in Scripture and were initially standardized during the biblical era. Liturgical calendars and lectionaries provide music directors with a road map so they can anticipate which songs to prepare long in advance. This is because certain prayers, melodies, and pieces of music are only appropriate during certain times of year or during particular holidays and festivals. "Ma Nishtana (The Four Questions)" and "O Come All Ye Faithful" have times of year when they are appropriate. Hearing either song over summer would seem very obviously out of place.

Tonality

Music tonality, the notes and scales used in the composition and performance of music, is one area in which there is the greatest divergence between modern Jewish and modern Christian worship practices. Jewish music by icons like Debbie Friedman and Julie Silver may be rooted in modern American and European tonality, but the Near Eastern musical influences rest just below the surface. Listen to, for example, the bridge of Friedman's 1989 recording of "V'sham'ru" to hear clear examples of vocal flourishes taken directly from the Hebraic Scale. Christian music, on the other hand, is firmly rooted in European and American musical traditions from the last three hundred years. One would need to search extensively to find ancient musical echoes in a modern Christian hymn or song by Elevation. This may be due to the fact that Christianity's inception was rooted in a Hellenized world that focused on assimilation into Western culture, while classical Judaism predates the Greco-Roman era.

Notation

Most Jews who have become Bar and Bat Mitzvah, were enrolled in Torah school, or even those who only attend services on Rosh Hashanah and Yom Kippur, know that the trope or *te'amim* found in the Torah inform the cantor as to how to chant the melodies of Scripture. Bar and Bat Mitzvah ceremonies even require that young adults read from Torah and chant the *te'amim* in front of their entire congregation. In this sense, the *te'amim* notation still plays an important, weekly role in synagogues around the world.

Other than the recitation of Torah and Haftarah, Jewish music is always notated using the conventional means of modern music: sheet music, lead sheets, etc. Today's Christian worship ensembles, musicians, and congregations use the modern modes of music notation exclusively. But again, remember that the ancient neumes of Christian liturgical music were strikingly similar to the *te'amim*. Contemporary sheet music is simply the modern descendant of the system that originated as neumes.

The Bible describes humanity's relationship with God throughout many generations. In this relationship, worship, and specifically *musical worship*, is one of man's primary means of communion and connection with God. Throughout the Hebrew Bible, the 547 biblical references that describe vocal and instrumental music, played on twenty-two confirmed instruments, suggest that music is a rich aspect of the human experience. It is therefore no surprise that biblical musical traditions continue to play an important role in the lives of worshipers around the world. The music of the Bible may at times seem like a relic of the ancient world, but echoes of the past ring out in the music of today.

DEFINITION OF TERMS

Alamot: (ah-lah-mote) Commonly understood to mean "young women" or in a musical setting, "young female musicians." One theory suggests that this may also be a variety of double-reed woodwind instrument with two barrels and one mouthpiece; possibly what Egyptians call a *yarghul*.

Asor: (ah-sor) An adjective indicating that an instrument has ten strings, or a noun meaning "ten-stringed instrument."

B.C.E.: "Before Common Era," referring to years before 1 C.E. A variant of "B.C." (Before Christ).

Bibliomusicology: The study of music in the Bible.

C.E.: "Common Era," referring to years after 0. A variant of "A.D." (*Anno Domini*, Latin for "The year of our Lord").

Chalil: (cha-leel) A double-reed woodwind instrument similar to the modern Turkish *ney* or the Western oboe.

Chatzotzerot: (chah-tzot-tzer-ote) [plural] Two valve-less trumpets made of hammered silver, similar to ancient Egyptian trumpets.

Dead Sea Scrolls: A set of scrolls containing Hebrew Scripture discovered in the mid-20th century, which date back to the 3rd or 4th centuries B.C.E. These are among the oldest examples of Scripture in existence, and support the notion that the Hebrew Bible has gone largely unchanged for at least 2,300 years.

Gittit: (gee-teet) A string instrument from Geth/Gath, a city in Philistia. This instrument may have been brought to Israel following David's military conquests.

Harp: A hand-held ancestor of the modern harp. Unlike a lyre, a harp does not have a bridge. See *kinnor* and *nevel*.

Hebrew Bible: Another term for the collection of books known in the Christian tradition as the "Old Testament." The name comes from the fact that the texts were written in Hebrew, with occasional sections in Aramaic, a language which is closely related to Hebrew.

Horn: See *shofar*.

Ivrit: (eev-reet) A transliteration of the Hebrew word for the Hebrew language, or a person who is a Hebrew.

Ketuvim: (ke-tu-veem) Hebrew for "Writings." This is the third section of the Hebrew Bible, and contains the Books of Psalms, Proverbs, Job, Song of Songs, Ruth, Lamentations, Ecclesiastes, Ester, Daniel, Ezra-Nehemiah, and Chronicles.

Karnah: A type of horn featured in King Nebuchadnezzar's court orchestra. This word is closely related to the *keren*.

Kateros: (kah-teh-ros) This lyre was an instrument of King Nebuchadnezzar's court orchestra and is a transliteration of the Greek *kithara*. It is also the namesake of the modern guitar. This is the only reference to a Greek instrument in the Hebrew Bible, which helps to date the composition, or at least the final redaction, of the book of Daniel.

Keren: The anatomical term for a ram's horn, as opposed to *shofar,* which means the horn has been fashioned into a musical instrument.

Kinnor: (kee-nor) This stringed instrument of David was similar to a harp or lyre. It had seven or ten strings made from the small intestine of a sheep, and was played either by hand or with a plectrum. This is the first musical instrument mentioned in the Bible.

Kle: Literally meaning "tool," this term is often used in Hebrew to refer to musical instruments.

Kle Oz: (clay-ohs) A loud or powerful musical instrument. This phrase literally translates to "powerful tool."

Kle Shir: (clay-sheer) The general term for a musical instrument. This phrase literally translates to "music tool."

Luthier: A maker of stringed instruments.

Lyre: A hand-held, stringed instrument similar to a harp. The key difference is that a lyre has a bridge (like a guitar or violin) and a harp does not. See *kinnor*.

Machol: The Hebrew word for "dance." One theory suggests this may also be the name of a woodwind instrument.

Mashrokita: A pipe that was featured in King Nebuchadnezzar's court orchestra.

Masoretes (mass-or-eets) A group of Jewish scribes and scholars from the sixth to tenth centuries C.E. who produced the definitive Hebrew text of the Hebrew Scripture by adding the *te'amim* (music notation/cantillation) and developing the modern Hebrew vowel system.

Masoretic Text: (mass-or-etic) The Hebrew Bible codex produced by the Masorites, which included vowels and *te'amim* (music notation/cantillation).

Maskil: A didactic song. Thirteen of the Psalms contain a heading indicating that they are *maskilim* (plural).

Mena'anim: A shaker or rattle, possibly a variety of *sistrum*, from either Egypt or Babylon.

Metzillot: Bells which adorned horses and jingled as they trotted.

Metziltayim: Finger cymbals.

Mishnah: A written record of the Jewish "Oral Law." Jewish tradition explains that when God gave the Israelites the Torah at Mount Sinai, He also gave oral explanations of the commandments detailed in the Bible. As a means of keeping the text's length reasonably short, only the Laws were recorded in the Bible, while their explanations were left to oral tradition. With the destruction of the Second Temple in 70 CE, rabbis felt they needed to produce a written record to preserve Jewish traditions, teachings, and history.

Nechilot: (neh-chee-lote) Wind instruments used as accompaniment. This term comes from the root *chalal,* meaning "to pierce, to hollow out." The woodwind instrument *chalil* shares this root as well.

Neginot: (neh-gee-note) Stringed instruments used for accompaniment.

Nevel: An ancestor of the harp. The *nevel* is usually referenced along with the *kinnor*, but the *nevel* is larger, with a tenor voice and up to twenty-two strings. *Nevel* strings are made from the large intestine of a sheep.

Nevi'im: (neh-vee-eem) Literally meaning "prophets," Nevi'im refers to the middle section of the Hebrew Bible, and includes the Books of Joshua, Judges, Samuel, Kings, Isaiah, Jeremiah, Ezekiel, Hosea, Joel, Amos, Obadiah, Jonah, Micah, Nahum, Habakkuk, Zephaniah, Haggai, Zechariah, and Malachi.

Oral Law: See *Mishnah*.

Pa'amonim: Bells made of gold that adorned the High Priest's robes and jingled as he walked.

Pesantarin: One of the instruments in King Nebuchadnezzar's court orchestra, this may be the Babylonian equivalent of the Hebrew *nevel*. See *nevel*.

Rabbi: A Jewish scholar or teacher. The rabbi is the religious leader of a synagogue or Jewish community. After the destruction of the Second Temple in 70 CE, rabbis displaced the priests, Pharisees, and Sadducees as the religious leaders.

Rabbinic Literature: Non-biblical writings produced by rabbis that offer a written record of the Oral Law or interpret the Bible or Oral Law.

Rashi: An abbreviation for "Rabbi Shlomo Yitzchaki," Rashi was a leading French rabbi in the 11th and 12th centuries C.E. He is recognized as a prolific writer and Jewish commentator.

Rosh Hashanah: *Rosh Hashanah* means "head of the year" in Hebrew and is the Jewish celebration of the new year. (Leviticus 23:23-32)

Sebbekha: Despite its King James translation as a sackbut, this is a stringed instrument played both as part of King Nebuchadnezzar's court orchestra. (Spelled differently in Daniel 3:5 than in 3:7,10,15.)

Septuagint (LXX): This translation in Koine Greek is the earliest attempt at translating of the Hebrew Bible. It is dated around the 3rd to 2nd century BCE. *Septuagint* literally means "seventy." It was given this moniker since tradition dictates that seventy translators were thought to have contributed to its creation.

Shabbat: The Sabbath. Also, "Saturday."

Shalishim: A *sistrum*, which is a metallic rattle or percussion instrument similar in sound to a modern headless tambourine.

Shir: (sheer) Music or song.

Shofar: The horn of an adult male sheep that has been hollowed out so it can be played as a musical instrument. This instrument is used in religious, ritual, cultic, civil, and military settings.

Shushan: (shoo-shawn) A borrowed melody from a secular song. The *shushan* is the first word of a song whose melody has been borrowed in order to set a psalm to music. (Modern examples include the album "A Shabbat in Liverpool" by Lenny Solomon and Shlock Rock, in which they set Shabbat liturgies to the music of the Beatles. Another example is the melody to the Christian hymn "Because He Lives," which was borrowed from "Any Dream Will Do" from Lord Andrew Lloyd Webber's and Sir Tim Rice's musical *Joseph and the Amazing Technicolor Dreamcoat.*) Unrelated, this is also the name of the city setting of the Book of Esther.

Sumponyah: An instrument in King Nebuchadnezzar's court orchestra. Possibly a bagpipe or a double-barreled lute. This instrument is mentioned four times in Daniel 3, and is spelled differently every time.

Talmud: A central text in Judaism, the Talmud is a combination of the Mishnah, or Oral Law, and the Gemara (many centuries of rabbinic commentary). There are two versions: The Babylonian Talmud and the Jerusalem Talmud. Unless otherwise stated, this book will always refer to the Babylonian version.

Tanakh: (tah-nah-kh) The term used by the Jews for the Hebrew Bible. It is an acronym of three Hebrew letters which represents the three sections of the Hebrew Bible (Torah, Nevi'im, and Ketuvim) that comprise its contents. Christians refer to this as the Old Testament.

Timbrel: A common English translation of *tof*. This is a type of small frame drum or tambourine.

Te'amim: (tay-ah-meem) The music notation or cantillation markings found throughout the text of the Hebrew Bible. The *te'amim* were added by the Masoretes in an effort to preserve Jewish oral tradition.

Tof: The generic term for any drum. Often a handheld frame drum.

Torah: Instruction, teaching, or law. "Torah" refers to the collection of Genesis, Exodus, Leviticus, Numbers, and Deuteronomy, as well as the laws given to Moses and the Israelites as described within these five books.

Tzeltzelim: Finger cymbals.

Ugav: One of the more difficult biblical instruments to define due to minimal context, this was most likely a type of pipe. This may also be the collective name for a family of wind instruments.

Vulgate: The first Latin translation of the Bible, dating to the late 4th century C.E.

Yobel: 1. The Year of Jubilee, or the seventh Sabbatical year. This celebration is marked with a *shofar* blast. 2. Another name for a *shofar*. See *shofar*.

Yom Kippur: The Day of Atonement. (Leviticus 16:29)

Appendix

Reading the Appendix:

- The first column lists every musical reference or term in the Bible in chronological order based on the traditional Jewish canon structure.
- The second column shows the original Hebrew.
- The third column shows the English transliteration of the Hebrew.
- The fourth column shows the Jewish Publication Society translation of each reference.
- The fifth column shows the New Revised Standard Version Translation of each reference.
- The sixth column shows the King James Version translation of each verse.
- The seventh column describes how music functions in the Bible in each instance.
- Verses are displayed "Book Chapter:Verse"

- Verses with a letter after the verse (Ex. Genesis 4:21 A) indicate that that verse contains more than one musical reference or term. They will always be listed in order of appearance.
- Verses in parentheses indicate that some translations have separated that chapter's sentences into verses differently than others. Depending on which translation you're reading from, the musical reference may be in the first verse listed, or it may be in the second verse listed inside of the parentheses.
- Throughout the Appendix, only proper nouns are capitalized. Words at the beginning of sentences are written in lower-case to offer greater clarity as to which words are proper nouns.
- Prefixes/suffixes have been included in the original Hebrew so that readers may more easily locate verses in the Bible when reading a Hebrew edition.

1. Any English translation marked with three asterisks (***) indicates that the translation has a discrepancy or is strange or noteworthy in some way. This may represent an inconsistency or a misleading or unreasonable translation. An explanation of the discrepancy was specifically identified and provided in the chapter and section of this book that was dedicated to the instrument or term in question.
2. Any time a hyphen (-) is positioned in an otherwise empty cell, it indicates that the word was not translated and was omitted from that English version.
3. Consecutive pairs of verses which end/begin with an ellipsis (. . .) indicate that what was originally two sentences in Hebrew has been combined into one sentence in that English translation.

4. Cells with "(2x)" contain a word that appeared only once in the original Hebrew but was written twice in the translation.
5. If your version of the Bible contains a musical verse not listed in this Appendix, such as 1 Chronicles 16:7 in the NRSV (which describes "singing priests"), that means that the musical terminology was added by the translators or editors of that English edition and is <u>not</u> in the original Hebrew.

CHARLES JIRKOVSKY

	Bible Verse	עברית Hebrew Transliteration	JPS
1	Genesis 4:21 A	כִּנּוֹר kinnor	lyre
2	Genesis 4:21 B	וְעוּגָב v' ugav	pipe
3	Genesis 31:27 A	בְּשִׂמְחָה וּבְשִׁרִים b' shimtah u'v' shirim	festive music
4	Genesis 31:27 B	בְּתֹף b' tof	timbrel
5	Genesis 31:27 C	וּבְכִנּוֹר u'v' khinnor	lyre
6	Exodus 15:1 A	יָשִׁיר ya' shir	sang
7	Exodus 15:1 B	אֶת־הַשִּׁירָה et-ha' shirah	song
8	Exodus 15:2	וְזִמְרָת v' zimrat	might
9	Exodus 15:20 A	אֶת־הַתֹּף et-ha' tof	timbrel
10	Exodus 15:20 B	בְּתֻפִּים b' tuppim	timbrels
11	Exodus 15:21 A	וַתַּעַן rata'an	chanted
12	Exodus 15:21 B	שִׁירוּ shiru	sing
13	Exodus 19:13	הַיֹּבֵל ha' yobel	ram's horn
14	Exodus 19:16	שֹׁפָר shofar	horn
15	Exodus 19:19	הַשּׁוֹפָר ha' shofar	horn
16	Exodus 20:15(18)	הַשֹּׁפָר ha' shofar	horn
17	Exodus 39:25 A	פַּעֲמֹנֵי pa'amon	bells
18	Exodus 39:25 B	אֶת־הַפַּעֲמֹנִים et-ha' pa'amonim	bells
19	Exodus 39:26 A	פַּעֲמֹן pa'amon	bell
20	Exodus 39:26 B	פַּעֲמֹן pa'amon	bell
21	Leviticus 23:24	תְּרוּעָה teruah	loud blasts
22	Leviticus 25:9 A	שׁוֹפָר shofar	horn
23	Leviticus 25:9 B	שׁוֹפָר shofar	horn
24	Numbers 10:2	שְׁתֵּי חֲצוֹצְרֹת כֶּסֶף sh'tey chatzotzerot kesef	two silver trumpets
25	Numbers 10:3	וְתָקְעוּ v' taku	both are blown in long blasts
26	Numbers 10:4	וְאִם־בְּאַחַת יִתְקָעוּ v'im-b'achat v'noaru	if only one is blown
27	Numbers 10:5	תְּרוּעָה teruah	short blasts
28	Numbers 10:6 A	תְּרוּעָה teruah	short blasts
29	Numbers 10:6 B	תְּרוּעָה teruah	short blasts
30	Numbers 10:7	תִּתְקְעוּ וְלֹא תָרִיעוּ ti' tekiah v'lo tariu	long blasts, not short ones
31	Numbers 10:8 A	יִתְקְעוּ yi' tekeu	blown
32	Numbers 10:8 B	חֲצֹצְרוֹת chatzotzerot	trumpets
33	Numbers 10:9 A	וַהֲרֵעֹתֶם va'ha'reotem	short blasts
34	Numbers 10:9 B	חֲצֹצְרֹת chatzotzerot	trumpets
35	Numbers 10:10	חֲצֹצְרֹת chatzotzerot	trumpets
36	Numbers 29:1	תְּרוּעָה teruah	horn
37	Numbers 31:6 A	וַחֲצֹצְרוֹת va' chatzotzerot	trumpets
38	Numbers 31:6 B	תְּרוּעָה teruah	blasts
39	Deuteronomy 31:19 A	הַשִּׁירָה shirah	poem
40	Deuteronomy 31:19 B	הַשִּׁירָה shirah	poem
41	Deuteronomy 31:21	הַשִּׁירָה shirah	poem
42	Deuteronomy 31:22	הַשִּׁירָה shirah	poem
43	Joshua 6:4 A	שׁוֹפְרוֹת הַיּוֹבְלִים shofarot ha' yobelim	ram's horns
44	Joshua 6:4 B	בַּשּׁוֹפָרוֹת ba' shofarot	horns
45	Joshua 6:5 A	יִתְקְעוּ yi' tekeu	blowing
46	Joshua 6:5 B	בְּקֶרֶן הַיּוֹבֵל b' keren ha' yobel	horn
47	Joshua 6:5 C	הַשּׁוֹפָר ha' shofar	horn
48	Joshua 6:6	שׁוֹפְרוֹת יוֹבְלִים shofarot yobelim	horns
49	Joshua 6:8 A	שׁוֹפְרוֹת הַיּוֹבְלִים shofarot ha' yobelim	horns
50	Joshua 6:8 B	בַּשּׁוֹפָרוֹת ba' shofarot	horns

MUSIC IN THE BIBLE

	NRSV	KJV	Function
1	lyre	harp	historical
2	pipe	organ ***	historical
3	songs	songs	send-off
4	tambourine	tabret	send-off
5	lyre	harp	send-off
6	sang	sang	thanksgiving
7	song	song	thanksgiving
8	might	song	thanksgiving
9	tambourine	timbrel	thanksgiving
10	tambourines	timbrels	thanksgiving
11	sang	–	thanksgiving
12	sing	sing	thanksgiving
13	trumpet	trumpet	general signal
14	trumpet	trumpet	fanfare
15	trumpet	trumpet	fanfare
16	trumpet	trumpet	fanfare
17	bells	bells	priestly dress
18	bells	bells	priestly dress
19	bell	bell	priestly dress
20	bell	bell	priestly dress
21	trumpet blasts	blowing of trumpets	Rosh Hahanaah
22	trumpet	trumpet	Yom Kippur
23	trumpet	trumpet	Yom Kippur
24	trumpets	trumpets	civil
25	both are blown	blow	civil
26	if only one is blown	blow	civil
27	blow	blow	civil
28	blow	blow	civil
29	blown	blow	civil
30	blow	blow	civil
31	blow	blow	civil
32	trumpets	trumpets	civil
33	sound an alarm	blow	warfare
34	trumpets	trumpets	warfare
35	trumpets	trumpets	ritual
36	trumpets	blowing the trumpets	Rosh Hahanaah
37	trumpets	trumpets	warfare
38	sounding the alarm	blow	warfare
39	song	song	mnemonic / historical
40	song	song	mnemonic / historical
41	song	song	mnemonic / historical
42	song	song	mnemonic / historical
43	trumpets of rams' horns	trumpets of rams' horns	warfare
44	trumpets	trumpets	warfare
45	long blast	long blast	warfare
46	ram's horn	rams' horn	warfare
47	trumpet	trumpet	warfare
48	trumpets of rams' horns	trumpets of rams' horns	warfare
49	trumpets of rams' horns	trumpets of rams' horns	warfare
50	trumpets	trumpets	warfare

	Bible Verse	עברית	Hebrew Transliteration	JPS
51	Joshua 6:9 A	הַשּׁוֹפָרוֹת	ha' shofarot	horns
52	Joshua 6:9 B	בַּשּׁוֹפָרוֹת	ba' shofarot	horns
53	Joshua 6:13 A	שׁוֹפְרוֹת הַיּוֹבְלִים	shofarot ha' yobelim	ram's horns
54	Joshua 6:13 B	בַּשּׁוֹפָר	ba' shofar	horns
55	Joshua 6:13 C	בַּשּׁוֹפָר	ba' shofar	horns
56	Joshua 6:16	בַּשּׁוֹפָרוֹת	ba' shofarot	horns
57	Joshua 6:20 A	בַּשּׁוֹפָר	ba' shofar	horns
58	Joshua 6:20 B	הַשּׁוֹפָר	ha' shofar	horns
59	Judges 3:27	בַּשּׁוֹפָר	ba' shofar	ram's horn / shofar
60	Judges 5:1	לֵאמֹר	lemor	sang
61	Judges 5:3 A	אָשִׁירָה	ah' shirah	sing
62	Judges 5:3 B	אֲזַמֵּר	ah' zamer	hymn
63	Judges 6:34	בַּשּׁוֹפָר	ba' shofar	horn
64	Judges 7:8	שׁוֹפְרוֹתֵיהֶם	shofertehem	horns
65	Judges 7:16	שׁוֹפָרוֹת	shofarot	ram's horn
66	Judges 7:18 A	בַּשּׁוֹפָר	ba' shofar	rams' horn / shofar
67	Judges 7:18 B	בַּשּׁוֹפָרוֹת	ba' shofarot	rams' horns / shofarot
68	Judges 7:19	בַּשּׁוֹפָרוֹת	ba' shofarot	horns
69	Judges 7:20 A	בַּשּׁוֹפָרוֹת	ba' shofarot	horns
70	Judges 7:20 B	הַשּׁוֹפָרוֹת	ha' shofarot	horns
71	Judges 7:22	הַשּׁוֹפָרוֹת	ha' shofarot	horns
72	Judges 11:34	בְּתֻפִּים	b' tuppim	timbrel
73	1 Samuel 10:5 A	נֵבֶל	nevel	lyre ***
74	1 Samuel 10:5 B	וְתֹף	v' tof	timbrels
75	1 Samuel 10:5 C	וְחָלִיל	v' chalil	flutes
76	1 Samuel 10:5 D	וְכִנּוֹר	v' khinnor	harp ***
77	1 Samuel 13:3	בַּשּׁוֹפָר	b' shofar	ram's horn
78	1 Samuel 16:17 (16) A	מְנַגֵּן	me' nagen	playing
79	1Samuel 16:17 (16) B	בַּכִּנּוֹר	ba' kinnor	lyre
80	1 Samuel 16:18 (17)	נֹגֵן	nagan	play
81	1 Samuel 16:23	אֶת־הַכִּנּוֹר	et-ha' kinnor	lyre
82	1 Samuel 18:6 A	לָשִׁיר	la' shir	singing
83	1 Samuel 18:6 B	בְּתֻפִּים	b' tuppim	timbrels
84	1 Samuel 18:6 C	וּבְשָׁלִשִׁים	shalishim	sistrums
85	1 Samuel 18:10	מְנַגֵּן בְּיָדוֹ	me' nagen b' yadoh	playing [the lyre] (by hand)
86	1 Samuel 19:9	מְנַגֵּן בְּיָד	me' nagen b' yad	playing [the lyre] (by hand)
87	2 Samuel 2:28	בַּשּׁוֹפָר	ba' shofar	horn
88	2 Samuel 6:5 A	וּבְכִנֹּרוֹת	u'v' khinnorot	lyres
89	2 Samuel 6:5 B	וּבִנְבָלִים	u'v' nevalim	harps
90	2 Samuel 6:5 C	וּבְתֻפִּים	u'v' tuppim	timbrels
91	2 Samuel 6:5 D	וּבִמְנַעַנְעִים	u'v' mena'anim	sistrums
92	2 Samuel 6:5 E	וּבְצֶלְצֶלִים	tzeltzelim	cymbals
93	2 Samuel 6:15	שׁוֹפָר	shofar	horn
94	2 Samuel 15:10	הַשּׁוֹפָר	ha' shofar	horn
95	2 Samuel 18:16	בַּשּׁוֹפָר	ba' shofar	horn
96	2 Samuel 19:36 (35)	שָׁרִים	sharim	singing
97	2 Samuel 20:1	בַּשּׁוֹפָר	ba' shofar	horn
98	2 Samuel 20:22	בַּשּׁוֹפָר	ba' shofar	horn
99	2 Samuel 22:1	הַשִּׁירָה	ha' shirah	song
100	2 Samuel 22:1	הַשִּׁירָה	ha' shirah	song

Music in the Bible

	NRSV	KJV	Function
51	trumpets	trumpets	warfare
52	trumpets	trumpets	warfare
53	trumpets	trumpets	warfare
54	trumpets	trumpets	warfare
55	trumpets	trumpets	warfare
56	trumpets	trumpets	warfare
57	trumpets	trumpets	warfare
58	trumpets	trumpets	warfare
59	trumpet	trumpet	warfare
60	sang	sang	thanksgiving
61	sing	sing	general worship
62	melody	sing praise	general worship
63	trumpet	trumpet	warfare
64	trumpets	trumpets	warfare
65	trumpets	trumpet	warfare
66	trumpet	trumpet	warfare
67	trumpets	trumpets	warfare
68	trumpets	trumpets	warfare
69	trumpets	trumpets	warfare
70	trumpets	trumpets	warfare
71	trumpets	trumpets	warfare
72	timbrels	timbrels	homecoming
73	harp	psaltery	prophetic
74	tambourine	tabret	prophetic
75	flute	pipe	prophetic
76	lyre	harp	prophetic
77	trumpet	trumpet	warfare
78	playing	cunning player	music therapy
79	lyre	harp	music therapy
80	play	play	music therapy
81	lyre	harp	music therapy
82	singing	singing	victory
83	tambourines	tabrets	victory
84	musical instruments	instruments of music	victory
85	playing the lyre	played with his hand	music therapy
86	playing music	played with his hand	music therapy
87	trumpet	trumpet	warfare
88	lyres	harps	victory
89	harps	psalteries	victory
90	tambourines	timbrels	victory
91	castanets ***	cornets ***	victory
92	cymbals	cymbals	victory
93	trumpet	trumpet	celebration
94	trumpet	trumpet	insurrection
95	trumpet	trumpet	insurrection
96	singing	singing (2x)	metaphor
97	trumpet	trumpet	civil
98	trumpet	trumpet	warfare
99	song	song	thanksgiving
100	song	song	thanksgiving

Bible Verse	עברית	Hebrew Transliteration	JPS
101	2 Samuel 22:50 A	אוֹדְךָ	odekha	sing your praise
102	2 Samuel 22:50 B	אֲזַמֵּר	ah' zamer	hymn
103	1 Kings 1:34	בַּשּׁוֹפָר	ba' shofar	horn
104	1 Kings 1:39	בַּשּׁוֹפָר	ba' shofar	horn
105	1 Kings 1:40	בַּחֲלִלִים	ba' chalilim	flutes
106	1 Kings 1:41	הַשּׁוֹפָר	ha' shofar	horn
107	1 Kings 5:12 (4:32)	שִׁירוֹ	shiro	songs
108	1 Kings 10:12 A	וְכִנֹּרוֹת	v' khinnorot	harps
109	1 Kings 10:12 B	וּנְבָלִים	u' nevalim	lyres
110	1 Kings 10:12 C	לַשָּׁרִים	la' sharim	musicians
111	2 Kings 3:15 A	מְנַגֵּן	m' nagen	musician
112	2 Kings 3:15 B	הַמְנַגֵּן	ha' menagen	musician
113	2 Kings 9:13	בַּשּׁוֹפָר	ba' shofar	horn
114	2 Kings 11:14 A	וְהַחֲצֹצְרוֹת	v'ha' chatzotzerot	trumpets
115	2 Kings 11:14 B	בַּחֲצֹצְרוֹת	ba' chatzotzerot	trumpets
116	2 Kings 12:14 (13)	חֲצֹצְרוֹת	chatzotzerot	trumpets
117	Isaiah 5:1 A	אָשִׁירָה	ah' shirah	sing
118	Isaiah 5:1 B	שִׁירַת	shirah	song
119	Isaiah 5:12 A	כִּנּוֹר	khinnor	lyre
120	Isaiah 5:12 B	וָנֶבֶל	va' nevel	lute
121	Isaiah 5:12 C	תֹּף	tof	timbrel
122	Isaiah 5:12 D	וְחָלִיל	v' chalil	flute
123	Isaiah 16:11	כַּכִּנּוֹר	ka' kinnor	lyre
124	Isaiah 18:3	שׁוֹפָר	shofar	ram's horn
125	Isaiah 23:15	כְּשִׁירַת	k' shirah	ditty
126	Isaiah 23:16 A	כִּנּוֹר	khinnor	lyre
127	Isaiah 23:16 B	נַגֵּן	nagen	play
128	Isaiah 23:16 C	שִׁיר	shir	music
129	Isaiah 24:8 A	תֻּפִּים	tuppim	timbrels
130	Isaiah 24:8 B	כִּנּוֹר	kinnor	lyres
131	Isaiah 24:9	בַּשִּׁיר	ba' shir	song
132	Isaiah 27:13	בְּשׁוֹפָר גָּדוֹל	b' shofar gadol	a great ram's horn
133	Isaiah 30:29 A	הַשִּׁיר	ha' shir	song
134	Isaiah 30:29 B	בֶּחָלִיל	b' chalil	flute
135	Isaiah 30:29 (32) C	בְּתֻפִּים	b' tuppim	timbrels
136	Isaiah 30:29 (32) D	וּבְכִנֹּרוֹת	u'v' khinnorot	lyres
137	Isaiah 42:10 A	שִׁירוּ	shiru	sing
138	Isaiah 42:10 B	שִׁיר חָדָשׁ	shir chadash	a new song
139	Isaiah 51:3	זִמְרָה	zimrah	music
140	Isaiah 58:1	כַּשּׁוֹפָר	ka' shofar	ram's horn
141	Jeremiah 4:5	שׁוֹפָר	shofar	horn
142	Jeremiah 4:19	שׁוֹפָר	shofar	horns
143	Jeremiah 4:21	שׁוֹפָר	shofar	horns
144	Jeremiah 6:1	שׁוֹפָר	shofar	horn
145	Jeremiah 6:17	שׁוֹפָר	shofar	horn
146	Jeremiah 42:14	שׁוֹפָר	shofar	horn
147	Jeremiah 51:27	שׁוֹפָר	shofar	horn
148	Ezekiel 26:13 A	הֲמוֹן	ha'mon	murmur
149	Ezekiel 26:13 B	שִׁירָיִךְ	shirahyikh	songs
150	Ezekiel 26:13 C	כִּנּוֹרַיִךְ	kinnorayikh	lyres

	NRSV	KJV	Function
101	sing	sing	thanksgiving
102	praises	praises	thanksgiving
103	trumpet	trumpet	coronation
104	trumpet	trumpet	coronation
105	pipes	pipes	coronation
106	trumpet	trumpet	coronation
107	songs	songs	historical
108	lyres	harps	instrument construction
109	harps	psalteries	instrument construction
110	singers	singers	instrument construction
111	musician	minstrel	prophetic
112	musician	minstrel	prophetic
113	trumpet	trumpets	coronation
114	trumpeters	trumpeters	coronation
115	trumpets	trumpets	coronation
116	trumpets	trumpets	instrument construction
117	sing	sing	metaphor/love
118	love-song	song of my beloved	metaphor/love
119	lyre	harp	metaphor
120	harp	viol ***	metaphor
121	tambourine	tabret	metaphor
122	flute	pipe	metaphor
123	harp	harp	metaphor
124	trumpet	trumpet	metaphor
125	song	sing	metaphor
126	harp	harp	metaphor
127	melody	melody	metaphor
128	sing	sing many songs	metaphor
129	timbrels	tabrets	metaphor
130	lyre	harp	metaphor
131	singing	song	metaphor
132	a great trumpet	trumpet	homecoming
133	song	song	general worship / metaphor
134	flute	pipe	general worship / metaphor
135	timbrels	tabrets	general worship / metaphor
136	lyres	harps	general worship / metaphor
137	sing	sing	general worship
138	a new song	a new song	general worship
139	voice of song	voice of melody	parable / thanksgiving
140	trumpet	trumpet	metaphor
141	trumpet	trumpet	general worship
142	trumpet	trumpet	warfare
143	trumpet	trumpet	metaphor
144	trumpet	trumpet	warfare
145	trumpet	trumpet	metaphor
146	trumpet	trumpet	warfare
147	trumpet	trumpet	general worship
148	music	noise	warfare / metaphor
149	songs	songs	warfare / metaphor
150	lyres	harps	warfare / metaphor

#	Bible Verse	Hebrew עברית	Hebrew Transliteration	JPS
151	Ezekiel 33:3	בַּשּׁוֹפָר	ba' shofar	horn
152	Ezekiel 33:4	הַשּׁוֹפָר	ha' shofar	horn
153	Ezekiel 33:5	הַשּׁוֹפָר	ha' shofar	horn
154	Ezekiel 33:6	בַּשּׁוֹפָר	ba' shofar	horn
155	Hosea 5:8 A	שׁוֹפָר	shofar	ram's horn
156	Hosea 5:8 B	חֲצֹצְרָה	chatzotzerah	trumpet
157	Hosea 8:1	שֹׁפָר	shofar	ram's horn
158	Joel 2:1	שׁוֹפָר	shofar	horn
159	Joel 2:15	שׁוֹפָר	shofar	horn
160	Amos 2:2	שׁוֹפָר	shofar	horns
161	Amos 3:6	שׁוֹפָר	shofar	ram's horn
162	Amos 6:5 A	הַפֹּרְטִים	ha' portim	hum snatches of a song
163	Amos 6:5 B	עַל־פִּי	al-pi	to the tune of
164	Amos 6:5 C	הַנָּבֶל	ha' navel	lute
165	Amos 6:5 D	כְּלֵי־שִׁיר	kle-shir	musicians
166	Zephaniah 1:16	שׁוֹפָר	shofar	horn
167	Zechariah 9:14	בַּשּׁוֹפָר	ba' shofar	ram's horn
168	Zechariah 14:20	עַל־מְצִלּוֹת	al-metzilot	bells
169	Psalm 3:1	מִזְמוֹר לְדָוִד	mizmor l' David	a psalm of David
170	Psalm 4:1 A	בִּנְגִינוֹת	bi' neginot	with instrumental music
171	Psalm 4:1 B	מִזְמוֹר לְדָוִד	mizmor l' David	a psalm of David
172	Psalm 5:1	מִזְמוֹר לְדָוִד	mizmor l' David	a psalm of David
173	Psalm 6:1	מִזְמוֹר לְדָוִד	mizmor l' David	a psalm of David
174	Psalm 7:1 A	שִׁגָּיוֹן לְדָוִד	shiggaion l' David	a psalm of David
175	Psalm 7:1 B	שָׁר	shar	sang
176	Psalm 7:18 (17)	וַאֲזַמְּרָה	v' ah' zamrah	sing a hymn
177	Psalm 8:1 A	עַל־הַגִּתִּית	al-ha' gittit	gittith
178	Psalm 8:1 B	מִזְמוֹר לְדָוִד	mizmor l' David	a psalm of David
179	Psalm 9:1 A	מִזְמוֹר לְדָוִד	mizmor l' David	a psalm of David
180	Psalm 9:1 B	אוֹדֶה	oreh	praise
181	Psalm 12:1	מִזְמוֹר לְדָוִד	mizmor l' David	a psalm of David
182	Psalm 13:1	מִזְמוֹר לְדָוִד	mizmor l' David	a psalm of David
183	Psalm 15:1	מִזְמוֹר לְדָוִד	mizmor l' David	a psalm of David
184	Psalm 16:1	מִכְתָּם לְדָוִד	michtam l' David	a michtam of David
185	Psalm 18:1	הַשִּׁירָה	ha' shirah	song
186	Psalm 18:50 (49)	אֲזַמְּרָה	a'zamerah	hymn
187	Psalm 19:1	מִזְמוֹר לְדָוִד	mizmor l' David	a psalm of David
188	Psalm 20:1	מִזְמוֹר לְדָוִד	mizmor l' David	a psalm of David
189	Psalm 21:1	מִזְמוֹר לְדָוִד	mizmor l' David	a psalm of David
190	Psalm 22:1	מִזְמוֹר לְדָוִד	mizmor l' David	a psalm of David
191	Psalm 23:1	מִזְמוֹר לְדָוִד	mizmor l' David	a psalm of David
192	Psalm 24:1	לְדָוִד מִזְמוֹר	l' David mizmor	of David. a psalm.
193	Psalm 26:7	בְּקוֹל	b' kol	voice
194	Psalm 28:7	קוֹל	kol	song
195	Psalm 29:1	מִזְמוֹר לְדָוִד	mizmor l' David	a psalm of David
196	Psalm 30:1 A	מִזְמוֹר . . . לְדָוִד	mizmor . . . l' David	a psalm . . . of David
197	Psalm 30:1 B	שִׁיר־חֲנֻכַּת	shir-ha'beit	song of the dedication
198	Psalm 31:1	מִזְמוֹר לְדָוִד	mizmor l' David	a psalm of David
199	Psalm 32:1	לְדָוִד מַשְׂכִּיל	l' David mazkil	of David. a maskil.
200	Psalm 33:1	רַנְּנוּ	ran'nu	sing

	NRSV	KJV	Function
151	trumpet	trumpet	warfare / metaphor
152	trumpet	trumpet	warfare / metaphor
153	trumpet	trumpet	warfare / metaphor
154	trumpet	trumpet	warfare / metaphor
155	horn	cornet ***	warfare / metaphor
156	trumpet	trumpet	warfare / metaphor
157	trumpet	trumpet	warfare / metaphor
158	trumpet	trumpet	fanfare / metaphor
159	trumpet	trumpet	ritual / metaphor
160	trumpet	trumpet	warfare
161	trumpet	trumpet	metaphor
162	sing songs	chant	recreation
163	to the sound of	sound of the	recreation
164	harp	viol ***	recreation
165	instruments of music	instruments of musick	recreation
166	trumpet	trumpet	warfare
167	trumpet	trumpet	messianic
168	bells	bells	ritual
169	a psalm of David	a psalm of David	mizmor
170	with stringed instruments	to the chief musician on Negioth	general worship
171	a psalm of David	a psalm of David	mizmor
172	a psalm of David	a psalm of David	mizmor
173	a psalm of David	a psalm of David	mizmor
174	a psalm of David	shiggaion of David	shiggaion
175	sang	sang	general worship
176	sing praises	sing praise	general worship
177	gittith	gittith	general worship
178	a psalm of David	a psalm of David	mizmor
179	a psalm of David	a psalm of David	mizmor
180	sing praise	praise	mizmor
181	a psalm of David	a psalm of David	mizmor
182	a psalm of David	a psalm of David	mizmor
183	a psalm of David	a psalm of David	mizmor
184	a miktam of David	michtam of David	michtam
185	song	song	thanksgiving
186	sing the praises	sing praises	worship
187	a psalm of David	a psalm of David	mizmor
188	a psalm of David	a psalm of David	mizmor
189	a psalm of David	a psalm of David	mizmor
190	a psalm of David	a psalm of David	mizmor
191	a psalm of David	a psalm of David	mizmor
192	of David. a psalm	a psalm of David	mizmor
193	singing aloud a song	voice of thanksgiving	mizmor / thanksgiving
194	song	voice	general worship
195	a psalm of David	a psalm of David	mizmor
196	a psalm ... Of David	a psalm ... Of David	historical
197	a song at the dedication	song at the dedication	historical
198	a psalm of David	a psalm of David	mizmor
199	of David. a maskil.	maschil, a psalm of David	maskil
200	praise	praise	general worship

	Bible Verse	עברית Hebrew Transliteration	JPS
201	Psalm 33:2 A	בְּכִנּוֹר b' khinnor	lyre
202	Psalm 33:2 B (33:3 A)	בְּנֵבֶל עָשׂוֹר b' nevel asor	ten-stringed harp
203	Psalm 33:2 C (33:3 B)	זַמְּרוּ־לוֹ zamru-lo	sing
204	Psalm 33:3 A	שִׁירוּ־לוֹ shiru-lo	sing
205	Psalm 33:3 B	שִׁיר חָדָשׁ shir chadash	a new song
206	Psalm 38:1 A	מִזְמוֹר לְדָוִד mizmor l' David	a psalm of David
207	Psalm 38:1 B	לְהַזְכִּיר lehazkir	lehazkir
208	Psalm 39:1	לְדָוִד מִזְמוֹר l' David mizmor	a psalm of David
209	Psalm 40:1	לְדָוִד מִזְמוֹר l' David mizmor	a psalm of David
210	Psalm 41:1	מִזְמוֹר לְדָוִד mizmor l' David	a psalm of David
211	Psalm 42:1	מַשְׂכִּיל לִבְנֵי־קֹרַח maskil l'ben-Korah	a maskil of Korah
212	Psalm 42:5 (4)	בְּקוֹל־רִנָּה וְתוֹדָה b' kol-rinah v'todah	shouts of praise
213	Psalm 43:4	בְּכִנּוֹר b' khinnor	lyre
214	Psalm 44:1	לִבְנֵי־קֹרַח מַשְׂכִּיל li'ben-Korah maskil	of the Korahites. a maskil.
215	Psalm 45:1 A	לִבְנֵי־קֹרַח מַשְׂכִּיל li'ben-Korah maskil	of the Korahites. a maskil.
216	Psalm 45:1 B	שִׁיר יְדִידֹת shir y'didot	a love song
217	Psalm 45:1 C	עַל־שֹׁשַׁנִּים al-shoshannim	shoshannim
218	Psalm 45:9 (8)	מִנִּי minni	lutes
219	Psalm 46:1	שִׁיר shir	song
220	Psalm 47:1	מִזְמוֹר mizmor	psalm
221	Psalm 47:2 (47:1 B)	תִּקְעוּ־כָף tiku-kaf	clap your hands
222	Psalm 47:6 (5)	שׁוֹפָר shofar	horn
223	Psalm 47:7 A (47:6)	זַמְּרוּ zameru	sing
224	Psalm 47:7 B (47:6)	זַמְּרוּ zameru	sing
225	Psalm 47:7 C (47:6)	זַמְּרוּ zameru	sing
226	Psalm 47:7 D (47:6)	זַמְּרוּ zameru	sing
227	Psalm 47:8 A (47:7)	זַמְּרוּ zameru	sing
228	Psalm 47:8 B (47:7)	מַשְׂכִּיל maskil	hymn
229	Psalm 48:1 A	שִׁיר shir	song
230	Psalm 48:1 B	מִזְמוֹר לִבְנֵי־קֹרַח mizmor li'ben-Korah	a psalm of the Korahites
231	Psalm 49:1	מִזְמוֹר mizmor	psalm
232	Psalm 49:5 (4)	בְּכִנּוֹר khinnor	lyre
233	Psalm 50:1	מִזְמוֹר לְאָסָף mizmor l' Asaph	a psalm of Asaph
234	Psalm 51:1	מִזְמוֹר לְדָוִד mizmor	a psalm of David
235	Psalm 52:1	מַשְׂכִּיל לְדָוִד maskil l' David	a maskil of David
236	Psalm 53:1	מַשְׂכִּיל לְדָוִד maskil l' David	a maskil of David
237	Psalm 54:1 A	בִּנְגִינֹת bi' neginot	with instrumental music
238	Psalm 54:1 B	מַשְׂכִּיל לְדָוִד maskil l' David	a maskil of David
239	Psalm 55:1 A	בִּנְגִינֹת bi' neginot	with instrumental music
240	Psalm 55:1 B	מַשְׂכִּיל לְדָוִד maskil l' David	a maskil of David
241	Psalm 56:1	לְדָוִד מִכְתָּם l' David michtam	of David. a michtam.
242	Psalm 57:1	לְדָוִד מִכְתָּם l' David michtam	of David. a michtam.
243	Psalm 57:9 A (8)	הַנֵּבֶל ha' nevel	harp
244	Psalm 57:9 B (8)	וְכִנּוֹר v' khinnor	lyre
245	Psalm 57:10 (9)	אֲזַמֶּרְךָ ah' zamerkhah	sing a hymn
246	Psalm 58:1	לְדָוִד מִכְתָּם l' David michtam	of David. a michtam.
247	Psalm 59:1	לְדָוִד מִכְתָּם l' David michtam	of David. a michtam.
248	Psalm 60:1 A	עַל־שׁוּשַׁן עֵדוּת al-shushan edut	on shushan eduth
249	Psalm 60:1 B	מִכְתָּם לְדָוִד l' David michtam	of David. a michtam.
250	Psalm 61:1	עַל־נְגִינַת al-neginat	with instrumental music

	NRSV	KJV	Function
201	lyre	harp	general worship
202	harp of ten strings	instrument of ten strings	general worship
203	melody	sing	general worship
204	sing	sing	general worship
205	a new song	a new song	general worship
206	a psalm of David	a psalm of David	mizmor
207	memorial offering	remembrance	lehazkir
208	a psalm of David	a psalm of David	mizmor
209	a psalm of David	a psalm of David	mizmor / thanksgiving
210	a psalm of David	a psalm of David	mizmor
211	a maskil of Korah	maschil, a psalm of David	maskil
212	praise	praise	thanksgiving
213	harp ***	harp	personal worship
214	of the Korahites. a maskil.	maschil, a psalm of David	maskil
215	of the Korahites. a maskil.	maschil, a psalm of David	maskil
216	a love song	a song for lovers	wedding / shushan
217	-	shoshannim	wedding / shushan
218	stringed instruments	-	wedding / shushan
219	song	song	general worship
220	psalm	psalm	mizmor
221	clap your hands	clap your hands	general worship
222	trumpet	trumpet	general worship
223	sing	sing	general worship
224	sing	sing	general worship
225	sing	sing	general worship
226	sing	sing	general worship
227	sing	sing	general worship
228	psalm	praises	maskil
229	song	song	general worship
230	a psalm of the Korahites	psalm for the sons of Korah	mizmor
231	psalm	a psalm	mizmor
232	lyre	harp	mizmor
233	a psalm of Asaph	a psalm of Asaph	mizmor
234	a psalm of David	a psalm of David	mizmor / lament
235	a maskil of David	maschil, a psalm of David	maskil
236	a maskil of David	maschil, a psalm of David	maskil
237	with stringed instruments	negioth	general worship
238	a maskil of David	maschil, a psalm of David	maskil
239	with stringed instruments	negioth	general worship
240	a maskil of David	maschil, a psalm of David	maskil
241	of David. a miktam.	michtam of David	michtam
242	of David. a miktam.	michtam of David	michtam
243	harp	pslatery	general worship
244	lyre	harp	general worship
245	sing praises	sing	general worship
246	of David. a miktam	michtam of David	michtam
247	of David. a miktam	michtam of David	michtam
248	-	shushan-eduth	shushan
249	of David. a miktam	michtam of David	michtam
250	with stringed instruments	negioth	general worship

	Bible Verse	עברית	Hebrew Transliteration	JPS
251	Psalm 62:1	מִזְמוֹר לְדָוִד	mizmor l' David	a psalm of David
252	Psalm 63:1	מִזְמוֹר לְדָוִד	mizmor l' David	a psalm of David
253	Psalm 64:1	מִזְמוֹר לְדָוִד	mizmor l' David	a psalm of David
254	Psalm 65:1 A	מִזְמוֹר לְדָוִד	mizmor l' David	a psalm of David
255	Psalm 65:1 B	שִׁיר	shir	song
256	Psalm 66:1 A	שִׁיר	shir	song
257	Psalm 66:1 B	מִזְמוֹר	mizmor	psalm
258	Psalm 67:1 A	בִּנְגִינֹת	bi' neginot	with instrumental music
259	Psalm 67:1 B	מִזְמוֹר	mizmor	psalm
260	Psalm 67:1 C	שִׁיר	shir	song
261	Psalm 68:1 A	לְדָוִד מִזְמוֹר	l' David mizmor	a psalm of David
262	Psalm 68:1 B	שִׁיר	shir	song
263	Psalm 68:26 A	שָׁרִים	shirim	singers
264	Psalm 68:26 B	נֹגְנִים	naggim	musicians
265	Psalm 68:26 C	תּוֹפֵפוֹת	toffot	timbrels
266	Psalm 69:1	עַל־שׁוֹשַׁנִּים לְדָוִד	al-shoshannim l' David	on shoshannim. Of David
267	Psalm 70:1	לְהַזְכִּיר	lehazkir	memorial offering
268	Psalm 71:22 A	בִכְלִי־נָבֶל	bi' kli-nevel	music of the lyre ***
269	Psalm 71:22 B	אֲזַמְּרָה	ah' zamrah	sing a hymn
270	Psalm 71:22 C	בְּכִנּוֹר	b' khinnor	harp ***
271	Psalm 71:23	אֲזַמְּרָה	ah' zamrah	sing a hymn
272	Psalm 73:1	מִזְמוֹר לְאָסָף	mizmor l' Asaph	a psalm of Asaph
273	Psalm 74:1	מַשְׂכִּיל לְאָסָף	maskil l' Asaph	a maskil of Asaph
274	Psalm 75:1 A	מִזְמוֹר לְאָסָף	mizmor l' Asaph	a psalm of Asaph
275	Psalm 75:1 B	שִׁיר	shir	song
276	Psalm 76:1 A	בִּנְגִינֹת	bi' neginot	with instrumental music
277	Psalm 76:1 B	מִזְמוֹר לְאָסָף	mizmor l' Asaph	a psalm of Asaph
278	Psalm 76:1C	שִׁיר	shir	song
279	Psalm 77:1	לְאָסָף מִזְמוֹר	l' Asaph mizmor	of Asaph. a psalm.
280	Psalm 78:1	מַשְׂכִּיל לְאָסָף	maskil l' Asaph	a maskil of Asaph
281	Psalm 79:1	מִזְמוֹר לְאָסָף	mizmor l' Asaph	a psalm of Asaph
282	Psalm 80:1	אֶל־שֹׁשַׁנִּים עֵדוּת	el-shoshannim edut	on shoshannim, eduth
283	Psalm 80:1	לְאָסָף מִזְמוֹר	l' Asaph mizmor	of Asaph. a psalm.
284	Psalm 81:1	עַל־הַגִּתִּית	al-ha' gittit	gittith
285	Psalm 81:2 (1)	הַרְנִינוּ	harninu	sing
286	Psalm 81:3 A (2)	שְׂאוּ־זִמְרָה	su-zimrah	song
287	Psalm 81:3 B (2)	וּתְנוּ־תֹף	u'tenu-tof	sound the timbrel
288	Psalm 81:3 C (2)	כִּנּוֹר	kinnor	lyre
289	Psalm 81:3 D (2)	עִם־נָבֶל	yim-navel	harp
290	Psalm 81:4 (3)	שׁוֹפָר	shofar	horn
291	Psalm 82:1	מִזְמוֹר לְאָסָף	mizmor l' Asaph	a psalm of Asaph
292	Psalm 83:1 A	שִׁיר	shir	song
293	Psalm 83:1 B	מִזְמוֹר לְאָסָף	mizmor	a psalm of Asaph
294	Psalm 84:1 A	עַל־הַגִּתִּית	al-ha' gittit	gittith
295	Psalm 84:1 B	לִבְנֵי־קֹרַח מִזְמוֹר	li' ben-Korah mizmor	of the Korahites. a psalm.
296	Psalm 85:1	לִבְנֵי־קֹרַח מִזְמוֹר	li' ben-Korah mizmor	of the Korahites. a psalm.
297	Psalm 87:1 A	לִבְנֵי־קֹרַח מִזְמוֹר	li' ben-Korah mizmor	of the Korahites. a psalm.
298	Psalm 87:1 B	שִׁיר	shir	song
299	Psalm 88:1 A	שִׁיר	shir	song
300	Psalm 88:1 B	מִזְמוֹר לִבְנֵי־קֹרַח	mizmor li'ben-Korah	a psalm of the Korahites

MUSIC IN THE BIBLE

	NRSV	KJV	Function
251	a psalm of David	a psalm of David	mizmor
252	a psalm of David	a psalm of David	mizmor
253	a psalm of David	a psalm of David	mizmor
254	a psalm of David	a psalm of David	mizmor / thanksgiving
255	song	song	thanksgiving
256	song	song	general worship
257	psalm	psalm	mizmor
258	with stringed instruments	negioth	general worship
259	psalm	psalm	mizmor
260	song	song	general worship
261	a psalm of David	a psalm ...	mizmor
262	song	... or song of David	general worship
263	singers	singers	general worship
264	musicians	players on instruments	general worship
265	tambourines	timbrels	general worship
266	of David	shoshannim, a psalm of David	shushan
267	memorial offering	remembrance	lehazkir
268	harp	psaltery	general worship
269	sing praises	sing	general worship
270	lyre	harp	general worship
271	sing praises	sing	general worship
272	a psalm of Asaph	a psalm of Asaph	mizmor
273	a maskil of Asaph	maschil of Asaph	maskil
274	psalm of Asaph	a psalm ...	mizmor / thanksgiving
275	song	... song of Asaph	thanksgiving
276	with stringed instruments	negioth	general worship
277	a psalm of Asaph	a psalm ...	mizmor
278	song	... or song of Asaph	general worship
279	of Asaph. a psalm	a psalm of Asaph	mizmor
280	a maskil of Asaph	maschil of Asaph	maskil
281	a psalm of Asaph	a psalm of Asaph	mizmor
282	-	shoshannim	shushan
283	of Asaph. a psalm	a psalm of Asaph	mizmor
284	gittith	gittith	general worship
285	sing	sing	general worship
286	song	psalm	general worship
287	tambourine	timbrel	general worship
288	lyre	harp	general worship
289	harp	psaltery	general worship
290	trumpet	trumpet	general worship
291	a psalm of Asaph	a psalm of Asaph	mizmor / historical
292	song	a song ...	general worship
293	a psalm of Asaph	... or psalm of Asaph	mizmor
294	gittith	gittith	Temple worship
295	of the Korahites. a psalm.	a psalm for the sons of Korah	mizmor
296	of the Korahites. a psalm.	a psalm for the sons of Korah	mizmor
297	of the Korahites. a psalm.	a psalm ...	mizmor
298	song	... or song for the sons of Korah	general worship
299	song	song ...	general worship
300	a psalm of the Korahites	... or song for the sons of Korah	mizmor

#	Bible Verse	עברית Hebrew Transliteration	JPS
301	Psalm 88:1 C	מַשְׂכִּיל לְהֵימָן maskil l' Heman	a maskil of Heman
302	Psalm 89:1	מַשְׂכִּיל לְאֵיתָן maskil l' Etan	a maskil of Ethan
303	Psalm 92:1 A	מִזְמוֹר mizmor	psalm
304	Psalm 92:1 B	שִׁיר shir	song
305	Psalm 92:2 (92:1 C)	וּלְזַמֵּר u'l' zamer	sing hymns
306	Psalm 92:4 A (92:3)	עֲלֵי־עָשׂוֹר וַעֲלֵי־נָבֶל ale-asor v'al navel	ten-stringed harp
307	Psalm 92:4 B (92:3)	הִגָּיוֹן higayin	voice
308	Psalm 92:4 C (92:3)	בְּכִנּוֹר b' khinnor	lyre
309	Psalm 95:1	נְרַנְּנָה nerannah	sing
310	Psalm 95:2	בִּזְמִרוֹת bi' zimrot	song
311	Psalm 96:1 A	שִׁירוּ shiru	sing
312	Psalm 96:1 B	שִׁיר חָדָשׁ shir chadash	a new song
313	Psalm 96:1 C	שִׁירוּ shiru	sing
314	Psalm 96:2	שִׁירוּ shiru	sing
315	Psalm 98:1 A	מִזְמוֹר mizmor	psalm
316	Psalm 98:1 B	שִׁירוּ shiru	sing
317	Psalm 98:1 C	שִׁיר חָדָשׁ shir chadash	a new song
318	Psalm 98:4	זַמֵּרוּ v' zameru	song
319	Psalm 98:5 A	זַמְּרוּ zamru	sing
320	Psalm 98:5 B	בְּכִנּוֹר b' khinnor	lyre
321	Psalm 98:5 C	בְּכִנּוֹר b' khinnor	lyre
322	Psalm 98:5 D	וְקוֹל זִמְרָה v' kol zimrah	melodious song
323	Psalm 98:6 A	בַּחֲצֹצְרוֹת b' chatzotzerot	trumpets
324	Psalm 98:6 B	שׁוֹפָר shofar	horn
325	Psalm 100:1	מִזְמוֹר mizmor	psalm
326	Psalm 101:1 A	לְדָוִד מִזְמוֹר l' David mizmor	of David. a psalm
327	Psalm 101:1 B	אָשִׁירָה ah' shirah	sing
328	Psalm 101:1 C	אֲזַמֵּרָה ah' zamerah	hymn
329	Psalm 105:2 A	שִׁירוּ־לוֹ shiru-lo	sing praises
330	Psalm 105:2 B	זַמְּרוּ־לוֹ zamru-lo	speak
331	Psalm 108:1 A	שִׁיר shir	song
332	Psalm 108:1 B	מִזְמוֹר לְדָוִד mizmor	psalm
333	Psalm 108:2 A	אָשִׁירָה a' shirah	sing
334	Psalm 108:2 B	וַאֲזַמְּרָה va'a' zamrah	chant a hymn
335	Psalm 108:3 (2)A	הַנֵּבֶל ha' nevel	harp
336	Psalm 108:3 (2)B	וְכִנּוֹר v' khinnor	lyre
337	Psalm 109:1	לְדָוִד מִזְמוֹר l' David mizmor	of David. a psalm.
338	Psalm 110:1	לְדָוִד מִזְמוֹר l' David mizmor	of David. a psalm
339	Psalm 118:14	זִמְרָת v' zimrat	might
340	Psalm 120:1 A	שִׁיר shir	song
341	Psalm 120:1 B	הַמַּעֲלוֹת ha' ma'alot	ascents
342	Psalm 121:1 A	שִׁיר shir	a song …
343	Psalm 121:1 B	לַמַּעֲלוֹת la' ma'alot	ascents
344	Psalm 122:1 A	שִׁיר shir	a song …
345	Psalm 122:1 B	הַמַּעֲלוֹת לְדָוִד ha' ma'alot l' David	… of ascents. of David.
346	Psalm 123:1 A	שִׁיר shir	a song …
347	Psalm 123:1 B	הַמַּעֲלוֹת ha' ma'alot	… of ascents
348	Psalm 124:1 A	שִׁיר shir	a song …
349	Psalm 124:1 B	הַמַּעֲלוֹת לְדָוִד ha' ma'alot l' David	… of ascents. of David.
350	Psalm 125:1 A	שִׁיר shir	a song …

MUSIC IN THE BIBLE

	NRSV	KJV	Function
301	a maskil of Heman	maschil of Heman	maskil
302	a maskil of Ethan	maschil of Ethan	maskil
303	psalm	psalm	mizmor / Shabbat
304	song	song	Shabbat
305	sing praises	sing praises	Shabbat
306	lute, harp	instrument of ten strings	Shabbat
307	melody	psaltery ***	Shabbat
308	lyre	harp	Shabbat
309	sing	joyful noise	Shabbat
310	songs of praise	joyful noise	Shabbat
311	sing	sing	general worship
312	a new song	a new song	general worship
313	sing	sing	general worship
314	sing	sing	general worship
315	psalm	psalm	mizmor
316	sing	sing	general worship
317	a new song	a new song	general worship
318	song and sing	joyful noise and sing	general worship
319	sing	sing	general worship
320	lyre	harp	general worship
321	lyre	harp	general worship
322	melody	voice	general worship
323	trumpets	trumpets	general worship
324	horn	cornet ***	general worship
325	psalm	psalm	mizmor / thanksgiving
326	of David. a psalm	a psalm of David	mizmor
327	sing	sing	general worship
328	sing	sing	general worship
329	sing	sing	general worship
330	sing	sing psalms	general worship
331	song	a song . . .	general worship
332	psalm	. . . or psalm of David	mizmor
333	sing	sing	general worship
334	melody	give praise	general worship
335	harp	psaltery	general worship
336	lyre	harp	general worship
337	of David. a psalm	a song or psalm of David	mizmor
338	of David. a psalm	a psalm of David	mizmor
339	might	song	general worship
340	song	a song . . .	general worship
341	ascents	. . . of degrees	general worship
342	a song . . .	a song . . .	general worship
343	ascents	. . . of degrees	general worship
344	a song . . .	a song . . .	general worship
345	. . . of ascents. of David.	. . . of degrees of David	general worship
346	a song . . .	a song . . .	general worship
347	. . . of ascents	. . . of degrees	general worship
348	a song . . .	a song . . .	general worship
349	. . . of ascents. of David.	. . . of degrees of David	general worship
350	a song . . .	a song . . .	general worship

Bible Verse	עברית	Hebrew Transliteration	JPS
351	Psalm 125:1 B	הַמַּעֲלוֹת	ha' ma'alot	... of ascents
352	Psalm 126:1 A	שִׁיר	shir	a song ...
353	Psalm 126:1 B	הַמַּעֲלוֹת	ha' ma'alot	... of ascents
354	Psalm 127:1 A	שִׁיר	shir	a song ...
355	Psalm 127:1 B	הַמַּעֲלוֹת לִשְׁלֹמֹה	ha' ma'alot l' Shlomo	... of ascents. of Solomon.
356	Psalm 128:1 A	שִׁיר	shir	a song ...
357	Psalm 128:1 B	הַמַּעֲלוֹת	ha' ma'a lot	... of ascents
358	Psalm 129:1 A	שִׁיר	shir	a song ...
359	Psalm 129:1 B	הַמַּעֲלוֹת	ha' ma'a lot	... of ascents
360	Psalm 130:1 A	שִׁיר	shir	a song ...
361	Psalm 130:1 B	הַמַּעֲלוֹת	ha' ma'alot	... of ascents
362	Psalm 131:1 A	שִׁיר	shir	a song ...
363	Psalm 131:1 B	הַמַּעֲלוֹת לְדָוִד	ha' ma'alot l' David	... of ascents. of David.
364	Psalm 132:1 A	שִׁיר	shir	a song ...
365	Psalm 132:1 B	הַמַּעֲלוֹת	ha' ma'alot	... of ascents
366	Psalm 133:1 A	שִׁיר	shir	a song ...
367	Psalm 133:1 B	הַמַּעֲלוֹת לְדָוִד	ha' ma'alot l' David	... of ascents. of David.
368	Psalm 134:1 A	שִׁיר	shir	a song ...
369	Psalm 134:1 B	הַמַּעֲלוֹת	ha' ma'alot	... of ascents
370	Psalm 137:2	כִּנֹּרוֹתֵינוּ	kinnorotnu	lyres
371	Psalm 137:3 A	דִּבְרֵי־שִׁיר	divre-shir	songs
372	Psalm 137:3 B	שִׁירוּ	shiru	sing
373	Psalm 137:3 C	מִשִּׁיר	mi' shir	songs
374	Psalm 137:4 A	נָשִׁיר	na' shir	sing
375	Psalm 137:4 B	אֶת־שִׁיר	et-shir	song
376	Psalm 139:1	לְדָוִד מִזְמוֹר	l' David mizmor	of David. a psalm
377	Psalm 140:1	מִזְמוֹר לְדָוִד	mizmor l' David	a psalm of David
378	Psalm 141:1	מִזְמוֹר לְדָוִד	mizmor l' David	a psalm of David
379	Psalm 142:1	מַשְׂכִּיל לְדָוִד	maskil l' David	a maskil of David
380	Psalm 143:1	מִזְמוֹר לְדָוִד	mizmor l' David	a maskil of David
381	Psalm 144:9 A	שִׁיר חָדָשׁ	shir chadash	sing a new song
382	Psalm 144:9 B	אֲשִׁירָה	ah' shirah	sing a hymn
383	Psalm 144:9 C	עָשׂוֹר	asor	ten-stringed harp
384	Psalm 144:9 D	אֲזַמְּרָה־לָּךְ	ah' zamrah-lach	hymn
385	Psalm 145:1	תְּהִלָּה לְדָוִד	tehillah l' David	a song of praise. of David.
386	Psalm 146:2	אֲזַמְּרָה	ah' zamerah	sing hymns
387	Psalm 147:1 A	זַמְּרָה	ah' zamrah	chant hymns
388	Psalm 147:1 B	תְּהִלָּה	tehillah	sing glorious praise
389	Psalm 147:7 A	זַמְּרוּ	zamru	song of praise, chant a hymn
390	Psalm 147:7 B	בְּכִנּוֹר	b' khinnor	lyre
391	Psalm 149:1 A	שִׁירוּ	shiru	sing
392	Psalm 149:1 B	שִׁיר חָדָשׁ	shir chadash	a new song
393	Psalm 149:3 A	בְּתֹף	b' tof	timbrel
394	Psalm 149:3 B	וְכִנּוֹר	v' khinnor	lyre
395	Psalm 149:5	יְרַנְּנוּ	yeranu	shout
396	Psalm 150:3 A	שׁוֹפָר	shofar	horn
397	Psalm 150:3 B	בְּנֵבֶל	b' nevel	harp
398	Psalm 150:3 C	וְכִנּוֹר	v' khinnor	lyre
399	Psalm 150:4 A	בְתֹף	b' tof	timbrel
400	Psalm 150:4 B	בְּמִנִּים	b' minnim	lute

	NRSV	KJV	Function
351	... of ascents	... of degrees	general worship
352	a song ...	a song ...	general worship
353	... of ascents	... of degrees	general worship
354	a song ...	a song ...	general worship
355	... of ascents. of Solomon.	... of degrees of Solomon	general worship
356	a song ...	a song ...	general worship
357	... of ascents	... of degrees	general worship
358	a song ...	a song ...	general worship
359	... of ascents	... of degrees	general worship
360	a song ...	a song ...	mercy plea
361	... of ascents	... of degrees	mercy plea
362	a song ...	a song ...	lament
363	... of ascents. of David.	... of degrees of David	lament
364	a song ...	a song ...	general worship
365	... of ascents	... of degrees	general worship
366	a song ...	a song ...	general worship
367	... of ascents. of David.	... of degrees of David	general worship
368	a song ...	a song ...	general worship
369	... of ascents	... of degrees	general worship
370	harps ***	harps	lament
371	songs	song	lament
372	sing	sing	lament
373	songs	songs	lament
374	sing	sing	lament
375	song	song	lament
376	of David. a psalm	a psalm of David	mizmor
377	a psalm of David	a psalm of David	mizmor
378	a psalm of David	a psalm of David	mizmor / mercy plea
379	a maskil of David	maschil of David	maskil / lament
380	a psalm of David	a psalm of David	mizmor / mercy plea
381	sing a new song	sing a new song	general worship
382	song	psaltery ***	general worship
383	ten-stringed harp	instrument of ten strings	general worship
384	play	sing praises	general worship
385	praise. of David.	David's psalm of praise	general worship
386	sing praises	sing praises	general worship
387	sing	praise	general worship
388	song of praise	sing praises	general worship
389	sing, make melody	sing, sing praise	general worship
390	lyre	harp	general worship
391	sing	sing	general worship
392	a new song	a new song	general worship
393	melody with tambourine	timbrel	general worship
394	lyre	harp	general worship
395	sing	sing	general worship
396	trumpet	trumpet	general worship
397	lute	psaltery ***	general worship
398	harp	harp	general worship
399	tambourine	timbrel	general worship
400	strings	stringed instruments	general worship

	Bible Verse	עברית Hebrew Transliteration	JPS
401	Psalm 150:4 C	וְעוּגָב v' ugav	pipe
402	Psalm 150:5 A	בְצִלְצְלֵי־שָׁמַע b' tziltzel-shema	resounding cymbals
403	Psalm 150:5 B	בְצִלְצְלֵי b' tziltzel	cymbals
404	Psalm 150:5 C	תְרוּעָה teruah ***	loud-crashing
405	Job 21:12 A	יִשְׂאוּ yisu	sing to the music
406	Job 21:12 B	כְּתֹף k' tof	timbrel
407	Job 21:12 C	וְכִנּוֹר v' khinnor	lyre
408	Job 21:12 D	לְקוֹל l'kol	tune
409	Job 21:12 E	עוּגָב ugav	pipe
410	Job 30:31 A	כִנֹּרִי kinnori	lyre
411	Job 30:31 B	וְעֻגָבִי v' ugavi	pipe
412	Job 39:24	שׁוֹפָר shofar	trumpet
413	Job 39:25	שֹׁפָר shofar	trumpet
414	Song of Songs 1:1	שִׁיר הַשִּׁירִים shir ha' shirim	Song of Songs
415	Daniel 3:5 A	קַרְנָא karnah	horn
416	Daniel 3:5 B	מַשְׁרוֹקִיתָא mashrokita	pipe
417	Daniel 3:5 C	קַתְרֹס kateros	zither
418	Daniel 3:5 D	סַבְּכָא sebbekha	lyre
419	Daniel 3:5 E	פְּסַנְתֵּרִין pesantarin	psaltery
420	Daniel 3:5 F	סוּמְפֹּנְיָה sumponyah	bagpipe
418	Daniel 3:5 G	וְכֹל זְנֵי זְמָרָא v'kol zene zemarah	and all types of instruments
419	Daniel 3:7 A	קַרְנָא karnah	horn
420	Daniel 3:7 B	מַשְׁרוֹקִיתָא mashrokita	pipe
421	Daniel 3:7 C	קַתְרֹס kateros	zither
422	Daniel 3:7 D	שַׂבְּכָא sebbekha	lyre
423	Daniel 3:7 E	פְּסַנְטֵרִין pesantarin	psaltery
424	Daniel 3:7 F	וְכֹל זְנֵי זְמָרָא v'kol zene zemarah	and all types of instruments
425	Daniel 3:10 A	קַרְנָא karnah	horn
426	Daniel 3:10 B	מַשְׁרוֹקִיתָא mashrokita	pipe
427	Daniel 3:10 C	קַתְרֹס kateros	zither
428	Daniel 3:10 D	שַׂבְּכָא sebbekha	lyre
429	Daniel 3:10 E	פְּסַנְטֵרִין pesantarin	psaltery
430	Daniel 3:10 F	וְסוּמְפֹּנְיָה v' suponyah	bagpipe
431	Daniel 3:10 G	וְכֹל זְנֵי זְמָרָא v'kol zene zemarah	and all types of instruments
432	Daniel 3:15 A	קַרְנָא karnah	horn
433	Daniel 3:15 B	מַשְׁרוֹקִיתָא mashrokita	pipe
434	Daniel 3:15 C	קַתְרֹס kateros	zither
435	Daniel 3:15 D	שַׂבְּכָא sebbekah	lyre
436	Daniel 3:15 E	פְּסַנְתֵּרִין pesantarin	psaltery
437	Daniel 3:15 F	וְסוּמְפֹּנְיָה v' sumponyah	bagpipe
438	Daniel 3:15 G	וְכֹל זְנֵי זְמָרָא v'kol zene zemarah	and all types of instruments
439	Ezra 3:10 A	בַּחֲצֹצְרוֹת ba' chatzotzerot	trumpets
440	Ezra 3:10 B	בִּמְצִלְתַּיִם metziltayim	cymbals
441	Ezra 3:11	בְּהַלֵּל b' hallel	sang songs
442	Nehemiah 4:12 (18)	בַּשּׁוֹפָר ba' shofar	trumpeter
443	Nehemiah 4:14 (20)	הַשּׁוֹפָר ha' shofar	trumpet
444	Nehemiah 12:8	הֻיְדוֹת huyedot	thanksgiving songs
445	Nehemiah 12:27 A	וּבְשִׁיר u'v' shir	song
446	Nehemiah 12:27 B	מְצִלְתַּיִם metziltayim	cymbals
447	Nehemiah 12:27 C	נְבָלִים nevalim	harps
448	Nehemiah 12:27 D	וּבְכִנֹּרוֹת u'v' khinnorot	lyres
449	Nehemiah 12:28	הַמְשֹׁרְרִים ha' mesher'rim	singers
450	Nehemiah 12:29	הַמְשֹׁרְרִים ha' mesher'rim	singers

	NRSV	KJV	Function
401	pipe	organs***	general worship
402	clanging cymbals	loud cymbals	general worship
403	cymbals	high sounding cymbals	general worship
404	loud crashing	high sounding	general worship
405	sing	-	celebration
406	tambourine	timbrel	celebration
407	lyre	harp	celebration
408	sound	sound	celebration
409	pipe	organ***	celebration
410	lyre	harp	lament
411	pipe	organ***	lament
412	trumpet	trumpet	warfare
413	trumpet	trumpets	warfare
414	Song of Songs	Song of Solomon	love
415	horn	cornet***	Babylonian Court
416	pipe	flute	Babylonian Court
417	lyre	harp	Babylonian Court
418	trigon	sackbut***	Babylonian Court
419	harp	psaltery	Babylonian Court
420	drum	dulcimer***	Babylonian Court
418	entire musical ensemble	all kinds of musick	Babylonian Court
419	horn	cornet***	Babylonian Court
420	pipe	flute	Babylonian Court
421	lyre	harp	Babylonian Court
422	trigon	sackbut***	Babylonian Court
423	harp	psaltery	Babylonian Court
424	entire musical ensemble	all kinds of musick	Babylonian Court
425	horn	cornet***	Babylonian Court
426	pipe	flute	Babylonian Court
427	lyre	harp	Babylonian Court
428	trigon	sackbut***	Babylonian Court
429	harp	psaltery	Babylonian Court
430	drum	dulcimer***	Babylonian Court
431	entire musical ensemble	all kinds of musick	Babylonian Court
432	horn	cornet***	Babylonian Court
433	pipe	flute	Babylonian Court
434	lyre	harp	Babylonian Court
435	trigon	sackbut***	Babylonian Court
436	harp	psaltery	Babylonian Court
437	drum	dulcimer***	Babylonian Court
438	entire musical ensemble	all kinds of musick	Babylonian Court
439	trumpets	trumpets	celebration / general worship
440	cymbals	cymbals	celebration / general worship
441	sang	sang	thanksgiving
442	trumpet	trumpet	civil
443	trumpet	trumpet	civil
444	songs of thanksgiving	thanksgiving	thanksgiving
445	singing	singing	dedication
446	cymbals	cymbals	dedication
447	harps	psalteries	dedication
448	lyres	harps	dedication
449	singers	singers	dedication
450	singers	singers	dedication

	Bible Verse	עברית Hebrew Transliteration	JPS
451	Nehemiah 12:35	בַּחֲצֹצְרוֹת ba' chatzotzerot	trumpets
452	Nehemiah 12:36	בִּכְלֵי־שִׁיר דָּוִיד bi' kle-shir David	musical instruments of David
453	Nehemiah 12:41	בַּחֲצֹצְרוֹת ba' chatzotzerot	trumpets
454	Nehemiah 12:42	הַמְשֹׁרְרִים ha' mesher'rim	singers sang
455	Nehemiah 12:46 A	הַמְשֹׁרְרִים ha' mesher'rim	singers
456	Nehemiah 12:46 B	שִׁיר־תְּהִלָּה v' shir-tehillah	songs
457	1 Chronicles 6:16 (31)	שִׁיר shir	song
458	1 Chronicles 6:17 (32)	בַּשִּׁיר ba' shir	song
459	1 Chronicles 13:8 A	וּבְשִׁירִים u'v' shirim	songs
460	1 Chronicles 13:8 B	וּבְכִנֹּרוֹת u'v' khinnorot	lyres
461	1 Chronicles 13:8 C	וּבִנְבָלִים u'v' nevalim	harps
462	1 Chronicles 13:8 D	וּבְתֻפִּים u'v' tuppim	timbrels
463	1 Chronicles 13:8 E	וּבִמְצִלְתַּיִם u'v' metziltayim	cymbals
464	1 Chronicles 13:8 F	וּבַחֲצֹצְרוֹת u'v' chatzotzerot	trumpets
465	1 Chronicles 15:16 A	הַמְשֹׁרְרִים ha' mesher'rim	singers
466	1 Chronicles 15:16 B	בִּכְלֵי־שִׁיר bi' kle-shir	musical instruments
467	1 Chronicles 15:16 C	נְבָלִים nevalim	harps
468	1 Chronicles 15:16 D	וְכִנֹּרוֹת v' khinnorot	lyres
469	1 Chronicles 15:16 E	וּמְצִלְתָּיִם u' metziltayim	cymbals
470	1 Chronicles 15:19	בִּמְצִלְתַּיִם b' metziltayim	cymbals
471	1 Chronicles 15:20	בִּנְבָלִים bi' nevalim	harps
472	1 Chronicles 15:21	בְּכִנֹּרוֹת b' khinnorot	lyres
473	1 Chronicles 15:24	בַּחֲצֹצְרוֹת ba' chatzotzerot	trumpets
474	1 Chronicles 15:27 A	וְהַמְשֹׁרְרִים v' ha' mesher'rim	singers
475	1 Chronicles 15:27 B	הַמְשֹׁרְרִים ha' mesher'rim	song of the singers
476	1 Chronicles 15:28 A	שׁוֹפָר shofar	horn
477	1 Chronicles 15:28 B	וּבַחֲצֹצְרוֹת u'va' chatzotzerot	trumpets
478	1 Chronicles 15:28 C	וּבִמְצִלְתַּיִם u'vi' metziltayim	cymbals
479	1 Chronicles 15:28 D	מַשְׁמִעִים mashem'im	playing
480	1 Chronicles 15:28 E	בִּנְבָלִים bi' nevalim	harps
481	1 Chronicles 15:28 F	וְכִנֹּרוֹת v' khinnorot	lyres
482	1 Chronicles 16:5 A	נְבָלִים nevalim	harps
483	1 Chronicles 16:5 B	וּבְכִנֹּרוֹת u'v' kinnorot	lyres
484	1 Chronicles 16:5 C	בִּמְצִלְתַּיִם ba' metziltayim	cymbals
485	1 Chronicles 16:6	בַּחֲצֹצְרוֹת ba' chatzotzerot	trumpets
486	1 Chronicles 16:9 A	שִׁירוּ shiru	sing
487	1 Chronicles 16:9 B	זַמְּרוּ zameru	speak
488	1 Chronicles 16:23	שִׁירוּ shiru	sing
489	1 Chronicles 16:33	יְרַנְּנוּ yeranu	shout
490	1 Chronicles 16:42 A	חֲצֹצְרוֹת chatzotzerot	trumpets
491	1 Chronicles 16:42 B	וּמְצִלְתַּיִם u'v' metziltayim	cymbals
492	1 Chronicles 16:42 C	לְמַשְׁמִיעִים l' mashem'im	sound
493	1 Chronicles 16:42 D	וּכְלֵי u' kle	instruments
494	1 Chronicles 16:42 E	שִׁיר shir	songs
495	1 Chronicles 23:5 A	בַּכֵּלִים ba' kelim	instruments
496	1 Chronicles 23:5 B	לְהַלֵּל l' hallel	singing praises
497	1 Chronicles 25:1 A	בְּכִנֹּרוֹת b' khinnorot	lyres
498	1 Chronicles 25:1 B	בִּנְבָלִים bi' nevalim	harps
499	1 Chronicles 25:1 C	וּבִמְצִלְתָּיִם u'vi' metziltayim	cymbals
500	1 Chronicles 25:3	בְּכִנּוֹר ba' kinnor	harp ***

Music in the Bible

	NRSV	KJV	Function
451	trumpets	trumpets	dedication
452	musical instruments of David	musical instruments of David	corporate worship
453	trumpets	trumpets	warfare
454	singers sang	singers sang	general worship
455	singers	singers	thanksgiving
456	songs	songs	thanksgiving
457	song	song	Temple Orchestra
458	song	singing	Temple Orchestra
459	song	singing	Temple Orchestra
460	lyres	harps	Temple Orchestra
461	harps	psalteries	Temple Orchestra
462	tambourines	timbrels	Temple Orchestra
463	cymbals	cymbals	Temple Orchestra
464	trumpets	trumpets	Temple Orchestra
465	singers	singers	Temple Orchestra
466	musical instruments	instruments of musick	Temple Orchestra
467	harps	psalteries	Temple Orchestra
468	lyres	harps	Temple Orchestra
469	cymbals	cymbals	Temple Orchestra
470	cymbals	cymbals	Temple Orchestra
471	harps	psalteries	Temple Orchestra
472	lyres	harps	Temple Orchestra
473	trumpets	trumpets	Temple Orchestra / fanfare
474	singers	singers	Temple Orchestra
475	music of the singers	song with the singers	Temple Orchestra
476	horn	cornet ***	Temple Orchestra
477	trumpets	trumpets	Temple Orchestra
478	cymbals	cymbals	Temple Orchestra
479	loud music	noise	Temple Orchestra
480	harps	psalteries	Temple Orchestra
481	lyres	harps	Temple Orchestra
482	harps	psalteries	Temple Orchestra
483	lyres	harps	Temple Orchestra
484	cymbals	cymbals	Temple Orchestra
485	trumpets	trumpets	Temple Orchestra
486	sing	sing	thanksgiving
487	sing	sing psalms	thanksgiving
488	sing	sing	thanksgiving
489	sing	sing	metaphor
490	trumpets	trumpets	Temple Orchestra
491	cymbals	cymbals	Temple Orchestra
492	music	sound	Temple Orchestra
493	instruments	instruments	Temple Orchestra
494	song	musical	Temple Orchestra
495	instruments	instruments	Temple Orchestra
496	praise	praises	Temple Orchestra
497	lyres	harps	Temple Orchestra
498	harps	psalteries	Temple Orchestra
499	cymbals	cymbals	Temple Orchestra
500	lyre	harp	thanksgiving

	Bible Verse	עברית Hebrew Transliteration	JPS
501	1 Chronicles 25:6 A	בַּשִּׁיר ba' shir	singers
502	1 Chronicles 25:6 B	בִּמְצִלְתַּיִם bi' mitzltayim	cymbals
503	1 Chronicles 25:6 C	נְבָלִים nevalim	harps
504	1 Chronicles 25:6 D	וְכִנֹּרוֹת v' khinnorot	lyres
505	1 Chronicles 25:7	מְלֻמְּדֵי־שִׁיר m' lumde-shir	trained singers
506	2 Chronicles 5:12 A	וְהַלְוִיִּם הַמְשֹׁרֲרִים v'ha' leviyim ha' meshre'ri	Levite singers
507	2 Chronicles 5:12 B	בִּמְצִלְתַּיִם bi' mitzltayim	cymbals
508	2 Chronicles 5:12 C	וּבִנְבָלִים u'vi' nevalim	harps
509	2 Chronicles 5:12 D	וְכִנֹּרוֹת v' khinnorot	lyres
510	2 Chronicles 5:12 E	בַּחֲצֹצְרוֹת ba' chatzotzerot	trumpets
511	2 Chronicles 5:13 A	לַמְחַצְּרִים lam' chatzerim	trumpeters
512	2 Chronicles 5:13 B	וְלַמְשֹׁרֲרִים v'lam' shirim	singers
513	2 Chronicles 5:13 C	בַּחֲצֹצְרוֹת ba' chatzotzerot	trumpets
514	2 Chronicles 5:13 D	וּבִמְצִלְתַּיִם u'vi' metziltayim	cymbals
515	2 Chronicles 5:13 E	וּבִכְלֵי הַשִּׁיר u'vi' khelim ha' shir	other musical instruments
516	2 Chronicles 7:6 A	בִּכְלֵי־ bi' khle	instruments
517	2 Chronicles 7:6 B	שִׁיר shir	music
518	2 Chronicles 7:6 C	מַחְצְרִים ma' chetzerim	trumpets
519	2 Chronicles 9:11 A	וְכִנֹּרוֹת v' khinnorot	lyres
520	2 Chronicles 9:11 B	וּנְבָלִים v' nevalim	harps
521	2 Chronicles 9:11 C	לַשָּׁרִים la' sharim	musicians
522	2 Chronicles 13:12	וַחֲצֹצְרוֹת va' chatzotzerot	trumpets
523	2 Chronicles 13:14	בַּחֲצֹצְרוֹת ba' chatzotzerot	trumpets
524	2 Chronicles 15:14 A	וּבַחֲצֹצְרוֹת u'va' chatzotzerot	trumpeting
525	2 Chronicles 15:14 B	וּבְשׁוֹפָרוֹת u'v' shofarot	horn
526	2 Chronicles 20:21	מְשֹׁרֲרִים meshrarim	singers
527	2 Chronicles 20:28 A	בִּנְבָלִים bi' nevalim	harps
528	2 Chronicles 20:28 B	וּבְכִנֹּרוֹת u'v' khinnorot	lyres
529	2 Chronicles 20:28 C	וּבַחֲצֹצְרוֹת u'va' chatzotzerot	trumpets
530	2 Chronicles 23:13 A	וְהַחֲצֹצְרוֹת v'ha' chatzotzerot	trumpets
531	2 Chronicles 23:13 B	בַּחֲצֹצְרוֹת ba' chatzotzerot	trumpets
532	2 Chronicles 23:13 C	וְהַמְשׁוֹרֲרִים v'ha' meshorarim	singers
533	2 Chronicles 23:13 D	בִּכְלֵי הַשִּׁיר bi' kle ha' shir	musical instruments
534	2 Chronicles 23:13 E	לְהַלֵּל l' hallel	hymns
535	2 Chronicles 23:18	וּבְשִׁיר u'v' shir	song
536	2 Chronicles 29:25 A	בִּמְצִלְתַּיִם bi' mitzltayim	cymbals
537	2 Chronicles 29:25 B	בִּנְבָלִים bi' nevalim	harps
538	2 Chronicles 29:25 C	וּבְכִנֹּרוֹת u'v' khinnorot	lyres
539	2 Chronicles 29:26 A	בִּכְלֵי דָוִיד bi' kle David	instruments of David
540	2 Chronicles 29:26 B	בַּחֲצֹצְרוֹת ba' chatzotzerot	trumpets
541	2 Chronicles 29:27 A	שִׁיר־יְהוָה shir-YHVH	song for the LORD
542	2 Chronicles 29:27 B	וְהַחֲצֹצְרוֹת v'ha' chatzotzerot	trumpets
543	2 Chronicles 29:27 C	כְּלֵי דָּוִיד kle David	instruments of King David
544	2 Chronicles 29:28 A	וְהַשִּׁיר v' ha' shir	song
545	2 Chronicles 29:28 B	מְשׁוֹרֵר m' shorer	sung
546	2 Chronicles 29:28 C	וְהַחֲצֹצְרוֹת v' ha' chatzotzerot	trumpets
547	2 Chronicles 31:2	וּלְהֹדוֹת u' lehodot	sing hymns and praises

MUSIC IN THE BIBLE 321

	NRSV	KJV	Function
501	music	song	Temple Orchestra
502	cymbals	cymbals	Temple Orchestra
503	harps	psalteries	Temple Orchestra
504	lyres	harps	Temple Orchestra
505	trained in singing	instructed in the songs	Temple Orchestra
506	levitical singers	Levites which were the singers	Temple Orchestra
507	cymbals	cymbals	Temple Orchestra
508	harps	psalteries	Temple Orchestra
509	lyres	harps	Temple Orchestra
510	trumpeters	trumpets	Temple Orchestra
511	trumpeters	trumpeters	Temple Orchestra / thanksgiving
512	singers	singers	Temple Orchestra / thanksgiving
513	trumpets	trumpets	Temple Orchestra
514	cymbals	cymbals	Temple Orchestra
515	other musical instruments	instruments of musick	Temple Orchestra
516	instruments	instruments	Temple Orchestra
517	music	musick	Temple Orchestra
518	trumpets	trumpets	Temple Orchestra
519	lyres	harps	Temple Orchestra / inst. const.
520	harps	psalteries	Temple Orchestra / inst. const.
521	singers	singers	Temple Orchestra / inst. const.
522	trumpets	trumpets	metaphor
523	trumpets	trumpets	metaphor
524	trumpets	trumpets	covenant
525	horns	cornets ***	covenant
526	sing	singers	general worship / warfare
527	harps	psalteries	general worship / warfare
528	lyres	harps	general worship / warfare
529	trumpets	trumpets	general worship / warfare
530	trumpeters	trumpets	victory
531	trumpets	trumpets	victory
532	singers	singers	victory
533	musical instruments	instruments of musick	victory
534	celebration	sing praise	victory
535	singing	singing	victory
536	cymbals	cymbals	Temple Orchestra
537	harps	psalteries	Temple Orchestra
538	lyres	harps	Temple Orchestra
539	instruments of David	instruments of David	Temple Orchestra
540	trumpets	trumpets	Temple Orchestra
541	song for the LORD	song for the LORD	Temple Orchestra
542	trumpets	trumpets	Temple Orchestra
543	instruments of King David	instruments ordained by David	Temple Orchestra
544	singers	singers	Temple Orchestra
545	sang	sang	Temple Orchestra
546	trumpeters	trumpeters	Temple Orchestra
547	give thanks and praise	give thanks and to praise	Temple Orchestra / thanksgiving

Notes

[1] Joachim Braun, *Music in Ancient Israel/Palestine: Archaeological, Written, and Comparative Sources* (Grand Rapids: Wm. B. Eerdmans Publishing Co., 2002), 197.

[2] R.E. Allen, ed. *The Concise Oxford Dictionary* (Oxford: Clarendon Press, 1992), 781.

[3] Dale B. Martin, *New Testament History and Literature* (New Haven: Yale University Press, 2012), 28.

[4] Martin, 2.

[5] Bible Hub, "Psalm 23" Interlinear Bible. https://biblehub.com/interlinear/psalms/23.htm

[6] Adele Berlin and Marc Zvi Brettler, eds., *The Jewish Study Bible,* 2nd ed. (New York: Jewish Publication Society, 2014).

[7] Braun, 1.

[8] Norman M. Weinberger, "Music and the Brain," *SA Special Editions* 16, no.3s (September 2006): 36-43. https://www.scientificamerican.com/article/music-and-the-brain-2006-09/.

[9] Weinberger, 36-43.

[10] Anita Collins, "How Playing an Instrument Benefits Your Brain" TED-Ed (YouTube, July 22, 2014). https://www.youtube.com/watch?v=R0JKCYZ8hng

[11] Yingying Hou, Bei Song, Yingying Hu, and Yafeng Pam, "The Averaged Inter-Brain Coherence Between the Audience and a Violinist Predicts the Popularity of Violin Performance" *NeuroImage* vol. 211 (May 2020): 1-11. https://www.scientificamerican.com/article/music-synchronizes-the-brains-of-performers-and-their-audience/.

[12] "Music," Oxford English Dictionary.

[13] Benj Fried, "Erev Shabbat Sermon" (Sermon, January 14, 2022).

[14] Fried.

[15] Braun, 84, 120-121.

[16] Braun, 84, 120-121.

[17] W. F. Albright, "The Song of Deborah" *Bulletin of the American Schools of Oriental Research*, no. 62 (April 1936): 26.

[18] Francisco Del Rio Sanchez, "Where did the Queen of Sheba rule—Arabia or Africa?" *National Geographic:* June 7, 2021. https://www.nationalgeographic.co.uk/history-and-civilisation/2021/06/where-did-the-queen-of-sheba-rule-arabia-or-africa.

[19] "Ditty," Oxford Learner's Dictionaries. https://www.oxfordlearnersdictionaries.com/us/definition/english/ditty.

[20] Adele Berlin and Marc Zvi Brettler, *The Jewish Study Bible: Jewish Publication Society Tanakh Translation,* 2nd ed. (Oxford University Press: New York, 2014), 827.

[21] Berlin and Brettler, 93.

[22] Berlin and Brettler, 1265.

[23] Berlin and Brettler, 1265.

[24] Alfred Sendrey, *Music in Ancient Israel* (New York: Philosophy Press, 1969), 96.

[25] Braun, 98.

[26] Braun, 98.

[27] Sendrey, 98.

[28] Sendrey, 103-104.

[29] Sendrey, 102.

[30] Sendrey, 104.

[31] Sendrey, 104.

[32] Sendrey, 302.

[33] Sendrey, 302.

[34] "Syncretism," Oxford English Dictionary.

[35] John Benham, "Introduction to Ethnomusicology" (video lecture, Liberty University, 2015).

[36] Sendrey, 110.

[37] Sendrey, 109-111.

[38] Sendrey, 110-111.

[39] Sendrey, 110.

[40] Sendrey, 111.

[41] "Shigionoth," Definition, Sefaria.org. https://www.sefaria.org/Habakkuk.3.1?ven=Tanakh:_The_Holy_Scriptures,_published_by_JPS&vhe=Miqra_according_to_the_Masorah&lang=bi.

[42] Haïk-Vantoura, 402.

[43] Haïk-Vantoura, 402.

[44] Haïk-Vantoura, 402.

[45] "Yisu," Definition, https://www.sefaria.org/Job.21.12?ven=Tanakh:_The_Holy_Scriptures,_published_by_JPS&vhe=Miqra_according_to_the_Masorah&lang=bi&lookup=%D7%99%D6%B4%D6%AD%D7%A9%D7%82%D6%B0%D7%90%D7%95%D6%BC&with=Lexicon&lang2=en.

[46] Tim Mackie, "Overview: Song of Songs" (YouTube, Bible Project, Portland, 2016). https://www.youtube.com/watch?v=4KC7xE4fgOw&t=53s.

[47] Tim Mackie, "Overview: Song of Songs" (YouTube, Bible Project, Portland, 2016). https://www.youtube.com/watch?v=4KC7xE4fgOw&t=53s.

[48] Jose ben Halpetha, *Seder Olam Rabba* (Jerusalem: Gil Publishers, 1971), 107.

[49] Daniel Pioske, *David's Jerusalem: Between Memory and History* (London: Routledge, 2015), 180.

[50] Pioske, 210.

[51] Lawrence J. Myktiuk, *Identifying Biblical Persons in Northwest Semitic Inscriptions of 1200-539 B.C.E.* (Brill: Leiden, 2004), 214.

[52] Sendrey, 272.

[53] "Harp Strings," "How They Do It" (Discovery+, 2015).

[54] "Harp Strings."

[55] Siegmund Levarie, "Philo on Music." *The Journal of Musicology* 9, no. 1 (1991): 125. Accessed September 19, 2020. doi:10.2307/763837.

[56] Levarie, 125.

[57] Flavius Josephus, *Antiquities of the Jews* (Lexington: First Rate Publishers, reprinted in 2019), chapter 12, section 3.

[58] Sendrey, 290.

[59] Braun, 227.

[60] Sendrey, 267.

[61] Josephus, " Chapter 7: How Solomon Grew Rich, And Fell Desperately In Love With Women And How God, Being Incensed At It, Raised Up Ader And Jeroboam Against Him. Concerning The Death of Solomon."
https://www.gutenberg.org/files/2848/2848-h/2848-h.htm

[62] Sendrey, 272.

[63] "Silver Lyre," Museum of the World, web. Retrieved on November 20, 2022.
https://britishmuseum.withgoogle.com/object/silver-lyre.

[64] Braun, 72.

[65] Braun, 71.

[66] Braun, 71-72.

[67] Braun, 72.

[68] Braun, 72-73.

[69] Braun, 148.

[70] Joachim Braun, *Jar with Drawing of Lyre Player,* 2002, print image, Jerusalem from *Music in Ancient Israel/Palestine* (Grand Rapids: Eerdmans, 2002), 148.

[71] Braun, 148.

[72] Carl McTague, "The Lyres of Ur," Mctague.org (2022). http://www.mctague.org/carl/music/computer/pieces/lyre/.

[73] Andrew Lawyer, "City of Biblical Abraham Brimmed with Trade and Riches" *National Geographic,* March 11, 2016. https://www.nationalgeographic.com/news/2016/03/160311-ur-iraq-trade-royal-cemetery-woolley-archaeology/.

[74] McTague.

[75] McTague.

[76] McTague.

[77] McTague.

[78] McTague.

[79] McTague.

[80] Andy Lowings, *The Golden Lyre of Ur,* 2013, digital image, Baghdad. Accessed on November 27, 2020. http://www.tristanlegovic.eu/blog.php?pennad=lyre-of-ur#bookmark/5/.

[81] McTague.

[82] McTague.

[83] Virginia Greene, "Conservation of a Lyre from Ur: A treatment review." *Journal of the American Institute for Conservation*, no.2 (2003): 265-270.
doi:10.2307/3180072. ISSN 0197-1360. JSTOR 3180072.

[84] Green, 265-270.

[85] Image sourced from Wikimedia Commons. https://commons.wikimedia.org/wiki/File:Woolley_holding_the_hardened_plaster_mold_of_a_lyre.jpg.

[86] Michelle Jirkovsky, interview. July 29, 2022.

[87] McTague.

[88] Braun, 291.

[89] Braun, 23.

[90] Braun, 23.

[91] Sendrey, 278.

[92] Sendrey, 278.

[93] Sendrey, 290.

[94] Sendrey, 279.

[95] Shoshanna Harrari, "Harrari Harps," 2008. https://www.youtube.com/watch?v=bO5uA-IPV0E.

[96] Braun, 22-24.

[97] Sendrey, 289.

[98] Braun, 84.

[99] Timothy J. Cooley, "Europe/Central and Southeastern Regions," in *Worlds of Music* 6th ed, ed. Jeff Todd Titon (Boston: Cengage Learning, 2017), 502-504.

[100] Cooley, 245.

[101] Douglas Alton Smith, "A History of the Lute from Antiquity to the Renaissance," *Lute Society of America.* (2002): 9.

[102] Dumbrill, 321.

[103] Sendrey, 292.

[104] Sendrey, 292.

[105] Sendrey, 272.

[106] Braun, 81.

[107] Braun, 81.

[108] Sendrey, 272.

[109] Sendrey, 294.

[110] Sendrey, 342.

[111] Benham.

[112] Mark Rober, "World's Largest Horn Shatters Glass" (web video, YouTube, 2018). https://www.youtube.com/watch?v=pFEB0chiuJA.

[113] Sendrey, 344-345.

[114] Eli Ribak, "How to Make a Shofar: A Look Inside Israel's Biggest Factory" (web, Haaretz, Tel Aviv, 2017). https://www.youtube.com/watch?v=gpKviLJnV2E.

[115] Jennifer Sterling Snodgrass, *Contemporary Musicianship: Analysis and the Artist* (New York: Oxford University Press, 2018), 71.

[117] Stephanie Pappas, "Ram-Headed Sphinx Abandoned by King Tut's Grandfather Found in Egypt," *Live Science* (web, February 27, 2019). https://www.livescience.com/64870-ram-headed-sphinx-egypt.html.

[118] Sendrey, 342.

[119] Sendrey, 332.

[120] Sendrey, 332.

[121] Sendrey, 332-342.

[122] Iwan Fox, "The Tale of Tutankhamun's trumpets..." (web, 4BarsRest. June 21, 2020). https://www.4barsrest.com/articles/2020/1881.asp.

[123] Matthew Baker, "Egyptian Pharaohs Family Tree: Dynasties 18,19, and 20," UsefulCharts, 2019. https://www.youtube.com/watch?v=HaZmGPePdTg.

[124] Fox.

[125] Fox.

[126] Fox.

[127] Fox.

[128] Joe Kiernan, "King Tutankhamun's Trumpets played after 3,000 + Years" June 11, 2014. https://www.youtube.com/watch?v=Qt9AyV3hnlc&t=101s.

[129] Kiernan.

[130] Kiernan.

[131] Fox.

[132] Braun, 291.

[133] Braun, 28.

[134] Braun, 28.

[135] Braun, 9.

[136] Benham.

[137] Sendrey, 308-309.

[138] Sendrey, 308-309.

[139] Sendrey, 309.

[140] Sendrey, 309.

[141] Sendrey, 309.

[142] Cooley, 499-500.

[143] Sendrey, 266-268.

[144] McTague.

[145] Braun, 110-111.

[146] Braun, 110-111.

[147] Braun, 110-111.

[148] Braun, 110-111.

[149] Braun, 110-111.

[150] Braun, 110-111.

[151] Sendrey, 310.

[152] Sendrey, 310.

[153] Sendrey, 310.

[154] Sendrey, 310,

[155] Braun, 15.

[156] Cooley, 245.

[157] Sendrey, 322.

[158] Sendrey, 322.

[159] Sendrey, 322.

[160] Sendrey, 320.

[161] Sendrey, 320.

[162] Braun, 30.

[163] Braun, 30.

[164] Sendrey, 373.

[165] Sendrey, 409.

[166] Braun, 118-119.

[167] Manohar Laxman Varadpande, *History of Indian Theatre* (Abhinav Publications, 1987), 55.

[168] Suzanne Haïk-Vantoura, *The Music of the Bible Revealed* (Berkeley: Bibal Press, 1991), 22.

[169] Braun, 21.

[170] Sendrey, 375.

[171] Braun, 21.

[172] Braun, 20.

[173] Braun, 20.

[174] Paul Ilton, *The Bible Was My Treasure Map* (New York, Julian Messner, 1958), 90-93.

[175] Sendrey, 381.

[176] Braun, 88-90.

[177] Sendrey, 381.

[178] Sendrey, 385.

[179] Sendrey, 386.

[180] Sendrey, 375.

[181] Braun, 197.

[182] Braun, 197.

[183] Sendrey, 365.

[184] Sendrey, 365.

[185] Sendrey, 324.

[186] Sendrey, 324.

[187] Sendrey, 296-299.

[188] Amy C. Merrill Willis, "Introduction to Daniel" in *The Oxford Annotated Study Bible: New Revised Standard Version with Apocrypha* 5th ed., ed Michael D. Coogan (New York: Oxford University Press, 2018), 1249.

[189] Sendrey, 299.

[190] Joseph Kerman and Gary Tomlinson, *Listen* 9th ed. (New York: W.W. Norton and Company, 2019), 82.

[191] "Alto Sackbut Renaissance Trombone," Fine Art America, 2020. https://fineartamerica.com/featured/alto-sackbut-renaissance-trombone-unknown.html

[192] Sendrey, 294.

[193] Sendrey, 294.

[194] Anastasios Koumartzis, *Ancient Sambuca,* n.d., digital image, Europos, Greece. Accessed on October 31, 2020. https://luthieros.com/product/ancient-sambuca-ancient-harp-like-lyre-top-quality-handcrafted-musical-instrument/.

[195] Sendrey, 294.

[196] Sendrey, 296-299.

[197] Sendrey, 296.

[198] Sendrey, 325.

[199] Sendrey, 325.

[200] Sendrey, 326.

[201] Braun, 219.

[202] Sendrey, 326.

[203] Martin.

[204] Alan P. Merriam, *Anthropology of Music* (Chicago: Northwestern University Press, 1964), 209.

[205] Sendrey, 209.

[206] Sendrey, xxi.

[207] Sendrey, 98.

[208] Sendrey, 98.

[209] Sendrey, 98.

[210] "Lament," Oxford English Dictionary.

[211] Sendrey, 265.

[212] Sendrey, 104.

[213] Sendrey, 302.

[214] "Music Therapy," Cleveland Clinic. https://my.clevelandclinic.org/health/treatments/8817-music-therapy.

[215] "Fanfare," Oxford English Dictionary.

[216] Sarah Gibbens. "Roman Auditorium Unearthed Under Western Wall in Jerusalem." *National Geographic*, October 18, 2017. https://www.nationalgeographic.com/news/2017/10/ancient-roman-theater-discovery-jerusalem- video-spd/#close.

[217] Jonathan P.J. Stock, "Asia/China, Taiwan, Singapore, Overseas Chinese," in *Worlds of Music: An Introduction to the Music of the World's Peoples*, 6th ed., ed. Jeff Todd Titon (Boston: Cengage Learning, 2017), 399.

[218] Joey Weisenberg, "The Torah of Music," Lecture series, January 26, 2022.

[219] Weisenberg.

[220] Xiaoming Wang, Qiang Li, and Gary L. Takeuchi, "Out of Tibet: An Early Sheep from the Pliocene of Tibet, *Protovis himalayensis*, Genus and Species Nov. (Bovidae, Caprini), and Origin of Ice Age Mountain Sheep," *Journal of Vertebrate Paleontology* 36, no. 5 (2016).
https://www.tandfonline.com/doi/abs/10.1080/02724634.2016.1169190?journalCode=ujvp20.

[221] Braun, 110-111.

[222] Cooley, 245.

[223] Haïk-Vantoura, 31.

[224] Joshua R. Jacobson, *Chanting the Hebrew Bible: Student Edition* (Philadelphia: The Jewish Publication Society, 2005), 10.

[225] Haïk-Vantoura, 50.

[226] Haïk-Vantoura, 14.

[227] Haïk-Vantoura, 46.

[228] Haïk-Vantoura, 46.

[229] Joshua A. Jacobson, *Chanting the Hebrew Bible: Student Edition* (Philadelphia: The Jewish Publication Society, 2005), 10.

[230] Arianne Brown, "Tricks of the Trope," Hazzan Arianne Brown, YouTube.
https://www.youtube.com/watch?v=BUhGnuwmJ4E&t=38s.

[231] Haïk-Vantoura, 38.

[232] Haïk-Vantoura, 50.

[233] Haïk-Vantoura, 14.

[234] Haïk-Vantoura, 14.

[235] Haïk-Vantoura, 30.

[236] Haïk-Vantoura, 38.

[237] Haïk-Vantoura, 7-10.

[238] Haïk-Vantoura, 7-10.

[239] Haïk-Vantoura, 7-10.

[240] Haïk-Vantoura, 52.

[241] Haïk-Vantoura, 89.

[242] Saul Levin, "The Traditional Chironomy of the Hebrew Scriptures," *Journal of Biblical Literature* 87, no. 1 (March 1968): 59-70.

[243] Saul Levin, "The Traditional Chironomy of the Hebrew Scriptures" (video, State University of New York, Binghamton, NY, 1968).
 https://www.youtube.com/watch?v=75BTeS5WyPA.

[244] Levin.

[245] Haïk-Vantoura, 90.

[246] Levin, 60.

[247] Levin, 60.

[248] Levin, 60.

[249] Haïk-Vantoura, 79.

[250] Levin.

[251] Levin.

[252] Brown.

[253] Michael Mark and Patrice Madura, *Contemporary Music Education*, 4th ed. (Boston: Cengage, 2014), 110.

[254] Herman Berlinski, "Jewish Critic Disputes Theory on Hebrew Signs" *The Washington Post* (April 11, 1980). https://www.washingtonpost.com/archive/local/1980/04/11/jewish-critic-disputes-theory-on-hebrew-signs/766b736e-5b18-43af-ae11-df7d7d58112b/.

[255] Berlinski.

[256] Berlinski.

[257] Haïk-Vantoura, 97.

[258] Haïk-Vantoura, 7-10.

[259] Michael Mark and Patrice Madura, *Contemporary Music Education* 4th ed. (Boston: Cengage, 2014), 110.

[260] Jacobson, 10.

[261] Jacobson, 10.

[262] Willis, 1249.

[263] Elmer L. Towns and Vernon M. Whaley, *Worship Through the Ages: How the Great Awakenings Shape Evangelical Worship* (Nashville: B&H Publishing Group), 2012, 297.

Selected Bibliography

Albright, W.F. "The Song of Deborah" *Bulletin of the American Schools of Oriental Research*, no. 62 (April 1936): 26.

Allen, R.E., ed. *The Concise Oxford Dictionary*. Oxford: Clarendon Press, 1992.

Baker, Matthew. "Egyptian Pharaohs Family Tree: Dynasties 18,19, and 20," UsefulCharts, 2019. https://www.youtube.com/watch?v=HaZmGPePdTg.

Benham, John. "Introduction to Ethnomusicology" (video lecture, Liberty University, 2015).

Berlin, Adele, and Marc Zvi Brettler, eds. *The Jewish Study Bible*, 2nd ed. New York: Jewish Publication Society, 2014.

Berlinski, Herman. "Jewish Critic Disputes Theory on Hebrew Signs" *The Washington Post* (April 11, 1980). https://www.washingtonpost.com/archive/local/1980/04/11/jewish-critic-disputes-theory-on-hebrew-signs/766b736e-5b18-43af-ae11-df7d7d58112b/.

Braun, Joachim. *Music in Ancient Israel/Palestine: Archaeological, Written, and Comparative Sources*. Grand Rapids: Wm. B. Eerdmans Publishing Co., 2002.

Brown, Arianne. "Tricks of the Trope," Hazzan Arianne Brown, YouTube. https://www.youtube.com/watch?v=BUhGnuwmJ4E&t=38s.

Cooley, Timothy J. "Europe/Central and Southeastern Regions," in *Worlds of Music* 6th ed, ed. Jeff Todd Titon. Boston: Cengage Learning, 2017.

Dumbrill, Richard J. *The Archeomuiscology of the Ancient Near East*. London: Tadema Press, 1998.

Fox, Iwan. "The Tale of Tutankhamun's trumpets..." (web, 4BarsRest. June 21, 2020). https://www.4barsrest.com/articles/2020/1881.asp.

Fried, Benj. "Erev Shabbat Sermon" (Sermon, January 14, 2022).

Friedman, Richard Elliot. *How Wrote the Bible?* New York: Simon & Shuster, 1989, 2019.

Gibbens, Sarah. "Roman Auditorium Unearthed Under Western Wall in Jerusalem." *National Geographic*, October 18, 2017. https://www.nationalgeographic.com/news/2017/10/ancient-roman-theater-discovery-jerusalem-video-spd/#close.

Greene, Virginia. "Conservation of a Lyre from Ur: A treatment review." *Journal of the American Institute for Conservation*, no.2 (2003): 265-270. doi:10.2307/3180072. ISSN 0197-1360. JSTOR 3180072.

Haïk-Vantoura, Suzanne. *The Music of the Bible Revealed*. Berkeley: Bibal Press, 1991.

Halpetha, Jose ben. *Seder Olam Rabba*. Jerusalem: Gil Publishers, 1971.

"Harp Strings." How They Do It. Discovery+, 2015.

Hayes, Christine. *Introduction to the Bible*. New Haven: Yale University Press, 2012.

Harrari, Shoshanna. "Harrari Harps," 2008. https://www.youtube.com/watch?v=bO5uA-IPV0E.

Ilton, Paul. *The Bible Was My Treasure Map*. New York, Julian Messner, 1958.

Jacobson, Joshua R. *Chanting the Hebrew Bible: Student Edition* Philadelphia: The Jewish Publication Society, 2005.

Jirkovsky, Charles. *Music as Worship in the Hebrew Bible: Instrumentation, Function, Notation, and Tonality*. Doctoral Thesis, Liberty University, December 2020.

Jirkovsky, Michelle. Interview. July 29, 2022.

Josephus, Flavius. *Antiquities of the Jews*. Lexington: First Rate Publishers, reprinted in 2019.

Kerman, Joseph, and Gary Tomlinson. *Listen* 9th ed. New York: W.W. Norton and Company, 2019.

Kiernan, Joe. "King Tutankhamun's Trumpets Played After 3,000 + Years" June 11, 2014. https://www.youtube.com/watch?v=Qt9AyV3hnlc&t=101s.

Lawyer, Andrew. "City of Biblical Abraham Brimmed with Trade and Riches" *National Geographic,* March 11, 2016. https://www.nationalgeographic.com/news/2016/03/160311-ur-iraq-trade-royal-cemetery-woolley-archaeology/.

Levin, Saul. "The Traditional Chironomy of the Hebrew Scriptures," *Journal of Biblical Literature* 87, no. 1 (March 1968): 59-70.

-----. "The Traditional Chironomy of the Hebrew Scriptures" (video, State University of New York, Binghamton, NY, 1968). https://www.youtube.com/watch?v=75BTeS5WyPA.

Levarie, Siegmund. "Philo on Music." *The Journal of Musicology* 9, no. 1 (1991): 125. Accessed September 19, 2020. doi:10.2307/763837.

Lowings, Andy. *The Golden Lyre of Ur,* 2013, digital image, Baghdad. Accessed on November 27, 2020. http://www.tristanlegovic.eu/blog.php?pennad=lyre-of-ur#bookmark/5/.

Mackie, Tim. "Overview: Song of Songs" (YouTube, Bible Project, Portland, 2016). https://www.youtube.com/watch?v=4KC7xE4fgOw&t=53s.

Mark, Michael, and Patrice Madura. *Contemporary Music Education*, 4th ed. Boston: Cengage, 2014.

Martin, Dale B. *New Testament History and Literature.* New Haven: Yale University Press, 2012.

McTague, Carl. "The Lyres of Ur," Mctague.org (2022). http://www.mctague.org/carl/music/computer/pieces/lyre/.

Merriam, Alan P. *Anthropology of Music.* Chicago: Northwestern University Press, 1964.

Myktiuk, Lawrence J. *Identifying Biblical Persons in Northwest Semitic Inscriptions of 1200-539 B.C.E.* Brill: Leiden, 2004.

Pappas, Stephanie. "Ram-Headed Sphinx Abandonded By King Tut's Grandfather Found in Egypt," *Live Science* (web, February 27, 2019). https://www.livescience.com/64870-ram-headed-sphinx-egypt.html.

Pioske, Daniel. *David's Jerusalem: Between Memory and History.* London: Routledge, 2015.

Ribak, Eli. "How to Make a Shofar: A Look Inside Israel's Biggest Factory" (web, Haaretz, Tel Aviv, 2017). https://www.youtube.com/watch?v=gpKviLJnV2E.

Rober, Mark. "World's Largest Horn Shatters Glass" (web video, YouTube, 2018). https://www.youtube.com/watch?v=pFEB0chiuJA.

Sanchez, Francisco Del Rio. "Where did the Queen of Sheba rule—Arabia or Africa?" *National Geographic:* June 7, 2021. https://www.nationalgeographic.co.uk/history-and-civilisation/2021/06/where-did-the-queen-of-sheba-rule-arabia-or-africa.

Sendrey, Alfred. *Music in Ancient Israel.* New York: Philosophical Library, 1969.

Smith, Douglas Alton. "A History of the Lute from Antiquity to the Renaissance," *Lute Society of America.* (2002): 9.

Snodgrass, Jennifer Sterling. *Contemporary Musicianship: Analysis and the Artist.* New York: Oxford University Press, 2018.

Stock, Jonathan P.J. "Asia/China, Taiwan, Singapore, Overseas Chinese," in *Worlds of Music: An Introduction to the Music of the World's Peoples*, 6th ed., ed. Jeff Todd Titon. Boston: Cengage Learning, 2017.

Towns, Elmer L., and Vernon M. Whaley. *Worship Through the Ages: How the Great Awakenings Shape Evangelical Worship.* Nashville: B&H Publishing Group, 2012.

Varadpande, Manohar Laxman. *History of Indian Theatre.* Abhinav Publications, 1987.

Wang, Xiaoming, Qiang Li, and Gary L. Takeuchi. "Out of Tibet: An Early Sheep from the Pliocene of Tibet, *Protovis himalayensis*, Genus and Species Nov. (Bovidae, Caprini), and Origin of Ice Age Mountain Sheep," *Journal of Vertebrate Paleontology* 36, no. 5 (2016). https://www.tandfonline.com/doi/abs/10.1080/02724634.2016.1169190?journalCode=ujvp20.

Weinberger, Norman M. "Music and the Brain," *SA Special Editions* 16, no.3s (September 2006): 36-43. https://www.scientificamerican.com/article/music-and-the-brain-2006-09/.

Weisenberg, Joey. "The Torah of Music," Lecture series, January 26, 2022.

Willis, Amy C. Merrill. "Introduction to Daniel" in *The Oxford Annotated Study Bible: New Revised Standard Version with Apocrypha* 5th ed., ed Michael D. Coogan. New York: Oxford University Press, 2018.

www.ingramcontent.com/pod-product-compliance
Lightning Source LLC
Chambersburg PA
CBHW050851160426
43194CB00011B/2110